ISAAC DEUTSCHER was born in 1907 near Krakow and joined the Polish Communist Party in 1926. After his expulsion in 1932, he maintained his opposition to the general drift of Comintern policy in the 1930s. He moved to London in 1939 and continued his journalistic activity until 1946, devoting the rest of his life to historical research and the writing of books and essays.

Isaac Deutscher's prolific output includes *Stalin* (1948); a trilogy on Leon Trotsky: *The Prophet Armed* (1954), *The Prophet Unarmed* (1959) and *The Prophet Outcast* (1963); *The Unfinished Revolution* (1967), *The Non-Jewish Jew* (1968), and numerous essays on Russia, China and contemporary communism. Isaac Deutscher died in 1967.

TAMARA DEUTSCHER, who has edited several collections of her husband's essays, is herself a writer specializing in Soviet and East European affairs.

Isaac Deutscher

Verso

Marxism, Wars and Revolutions:

Essays from Four Decades

Edited and introduced by
Tamara Deutscher

With a preface by *Perry Anderson*

British Library
Cataloguing in Publication Data
Deutscher Isaac
  Marxism, Wars and Revolutions
  1. Communism — 1945- — Case studies
  2. Communist state — Case studies
  I. Title
  320.5'32'0722   HX44

First published 1984
ⓒ Tamara Deutscher and Verso 1984

Verso
15 Greek Street London W1

Filmset in Garamond by
PRG Graphics Ltd
Redhill, Surrey

Printed in Great Britain by
The Thetford Press Ltd
Thetford, Norfolk

ISBN 0 86901 095 4
     0 86091 803 3 pbk

Contents

IV. China

V. Marxism and Our Time

Preface

Isaac Deutscher, who died seventeen years ago, was one of the greatest socialist writers of this century. He was a Marxist and a historian. But in the way in which these two vocations were connected in his work, the place he occupies in the literature of each is unlike any other. Deutscher's fame rests above all, of course, on his political biographies of Stalin and Trotsky — two masterpieces on the fate of the Russian Revolution. In them, all Deutscher's powers were concentrated on the object of his life's study; and it is there that readers new to his legacy will continually start. This volume serves a complementary purpose. The collection of essays and addresses that it contains gives us the best intellectual portrait of the biographer himself — that is, of Deutscher as a mind. For the essayist, in the nature of the genre, could speak more directly and personally, and over a more various and unexpected range of topics, than the historian: subjective experience and conviction find greater expression in these interventions than in the major objective reconstructions of the past themselves. From them, we can see Deutscher as he was, a much more complex and multi-dimensional figure than the terms by which he became best known in his life-time would suggest: not simply a scholar, but a thinker, of the Left; and not only a commentator on events, but a committed participant in them. Thanks to the care of Tamara Deutscher, the symposium of texts below — which includes several that have never before been published, or collected, in English — presents a more comprehensive view of Isaac Deutscher, as a fighter and a critic, an intellectual and militant, than any previously available.

What do they reveal? In the first instance, through their prism, the original context that nurtured Deutscher comes into view. The universalism of the mature writer tended to conceal these origins: but it was in fact a very particular regional experience that made possible the later cosmopolitanism. However, like that of another master of English prose, Joseph Conrad, his Polish past long lay partly hidden from sight, and can easily be misunderstood. Deutscher was born in the province of Krakow in 1907, and as a boy grew up in natural sympathy with Polish traditions of literary experiment and political emancipation. But his family was not from the patriotic gentry, but from the Jewish middle-class, where his father owned a printing-business; and his youthful politics were early on socialist. A generation earlier, Rosa Luxemburg had come from a similar background in the neighbouring province of Lublin, where her father was in the timber-trade.[1] Like her, Deutscher entered the Polish revolutionary movement while still in his teens, joining the Polish Communist Party in early 1927. Between the experiences of the two lay, of course, the change that had confounded one of Luxemburg's life-long perspectives — the independence of Poland. But as Deutscher explains in *The Tragedy of the Polish Communist Party*, the predominant tradition in the political milieu in which he became a militant was still Luxemburgist. The way in which that tradition was weakened, compromised and finally snuffed out forms, in fact, the leitmotif of his moving evocation — at once analytically sharp and acutely felt — of the fate of pre-war communism in Poland. Deutscher's own formation, however, was in close continuity with Luxemburg's heritage. From it he took its moral independence, its spontaneous internationalism, its uncompromising revolutionary spirit — a Marxism that was as classical in ease with the theory of historical materialism (Luxemburg had been the first Marxist to criticize the schemas of reproduction in *Capital*), as it was vigorous in its connection with the practical life of the workers' movement.

To these historical bequests there was added a specific geographical endowment as well. Poland lay between Germany and Russia, the two great powers that had decisively shaped — or misshaped — its destiny since the days of Napoleon. Luxemburg's career as a socialist had passed in the ambience of all three nations: organizing the clandestine labour movement in Poland from her student days, intervening in the debates of the Russian movement during the Revolution of 1905-1907, and leading the Left in the German movement in the final decade of her life. Nor was her case an isolated one. Her contemporary Karl Radek, from Brest, was equally at home from Bremen to Moscow. For a socialist of Deutscher's generation, Versailles Poland no longer afforded this kind of possibility. But the

---

[1] The principal difference between the two was the language spoken at home: Polish in Luxemburg's case, Yiddish in Deutscher's.

geopolitical position of the country still ensured that any Polish Marxist would be formed against the immediate horizons of events in Germany and Russia: in some ways more so than ever, as the October Revolution had now given birth to the USSR, the first workers' state in the world, while the Communist International focused its greatest hopes and efforts on a second breakthrough in Weimar Germany. It was thus quite logical that Deutscher's service in the Polish Communist Party should have come to an end, not over national issues as such — tortuously mishandled though these were by the Party under Soviet pressures, as his retrospect recalls — but over the growth of fascism under the neighbouring capitalist state. In 1932, he formed part of a minority opposition that attacked the sectarian passivity of the German Communist Party, imposed by the Stalinist leadership of the Comintern, towards the rise of Nazism — while at the same time criticizing the results of the same 'third period' line, and the bureaucratic regime that accompanied it in the Polish party. These positions came to coincide with those of Trotsky in exile: and Deutscher was expelled from the Polish Communist Party, as Trotsky's warnings of the terrible threat posed by Hitler's gangs to the European working-class reached their crescendo.

If Germany was the immediate occasion for Deutscher's break with the official Communist movement, Russia was to be the abiding concern of his mature work as a Marxist. Already in 1931 he had travelled to the USSR for the Polish party, and witnessed at first hand the ravages of collectivization and famine, as well as the industrial feats of the first five-year plan. By this time, the policies of the Third International were entirely subordinated to the twists and turns of the Soviet party leadership, as Stalin remorselessly consolidated his power in Russia. With the victory of Nazism in Germany in 1933, the direction taken by the Russian Revolution would be decisive for the fate of the European labour movement as a whole. The text that opens this collection, the pamphlet Deutscher wrote in October 1936 on the first of the great Moscow Trials, set the agenda for the rest of his life. Written with searing indignation, his hand — as Tamara Deutscher puts it — 'trembling with rage', Deutscher's protest nonetheless already displayed some of the distinctive qualities that were to mark his later work as a Marxist historian. Thus he was not content with dismantling the circumstantial absurdities of Stalinist 'evidence' at the Trial: even more conclusively, he dwelt on the psychological impossibility of an alleged 'terrorism' that abased itself before its accusers, an audacious 'conspiracy' collapsing into abject self-flagellation, and surmised the real mechanisms which extracted the confessions of Zinoviev, Kamenev and the rest — the GPU's secret promises of post-trial pardon in exchange for their moral suicide in the dock, promptly discharged by their summary physical execution. The penetration of Deutscher's insight here — contrasting with the overblown speculations of so many of his contemporaries — has since been confirmed by the evidence that has subsequently emerged about the trials: a remarkable tribute to his gifts of historical reconstruction. He concluded the pamphlet with the ringing words: 'History still leaves socialism some time to save its burning edifice. Let us not lose faith in our ideals'.

Three years later, Deutscher left Warsaw for London. The small communist opposition in Poland was isolated and dispersed; he had rejected the formation of a new International by Trotsky, arguing that a 'period of intense reaction and depression' was 'wholly unfavourable' to the venture; a new European war was visibly imminent, as the ambitions of the Third Reich expanded. Deutscher settled down to master English and start a new journalistic career abroad.[2] War broke out a few months later, with the German invasion of Poland. Nazi victory in the West was followed by Soviet occupation of the East of the country, in accordance with the provisions of the Molotov-Ribbentrop Pact of 1939. With this partition, Deutscher's native land had once again disappeared from the map of Europe. Two years later, Hitler launched the Wehrmacht against the USSR itself, and within months was at the gates of Moscow. Deutscher, after a brief spell with Polish forces in Scotland, was now working as a journalist for *The Economist* in London. The second text in this collection is the record of his reaction to the titanic struggle under way in Russia. Written in February 1942, when the victory of Stalingrad still lay well ahead, Deutscher's article — addressed to Polish readers in exile — expresses, with impassioned eloquence, the other pole of his response to the drama of the Soviet Union under Stalin: after his scorn and disgust at the infamy of the Trials, his respect and admiration for the 'heroic resistance of the Russian workers and peasants' in which history had stripped off the mask of the bureaucracy and revealed 'the Revolution's true countenance: bleeding but dignified, suffering but fighting on'. Attacking both liberal myths of the 'solidarity of the two totalitarianisms', and the Stalinist crimes that had given rise to them, he underscored the

[2] For this period of Deutscher's life, as for the whole of his youth, see Daniel Singer's invaluable biographical essay 'Armed with a Pen', in David Horowitz (ed), *Isaac Deutscher –The Man and His Work*, London 1971, an essential volume for understanding Deutscher's work.

real historical significance of the conflict between the USSR and Germany — a 'battle for the very existence of the workers' movement and the freedom of the European peoples — a freedom without which socialism cannot be achieved'. 'The destiny of the world now hangs in the balance across the vast spaces of the USSR,' he wrote. 'In the terse war communiqués we socialists read not only the reports about "normal" war operations: we are also reading in them the fate of the deadly struggle between revolution and counter-revolution.'

Both these early Polish-language texts, on the Purges and the Red Army at bay, were written with an incandescent intensity, in the furnace of the events themselves. *Reflections on the Russian Revolution*, published in *The Political Quarterly* in early 1944, as the Nazi armies were in full retreat before the advancing Soviet forces, and the end of the German invasion was near, is quite different in mode. Here Deutscher, setting aside any reference to current events, looked at the development of the Russian Revolution as a whole in a long historical perspective, comparing it with the English Revolution and the French Revolution before it. Stalin's dictatorship, he concluded, was closer to the Cromwellian Protectorate than the Napoleonic Empire in the paradoxical continuity of a repressive and hierarchical regime with the insurgent origins of October. But no stabilization was yet in sight. The 'Pandora's box of the Revolution is still open' he wrote, releasing 'its monsters and its fears' — but also 'the hope at the bottom of it', which alone had made it possible to 'sustain and keep together a nation which had drained the cup of defeat almost to the last bitter dregs', in the first months of the Nazi invasion. What the future of the post-revolutionary bureaucracy formed under Stalin would be remained uncertain, once the struggle was over. 'Here the student of history can only put the question-mark without attempting to formulate any reply.' These concluding words announce the change in Deutscher's practice as a writer that was to occur in the years immediately following the peace. After 1945, Deutscher did not consider going back to Poland[3] (Marx never thought of resettling in Germany); renouncing immediate political engagements, he wrote *Stalin: A Political Biography* instead, which appeared in 1949. The fourth text devoted to the USSR below, *Two Revolutions*, is his introduction to the French edition. It extends his comparison of the Russian and French Revolutions, now with all the authority of that

---

[3] Save once, after the Polish October, in 1956 — when informal overtures were made to him by the authorities to return to Poland. His reply was that he would do so if he could deliver a series of lectures on the history of Polish Communism, to be subsequently written up into a book: whereupon no more was heard of the offer.

work, discussing in particular the analogy between their respective expansions beyond their borders, with the forcible creation of satellite states in Europe — hybrid products at once of emancipation and oppression. Revolt among his allies and satellites had contributed to the downfall of Napoleon, a precedent that should give 'grave warning' to Stalin as he constructed a Soviet order in Eastern Europe — already against the rebellion of Tito. One of Napoleon's client states, he noted, had been the Duchy of Poland, where his legend had lived on long after his defeat, and was still alive to Deutscher as a schoolboy. The French system had not been saved by its redeeming features. But the verdict of history on its Stalinist counter-part was unlikely to be more severe than on the Napoleonic original.

* * *

By the time Deutscher's biography of Stalin appeared, the political conjuncture in the West had, of course, changed. From 1946 onwards, the Cold War had set in: a virulent anti-communism now dominated official culture and politics in the advanced capitalist countries. In a climate of conformity and hysteria, the Soviet experience became the object of a vast ideological campaign, orchestrated through government agencies, political parties, trade-unions and intellectual institutions alike, depicting the Russian threat — of perpetual aggression and subversion — to the Free World. In other words, a period very like our own. Deutscher's response to it, which forms the theme of the second part of this collection, thus makes timely reading. *The Ex-Communist's Conscience* is a cool and devastating review of *The God That Failed*, a symposium of penitents with communist pasts. Deutscher compares their renegacies — liberal or conservative — with those of disillusioned early admirers of the French Revolution such as Wordsworth or Coleridge, who rallied to the counter-revolutionary cause of Tory oligarchy and Holy Alliance in the struggle against Napoleon. This demeaning path he contrasted with the examples of three very different figures — Jefferson, Goethe and Shelley, who refused to choose between the two armed camps of their time, and, whose judgement 'history has proved superior to the phobias and hatreds of their age'. The next essay deals directly with the centrepiece of the phobic literature of the Cold War, Orwell's *1984*. Deutscher, who knew Orwell quite well as a fellow-journalist, pens a brilliant psychological portrait of him, and the reasons for his compulsive vision of Stalinism as ultimately the expression of a primordial sadism, wielding power and inflicting

pain for their own sake, human evil detached from historical cause or
social reason. Amidst the contemporary apotheosis of Orwell, with
its suffuse tributes to his genius and solemn debates on his affili-
ations, wanting any sense of the proportions of their object, the
economy and severity of *1984 — The Mysticism of Cruelty* are a
reminder of the nature of true criticism. But if the celebrity of the
book was created, in Deutscher's words, by the 'social demand' of
the Cold War, what was the real character of the Cold War as an
international conflict itself? The third piece in this section provides a
broad historical retrospect, twenty years after Potsdam. Deutscher
prepared this text for a speech at a National Teach-In in Washington
during May 1965 on the war in Vietnam — a direct outcome of the
original conflict unleashed by Western intervention (French, British
and American) in Indochina in 1945. Accepting the inevitability of a
world-wide clash between capitalist and anti-capitalist regimes and
social forces, after their joint defeat of the Axis powers, Deutscher
pointed out, however, the drastic inequality of position and strength
between the leading victor states, the USA and USSR — 'two colossi,
one full-blooded, vigorous and erect, and the other prostrate and
bled white'; and the absurdity of the claims that Russia was bent on a
military assault on the West after its ordeal in the Second World War,
or that Stalin sought — rather than feared — the spread of revolutions abroad. Nevertheless, despite the asymmetry of economic
power and of political responsibility at the origins of the conflict,
whose onus lay essentially with Anglo–American imperialism,
'effects outlive their causes', and 'the danger is only too obvious that
this cold war may terminate in total nuclear war'. Moreover,
Deutscher went on, in another decisive respect 'the cold war has
already given us the foretaste of the fully-fledged nuclear war: its
fall-out cannot be confined to enemy territory; it contaminates the
moral texture, it destroys and warps the thinking processes of the
popular masses in our countries, in all the countries engaged in
waging the cold war.' To fight against the Cold War was not to
abandon class struggle, but to release it from the morass of 'hysteria
and insanity, myths and legends' in which it had become alienated
and obscured, to allow it — adapting a phrase of Marx's about the
Commune — to run through its different phases in the most rational
and humane way,[4] so that 'the divisions may once again run within

---

[4] 'The Commune does not do away with the class struggles through which the working-
classes strive to abolition of all classes and, therefore, all class rule, but it affords the
rational medium in which that class struggle can run through its different phases in the
most rational and humane way': Karl Marx, *The First International and After*, ed. David
Fernback, London 1974, p 253.

nations, rather than between them.'

* * *

Following the death of Stalin there opened a period in which there
seemed for a time to be a real prospect of such a rationalization of
East–West conflict. Deutscher was the first observer to predict the
ferment of destalinization in the USSR after 1953. His book *Russia
After Stalin* explored the different possible directions in which the
Soviet state and society might move, as the first signs of the Thaw
became visible. In these same years, which seemed to hold some
promise of a revival within the international communist movement
of pre-Stalinist traditions, he was preparing his monumental
biography of Trotsky, the first volume of which — *The Prophet
Armed* — appeared in 1954. The texts contained in part III reflect
these interlinked concerns, but also cast light on Deutscher's
attitudes to Poland and the crisis of Stalinism in Eastern Europe, to
Germany and the fate of socialism in Central Europe, and to
Scandinavian social-democracy in Western Europe. *The Tragedy of
the Polish Communist Party*, as we have seen, recreates the world of
pre-war Polish communism in which Deutscher was formed. But it
was prompted by the Polish renewal of 1956, when the reforming
current led by Gomulka defied Soviet intimidation with a significant
liberalization of political and intellectual controls in Poland.
Deutscher viewed these developments with a critical sympathy,
hoping for a return of the better traditions of the past. His conclusion
is striking testimony to the complete freedom of his spirit from all
national cant. He insisted on the 'indestructible links between the
Polish and Russian Revolutions' — links proved both 'negatively
and positively', in 1918-1920, in 1939, in 1954 and again in 1956.
Considering how often history had 'mocked and insulted Poland's
national dignity and, in the first place, the dignity and independence
of the Polish revolutionary movement', it was not surprising that the
Polish people 'sought refuge in the jungle of our nationalist legends'.
The Polish masses, he argued, would eventually understand that 'the
bonds which unite their destiny with that of the Russian and other
revolutions are indissoluble', but only 'after they have recovered
from the blows and shocks inflicted on them in the past, and when
they feel that nothing can ever again threaten their independence and
national dignity'. Ten years later, Deutscher addressed a scathing
Open Letter to Gomulka, denouncing the first trial of men who were
to be the leaders of KOR in the eighties, and warning that with such

persecutions Gomulka would be 'compromising the future of social-ism'. Deutscher's judgement on each occasion was vindicated. The final decline of the Gomulka regime into the squalid repressions of 1968 prepared the way for the moral discredit of communism in the country at large; and the subsequent rise of Solidarity proved unable to transform Polish state and society, in the absence of any corres-ponding popular movement against the bureaucratic order in the Soviet Union. The 'negative bonds' between Polish and Russian experience still prevail.

Deutscher's conversations and correspondence with Brandler re-present a very different kind of document, one of peculiar fascination within his work as a whole. For Heinrich Brandler embodied a living mediation between the epoch of Luxemburg and Lenin, and that of Deutscher. Born in 1881, as a young Saxon building-worker he had joined the German Social-Democratic Party, and become a friend and adherent of Rosa Luxemburg before the First World War. In 1918 he had participated in the founding of the German Communist Party, and found himself by 1921 at the head of it. In the following year there occurred the 'German October' — the ill-starred attempt at an insurrectionary rising in Central Germany by the KPD, on instructions from the Comintern in Moscow prompted by Zinoviev and Trotsky. Brandler, modest and cautious by temperament, neither believed in the prospects for a successful German Revolution in 1923, nor thought himself capable of leading one. But as a loyal Communist he obeyed instructions, and was then blamed for the failure of the enterprise. Expelled from the party for opposing the 'third period' line in 1929, he spent the Nazi period in exile in France and Cuba. Deutscher first met him on his return to Europe in 1948. Tamara Deutscher vividly evokes the friendship that ensued. During these initial encounters, Deutscher recorded his discussions with Brandler, in which the older man recollected the famous episodes of the twenties in which he had been a principal figure. Deutscher's ability to convey a personality — on this occasion obliquely — is once again notable. After his return to West Germany, Brandler organized a small Marxist formation, *Gruppe Arbeiterpolitik*, com-mitted to revolutionary socialism, and the two men continued to write to each other. Brandler had always been closer to Bukharin's Right Opposition in the twenties, while Deutscher's sympathies lay with Trotsky's Left Opposition, and this difference was reflected in the latter's more stringent overall hostility to Stalinism in the post-war years. When working-class riots erupted against the Ulbricht regime in East Germany in 1953, however, it was Brandler who viewed this upheaval with more unconditional approval, concentrating on its sociological character in the DDR itself, while Deutscher reminded him of the international context in which the rising was ideologically appropriated by the West, and of the setback to the cause of political reform in East Germany that it occasioned, paradoxically rescuing Ulbricht from the brink of political extinction as the Soviet leadership abandoned its intention of jettisoning him. The debate between the two over the significance of this contemporary crisis was conducted on both sides in terms of its position within German historical development as a whole, since the epoch of Tilsit. The exchange printed here concludes with Brandler's reaction to Deutscher's treatment of the 'German October' thirty years earlier, in the second volume of his biography of Trotsky, *The Prophet Unarmed*.[5] While admiring the character of the manuscript as a whole, he sought to clarify his own role in the disasters of that year, when many believed that the best single chance of a revolution in the West was missed. Deutscher's response to his objections is of especial interest, since here — in direct dialogue with an interlocutor of Lenin himself, both witness to the past and comrade-in-arms in the present — he sets out a memorable explanation of his practice as a Marxist historian, dealing with events in which his own revolutionary sympathies were fully engaged.

Deutscher's exchanges with the Norwegian Social-Democrat Trygve Lie provide a caustic contrast. Lie had been Minister of Justice in the Labour government that had first — grudgingly — given asylum to Trotsky in 1935, then isolated and harassed, and finally expelled him, under combined bourgeois and bureaucratic pressures, in 1937. In the course of his research for the third volume of his biography of Trotsky, *The Prophet Outcast*, Deutscher interviewed Lie in 1956 about these events. The notes that he took of his findings give a revealing glimpse of a certain kind of West European Social-Democracy, in all its repellent meanness and hypocrisy, as it confronted the grandeur of the Bolshevik tradition in the person of Trotsky in Norway. Trygve Lie, of course, incarnated all that was worst in such Scandinavian traditions, irresistibly recalling Ibsen's most savage portraits to Deutscher. Above and beyond his role during Trotsky's exile, he was of course one of the most servile functionaries of US policy in the Cold War, when as the American

---

[5] For a fuller selection of the Deutscher-Brandler correspondence, see *New Left Review*, no 105, September-October 1977. The complete original series of letters had been edited by Hermann Weber, *Unabhängige Kommunisten — Der Briefwechsel zwischen Heinrich Brandler und Isaac Deutscher 1949 bis 1967*, Berlin 1981.

appointee as Secretary-General of the United Nations, he introduced McCarthyism into the international civil service, demoralizing it for a decade to the disgust of even liberal colleagues. The moral and political gulf between a Brandler and a Lie brings home much of the real human meaning of the original separation of the Third from the Second International on the morrow of the First World War.

✳ ✳ ✳

The central focus of Deutscher's work was the fate of the Russian Revolution, the transformations of the Soviet state that emerged from it, and their impact on the European labour movement. Of all these, he had direct experience and first-hand knowledge, as a Marxist apprenticed in the Polish Communist Party, fluent in German and Russian, familiar with the Latin cultures, wielder of an astonishing command of English. This was the world of classical Marxism, native to Europe. The victory of the Chinese Revolution in 1949 transformed the boundaries of this universe, extending the problems of the transition to socialism to Asia, in the context of an ancient civilization with a longer continuous history than any in Europe, and a culture of traditional self-sufficiency. Deutscher immediately realized the world-historical significance of the overthrow of the Kuomintang. This was, indeed, the final emphasis of his essay *Two Revolutions* already mentioned, written within a few months of the entry of Mao's armies into Peking, where he argued that comparisons between the destiny of the French and Russian Revolutions found their natural stopping-place with the arrival of the Chinese Revolution. 'For this phenomenon we find no parallel in the epoch of the French revolution. To its very end the French revolution stood alone.' Deutscher watched with close interest the first years of Communist China, but it was not until the exhaustion of the reforming impetus in Khrushchevite Russia in the late fifties, and the Chinese challenge to Soviet direction of the international communist movement in the early sixties, that he turned his full attention to the specific historical character of Maoism. The result was one of his finest and most original essays, *Maoism — Its Origins and Outlook*, which surveyed the tensions and contradictions of the Chinese experience in the light of its Russian predecessor. The balance and complexity of his assessment, made without benefit of any specialized linguistic or area skills, has few equals in the subsequent literature. Maoism, he argued, could be seen as a kind of fulfilment of Marx's conjecture that late 19th-century Russia might develop directly from a primitive agrarian society to socialism, through a revolution based on the peasantry and its communal traditions, provided that the working-class had come to power in the advanced industrial countries of Western Europe, and so could exert a gravitational pull on backward Russia. *Mutatis mutandis*, just such a sequence had occurred in China, but — ironically — with newly industralized Russia playing the part Marx had assigned to Western Europe. Hence the paradoxes of Maoism. On the one hand, from its rural origins it rested more securely on the consent of the majority of the population than had Bolshevism, the movement of an urban minority: initially more confident relations with the peasantry were also assisted by coming to power after and not before a civil war, permitting the Maoist regime — unlike the Leninist — to proceed immediately to the constructive tasks of economic revival. On the other hand, the agrarian background of Maoism also meant a narrow cultural provincialism and uncontested political authoritarianism, in marked contrast to the broad internationalism and lively intellectual pluralism of the classical Bolshevik tradition. Socially, the Chinese regime was relatively more egalitarian than the Russian at a comparable stage of its post-revolutionary development; but its organizational monolithism, untouched by any more democratic past heritage, nevertheless gave it an unmistakable 'affinity with Stalinism'. Internationally, its preaching of the watchwords of irreconcilable class struggle and its campaign for radical resistance to imperalism, were formally appealing. But Deutscher pointed to the incongruity of the cult of Stalin that accompanied them, and presciently asked: how far 'Maoist professions of revolutionary internationalism' really reflected 'the frame of mind of the Chinese masses', and were 'not merely a response to Western provocation', with the continuing blockade of China by the USA? Thus already in 1964, at the height of apparent Maoist intransigence towards American imperialism, Deutscher lucidly foresaw the danger that if the 'Western powers were to try to play China against the Soviet Union' — 'might Peking not succumb to the temptation?' Less than a decade later, the answer was to be forthcoming.

Deutscher did not live to see the embrace with Washington of Mao's last years. But he did witness, and judge, the launching of the 'Cultural Revolution' in China that paved the way for it. Proclaimed in the name of the radical ideas of the Paris Commune, and a revolt against all hierarchy and bureaucracy, the Cultural Revolution was greeted with a wide range of indulgence and enthusiasm among the left intelligentsia of Europe and North America, forming a whole generation of *maoisant* sympathisers in the West. Credulity in the official propaganda of the Chinese regime, as purge succeeded purge in the ranks of party and state and of the population at large, often persisted until the death of Mao himself. Deutscher was totally untouched by such fashionable illusions. From the outset, as can be seen from his trenchant piece *The Meaning of the 'Cultural Revolution'*, he indicted the crude intellectual nihilism, the mindless xenophobia, and the brutal persecutions unleashed by the 'Great Helmsman' in 1966. For all its apparently farcical aspects, he warned, 'the Maoist "cultural revolution" is a deadly serious affair. Its effect on China's spiritual and intellectual life is, in all probability, going to be just as devastating and lasting as were the consequences of the Stalinist witch-hunts. Its political meaning is also comparable. Like Russia in the last years of the Stalin era, so China has now plunged headlong into a self-centred isolationism and nationalism.' The result would be 'an irreparable loss to the nation: a gap in its cultural consciousness, a lowering of standards, and an impoverishment of spiritual life. Post-Stalinist Russia is still smarting under the loss, and so will Maoist and post-Maoist China.' Deutscher's clairvoyance did not halt here. He went on to predict, again with arresting accuracy, that the deliberately lowered economic horizons of the regime — its failure to advance Chinese industralization with anything like Russian-style success under Stalin, its inability to resolve rural over-population and unemployment — were unlikely to provide a basis for political stabilization. 'Pressures for a more ambitious policy of economic progress will make themselves felt', and 'some reaction against the latest version of Maoism is all too likely to set in.' He concluded: 'Mao has been in one person China's Lenin and Stalin. But at the end of his road he shows more and more similarity to Stalin; and the latest orgy of his personality cult underlines the likeness. It is as if he had outlived himself and is already a relic of the past, an embodiment of China's backwardness and isolationism. When the reaction against these aspects of Maoism comes, his successor or successors, whoever they are, will have to act as its mouthpieces and agents'. The profile of Deng Xiaoping and his associates is already delineated.

*   *   *

The final group of texts collected here is distinct in character from the rest. In these, which date from the sixties, Deutscher posed four of the most general and fundamental questions confronting any socialist

in the second half of the twentieth century. How should the bureaucratic systems, that have emerged from every revolution in the backward countries so far, be viewed historically? What is the validity of
the classical theory of Marxism for an analysis of capitalism in the
advanced countries? Where does the role of violence lie in the transition to a society beyond capitalism? What would be the shaping
forms of a socialist civilization? The first of these issues Deutscher
explored in *The Roots of Bureaucracy*. It is often said that his con-
junctural writing on Russian political development in the Khrushchevite epoch was overly optimistic about the prospects of democratization in the USSR and in the Soviet bloc generally; and it is true
that he thought the failure of reforms in the early sixties was unlikely
to be a durable one, given the wider changes in Soviet social structure
as a whole. The protracted stabilization of Brezhnevism was a
process he did not live to dissect. But in his most considered
theoretical reflections on the historical phenomenon of bureaucracy
as a whole, he left little ground for confidence in any short-term
supersession of it in a society like the USSR, let alone China. For
there, in a *tour de force* of long-range interpretation, he located the
social origins of bureaucracy in the division between mental and
manual labour which lay 'buried on the border between the primitive
communistic tribe and civilized society', with the first embryonic
emergence of class society itself. After sketching the metamorphoses
of bureaucratic administration, and its relations to successive modes
of production from the Pharaohs and the Bourbons, Deutscher then
argued that under capitalism 'the political power of the bureaucracy
has always been in inverse proportion to the maturity, the vigour, the
capacity for self-government of the strata constituting a given bourgeois society. On the other hand, when in highly-developed
bourgeois societies class struggles have reached something like a
deadlock, when contending classes have lain as if prostrate after a
series of exhausting social and political struggles, then political
leadership has almost automatically passed into the hands of a
bureaucracy.' This was why Victorian England or Jacksonian
America, with their self-assured bourgeoisies, were the least bureaucratic of the major capitalist powers in the nineteenth century, while
the 'mutual exhaustion' of bourgeoisie and proletariat after 1848 gave
rise to the Second Empire in France, and the 'many-sided deadlock'
between junkers, industrialists and workers in Germany yielded the
dictatorship of Bismarck's officialdom. It was this logic, transposed
to societies where the capitalist class itself had been destroyed, yet the
working-class was still fragmented and weak, that explained the
enormous growth in the power and longevity of post-revolutionary

bureaucracies, against the background of the relentless hostility of the surrounding imperialism. These post-capitalist bureaucracies, however, for all their despotic arrogance and privilege, did not constitute new classes. To this day, Deutscher observed, 'the Soviet bureaucracy has not managed to acquire that social, economic and psychological identity of its own which would allow us to describe it as a new class. It is something like an amoeba covering post-revolutionary society with itself. It is an amoeba because it lacks a social backbone of its own, it is not a formed entity, not a historic force that comes on the scene in the way in which, for example, the old bourgeoisie came forth after the French Revolution.' Mined by its own contradictions, it would not last forever. In a society characterized by widespread automation, shorter working-hours, civilized leisure and cultural independence, 'the antagonism between brain-work and manual labour really will wither away, and so will the division between the organizers and the organized.' Then, he predicted, but only then, 'it will be seen that if bureaucracy was a faint prelude to class society, bureaucracy will mark the fierce, ferocious epilogue to class society — no more than an epilogue.'

The three remaining texts in this group are all products of Deutscher's practical political interventions within the Left, once a mass movement of semi-revolutionary temper arose among a younger generation in the West towards the end of his life, with the emergence of widespread opposition to the American war in Vietnam and the beginnings of revolt on the campuses. These addresses show him grappling with the problems of socialism in the richest capitalist nations of the time, and demonstrate how wrong it is to think of Deutscher as 'just' a historian, albeit of the major revolutionary experience of this century: for without ever ceasing to think historically, he also developed, and defended, original ethical and philosophical positions as well. *Marxism in Our Time* looks at the general situation of historical materialism as a theory of social emancipation, a century after *Capital*: one which he judged — in a typically dialectical formulation that is a far cry from current slogans — to be one of 'simultaneous ascendancy and decline'. To the question — is Marxism obsolete? — Deutscher replied: 'There is one, only one essential element in the Marxist critique of capitalism. It is very simple and very plain, but in it are focused all the many-faceted analyses of the capitalist order. It is this: there is is a striking contradiction between the increasingly social character of the process of production and the anti-social character of capitalist property. Our mode of existence, the whole manner of production, is becoming more and more social in the sense that the old free-lance producers can no longer go on producing in independence from each other, from generation to generation, as they did in the pre-capitalist system. Every element, every fraction, every tiny little organ of our society is dependent on all the rest. The whole process of production becomes one social process of production — and not only one national process of production but one international process of production. At the same time you have an anti-social kind of property, private property. This contradiction between the anti-social character of property and the social character of our production is the source of all anarchy and irrationality in capitalism.' The contradiction could not be reconciled in the long-run — a 'collision must come'. The nature of that collision could not be predicted in detail: but its general shape was not in doubt. On the one hand, Deutscher — at the height of the Kennedy-Johnson boom — expressed his disbelief in any 'further smooth, evolutionary development of Western capitalism': after twenty years of prosperity, slump would come again — as it did. On the other hand, the class struggle in the West had to be seen as a 'war against capitalism that has lasted many generations', and which had seen 'the mobilization of counter-revolution all over the world, in all its various forms, from fascism to the most refined social-democratic reformism, all mobilized in the defence of the existing social order.' Then, in a striking passage, Deutscher went on: 'Never yet, except in extraordinary moments like the Commune of Paris, has the working class mobilized itself even to a fraction of that intensity and strength at which the possessing and ruling classes have maintained their mobilization on an almost permanent footing. Even during the Commune the insurgents never really mobilized for a life-and-death struggle — we have all the descriptions showing their light-mindedness, their good-humoured and good-tempered optimism.'

It was the strengths, yet also the weaknesses, of such optimism that Deutscher reviewed in *The Dialectics of Violence and Non-Violence*, one of his sharpest and most unsettling pieces. In it, he started by stressing the traditional tension within the classical outlook of Marxism between the necessity of political violence as a means for overthrowing bourgeois class rule, and the aim of a classless society that for the first time in history would be truly free from violence. That essential and defensible dialectic was, however, overborn in the tragic vicissitudes of the Russian Revolution, when 'under overwhelming and inhuman pressures' terror was let loose and 'what was to have been but a glassful of violence became buckets and buckets full, and then rivers of violence,' so that 'in the end the non-violent meaning of Marxism was suppressed under the massive, crushing weight of Stalinism.' But the two could not be cleanly separated. For, Deutscher argued, 'it would show a lack of moral courage in Marxism to draw the formal line of dissociation and say that we are not responsible for Stalinism, that that wasn't what we aimed at' — 'we cannot delete Stalinism from our records although we are not responsible for Stalinist crimes'. Why was this so? In a rare personal avowal, Deutscher went on: 'To some extent we (and when I say we I mean that generation of Marxists with which I as an individual identify morally, I mean Lenin, Trotsky, Bukharin, Zinoviev, the early Communist leaders in Europe) participated in this glorification of violence as a self-defence mechanism. Rosa Luxemburg understood this when she criticized the first faint signs of this attitude.' Yet this was self-criticism, not repudiation. Revolutionary violence, regretted and unglorified, remained necessary against an enemy who had never shrunk from any extremity of it, as the murderous war in Vietnam that formed the context of his intervention demonstrated. But in advanced industrial societies like America itself, the potential balance of class forces was immensely more favourable to an undistorted outcome of revolutionary struggle than in backward and isolated Russia. There such violence could be 'rational and infinitesimal', if the vast majority of the exploited were ready to employ it to break the power of their exploiters, without making a virtue of it.

In the last text of the volume, *On Socialist Man*, Deutscher looked towards the future to ask what could be said, without relapse into utopian speculation, of human potential and limitation in a classless society once finally achieved. (The term 'man' should not deceive, as Deutscher's reference to the 'dependence of woman and child on the father' makes clear: it is gender-neutral, in the sense of the Russian *chelovek* or German *Mensch*.) Two features of his reply stand out. The first is the sobriety of his projection: socialism would not 'solve all predicaments of the human race' — indeed of Trotsky's trinity of 'hunger, sex and death', it could offer relief only for the first. Beyond class, human beings would still — *pace* Shelley — suffer guilt and pain, and feel the discomfort of civilizational restraints over instinctual drives. But these drives — and this is the second significant theme of his address — could in themselves be given neither the historical immobility nor the societal importance that Freud's theory attached to them. While respecting the warrant of psychoanalysis within its proper and restricted domain, Deutscher had no difficulty in dispatching its inflated claims for the interpretation of history, let alone intrusions of it into politics. As he drily pointed out, in discussing Freud's theory of aggression, 'throughout history men organized into armies have slaughtered each other over property or claims to property; but they have not so far, except in mythology, fought wars over "prerogative in the field of sexual relationships".' Whereas Marxism had tried to 'tackle from the right end the tasks confronting our society', and had moved mountains — both in victory and defeat — in so doing, the practical social effects of psychoanalysis were by comparison nugatory. In a period like the present, when an uncritical cult of psychoanalysis, often in its most ostentatiously idealist forms, correlates so closely with a retreat from historical materialism, Deutscher's calm reminder of the real relations of truth and force between the two could not be more salutary. Socialism, in his vision, would bring neither an impossible liberation from all human servitudes, nor stop at an imaginary immutability of all human instincts.

Isaac Deutscher died in August 1967. He was just 60. It is difficult to compute the loss his disappearance has meant to Marxist culture, and the socialist movement, since. His fellow-historian of the USSR, E.H. Carr, of whom he was a friend and critic, survived him for fifteen years, living to the age of 90. It is enough to think of what Carr accomplished in the last three decades of his life — all but one of the fourteen volumes of his *History of Soviet Russia* were written after he had passed his sixtieth year — to be conscious of the scale of what we have missed by the cutting short of Deutscher's career. Two volumes of biography of Lenin, certainly. The single chapter he left behind — a beautifully fresh and surprising *Lenin's Childhood* — suggest that this might have been the most unexpected of his Bolshevik portraits, bringing his powers of psychological insight to their height in the life of a man far less known, and more enigmatic, as a human being than either Stalin or Trotsky. But perhaps also that 'theoretical-historical survey of the European labour movement since 1848', of which he more than once spoke, in public and in private. Undoubtedly, at the same time, we would have possessed a rich and unbroken series of reflections on major changes in the world scene since 1968, whose upheavals came a few months after his death. In one vast cycle — the blossoming of the Czech spring, and the burial of chances for reform in the Soviet bloc with the invasion of Czechoslovakia; the upsurge of an international student revolt in the West, followed by working-class insurgence in France, Italy and Britain; the end of fascism in Portugal and Spain, and the defeat of the USA in Vietnam; and then in another cycle — the return of a slump to world capitalism; the swing to the right in the West, with the ascendancy of governments of militant reaction, and the fraying of the last communist ties to the intransigent traditions of the Third International; the rise of a new wave of socialist and anti-colonial revolutions in the Third World, and the gradual growth in the strategic weight of the USSR; mass explosion in Poland, decline of Brezhnevism in Russia, Bukharinite liberalization in China, fratricidal wars in Indochina; the conformation, finally, of a Second Cold War out of all these — such developments would have been explored, in their historical meaning and interrelations, by the same mind that had lived through the tragedy of pre-war Polish communism, analysed Stalin's power at its apogée, demystified the First Cold War, and followed the successive hopes and fiascos of Khrushchevism and Maoism. Our map of the present would look different if we had a continuity of that committed intelligence with us.

As it is, nearly two decades later, the political and intellectual scene is for the moment in many ways a bleak one: amidst renewed Cold War, and unended recession, much of the Western Left is prey to every kind of fashionable temptation and illusion purveyed by the Right — a post-1907 mood, as Deutscher might have put it. In the slogans of 'post-marxism' he would have seen mainly — the only novelty of the eighties, as opposed to his antithesis of the fifties — renegades posing as heretics. He would have mordantly analysed the continual reproduction by Brezhnevite bureaucrats of Bukovskyite dissidents, and the echo-chambers of 'gulagism'. But he would not have exaggerated the contemporary anti-cyclones, in either East or West. The new peace movements in Europe, and their opposition to the arms race and the division of the continent, would in particular have encouraged him. There, it is fitting that the best work confronting the current Cold War should have been produced out of direct inspiration from his example, by the editor of *Russia, China and the West*.[6] Cases such as this show what can be learnt from Deutscher, in a time whose dominant tone is so far from his. The historical conditions that produced this singular revolutionary socialist have passed away. Neither the palpable connection with the world of Lenin or Luxemburg, nor the natural cosmopolitanism of an older East-Central Europe, was available to subsequent generations. Yet Deutscher's work continues to represent an irreplaceable source for the culture and politics of socialism. The reasons lie in the eminent combination of its qualities. First of all, perhaps, the serene political fortitude with which Deutscher met the contingencies of his

---

[6] Fred Halliday, *The Making of the Second Cold War*, London 1983, who edited *Russia, China and the West*, the first collection of Deutscher's political journalism to appear after his death (Oxford, 1969).

own period — his unshakeable fidelity to the ideals of Marx and Engels, amidst so many conflagrations in which one edifice of the Left after another burnt down, or had to be rebuilt. That fortitude was the product of his absolute independence of thought — the complete freedom of his person and outlook from those fashions and phobias which have typically swayed the conformist intelligentsias of the West in one direction after another — successively Stalinist or Maoist, structuralist or post-structuralist, apostles of the New Working-Class or the New Social Movements, eurocommunism or eurosocialism. But this spiritual independence was the very opposite of sectarian or pharisaical isolation. Deutscher had a capacity to communicate with a greater audience than any other socialist writer of his time in English. His books were translated, his articles read, across the world. Such universality was given by literary power. But the peculiar splendour of his prose was not simply an aesthetic gift: it was the expression of a sovereign intellectual command of a classical Marxism, so close to its sources in the full range of European culture and enlightenment behind it, that it had no need of a specialized vocabulary — required not the slightest technical strain — to find its words. The adoption of biography as his mode of writing history had a related meaning — a genre that has always possessed the widest appeal among the different kinds of literature about the past. In Deutscher's case, however, the biographical form had an additional, deeper meaning. In the life of an individual, he could join the discourses of morality and necessity that Marxism has often found it so hard to hold together. His Stalin and Trotsky are preeminently products of history, subject to the determinations of wider social forces that they expressed or rejected: but they are also moral agents, accountable for their actions and the consequences of them. Ethics traditionally refers to persons; causal dynamics to groups. Deutscher's extraordinary psychological grasp was the medium in which the two — causality and responsibility — achieved synthesis in his writing. A socialist politics today needs to be informed by a sense of each in equal measure. Another way of putting this is to recall the actual contrasts between the Trio Deutscher selected for their resistance to conformity in the Napoleonic age. Goethe, Shelley, Jefferson — serene olympian, visionary iconoclast, shrewd politician. He had an element of each in his own make-up. A socialist movement will only flourish if it can encompass all of the ideals they represent.

Perry Anderson, August 1984

Introduction

The writings collected in this volume, spanning four decades, date from different periods of Isaac Deutscher's life as a political essayist and historian. They may seem to vary in their subject-matter and analytical approach, yet the main theme running through them like a strong thread is that which has so heavily marked (and marred) European thought in the decades of unfulfilled hopes following the Russian revolution. It is the theme of the degeneration of a revolutionary state. It was to the search for the deepest sources of this degeneration that Isaac Deutscher devoted most of his writings.

He remained a Marxist socialist all his adult life. He did not hold Marxist theory responsible for the history made in its name, and used classical Marxist methods of analysis to uncover the hidden springs of the degeneration of the state which, claiming allegiance to Marxism, so blatantly perverted it and made of it a lifeless dogma. Over half a century ago he was expelled from the Stalinist Church, and excommunicated; and like other heretics from other Churches, he made it his task to help in rescuing a great idea from dogmatic ossification.

Another kind of unity can also be claimed for this collection: that of the author's ability to place, and interpret, contemporary events within a broad historical perspective, and to draw analogies which consist not merely in 'assembling the points of formal resemblance between historical situations', but in discovering parallel motives, passions and aspirations behind each unique situation.

With the passing of time some of the essays — topical at the moment of writing — have acquired their own 'historical perspective'. What was not written as history has by now become history. It is therefore important to place at least some of the essays in the context of contemporary events and to bear in mind the political ambience prevalent at the time of writing.

✣   ✣   ✣

The volume opens with the earliest essay available to me. It is an impassioned indictment of Stalin's infamous 'trials', made all the more powerful by the high charge of emotion which it contains.

The Moscow Trial, written at great speed, was ready for publication on 1 September 1936, barely a few days after Moscow announced that the death sentence on Zinoviev, Kamenev and the other accused had been carried out. It was published in Warsaw as a pamphlet by a publishing cooperative 'Swiatlo'.

Isaac used to recall it quite often, but there was no way in which we could get hold of it. When the text finally reached me, it came too late for him to experience the emotion with which he would have read his own angry denunciation of Stalin's 'St Bartholomew Night' — the first of the bloody trials in which, amid the frenzy of the wildest accusations, Zinoviev, Kamenev, Mrachkowski, Smirnov and a score of other old Bolsheviks perished. One can feel that Isaac's hand had been trembling with rage. Yet he tried to control himself and to provide the reader not only with scathing denunciation, not only with an exposure of the absurdity and hollowness of the accusations, but also with a considerered analysis of the international background.

That this brochure not only remained in existence in Poland but was also read and distributed 'underground' during the worst period of Stalinism, Isaac learned in circumstances in which tragedy, sadness and residual satisfaction were inextricably bound together.

During our stay in Rome, at Easter 1959, Isaac was insistently urged to visit a Polish patient who, we were told, lay critically ill in a special clinic and wanted desperately to speak to him 'before it was too late'. The patient was Stefan Kurowski, the former President of the Polish Supreme Court. He was in the last stages of tuberculosis, and the Polish government had sent him to Rome in the vain hope that some newly discovered treatment might prolong his life. Isaac knew Kurowski's name: before the war he had gained tremendous respect as a brilliant lawyer specializing in the defence of members of the illegal Communist Party. What Isaac did not remember was that in 1918–19 Kurowski had been one of the founding members of the Communist Party, and that in the 1930s he had been very deeply engaged in clandestine political work. By that time, however, Isaac had already been expelled from the CP, and never, before the short and dramatic encounter in the Rome clinic, did he have a chance to meet Kurowski personally. During the years of Nazi occupation

Kurowski went 'underground' and earned his living as a manual labourer. After the Warsaw rising of 1944 Kurowski was imprisoned by the Germans. Only the end of hostilities brought him freedom. By that time, however, both his lungs were affected by tuberculosis and only an intensive treatment slowed down the progress of the disease. In 1945 he represented the Polish government at the Nuremberg trial; later he became the first Prosecutor General of the People's Republic of Poland, and in 1950 the President of the Supreme Court. Very soon, however, Kurowski demonstratively resigned from his post. He also announced that he would return to his old job of defending political prisoners and volunteered to act as Gomulka's counsel of defence in the quite likely event of a trial *à la* Rajk and Kostov. This was a gesture of extraordinary courage. How was it that he was allowed to resign and that no punishment was inflicted on him for what must have looked like a challenge of the former Attorney General to the Stalinist perverters of justice? I do not know the answer. Maybe he owed his immunity to the disease which was draining his life away.

Shortly after the 1956 upheaval Kurowski returned to the Supreme Court as its President and 'became the first to fight for the restoration . . . of the violated principles of legality'.[1] By this time, however, his health was completely ruined. With dwindling strength he urged a more open and honest break with the evils of Stalinism than that which Gomulka was prepared to carry out.

What was it that the dying man wanted to tell Isaac 'before it was too late'? Isaac returned from his visit to the clinic deeply shaken. He had spent two and a half hours by Kurowski's bedside. 'I did not ask any questions, I only let him talk, because I felt that he would not be at peace until he told me all that was on his mind.' With an oxygen bottle in his mouth, Kurowski spoke with difficulty, but curiously enough, the effort seemed to make him stronger and not weaker, as if a great burden was being lifted from his wasted body.

'For years and years I wanted to let you know,' he told Isaac, 'that when we expelled you from the Communist Party you were right and we were wrong; and we paid a terrible price for this. And we are still paying it.' Kurowski spoke of the communist movement of the late 1930s, of the nightmare of the purges in Russia, of Stalinism in the late 1940s and early 1950s, of the cynicism and lack of ideology in the Polish ruling circles. 'All these years,' he said, 'I have been conducting an inner dialogue with you. Gradually I took over as mine all

1. From the obituary of Kurowski published in the Polish journal *Polityka*.

your arguments, all those warnings, accusations, and invective which you threw in our faces and for which we excluded you from the party and went on abusing and slandering you.'

But there was something more Kurowski wanted to tell Isaac, something which had happened only a few months before. This is what he said: In 1948 a group of about ten people were caught and sentenced to ten years' imprisonment for illegally reproducing and distributing Isaac's pamphlet on the Moscow Trial written in August 1936. After the 'Polish October', in 1956, the case came up to the Supreme Court for revision. The verdict was quashed and the prisoners released. Subsequently, the President of the Supreme Court gave his ruling: 'In the People's Republic of Poland the writings of Isaac Deutscher cannot be considered as harmful or subversive.'

'This was my last act as President of the Supreme Court; it was also the one of which I am most proud', said the dying man to Isaac. The story was given me in accents in which deep emotion, grief, weariness, and a sense of achievement were all mixed together.

Ever since that evening in Rome we tried to find the pamphlet. But it was only in the spring of 1968 that Douglas Gill, a young student from Oxford doing research in the Library of Warsaw University, came upon it. 'To be read only in the Reading Room, not to be removed', proclaimed the library stamp; the Librarian gave it to him shrugging his shoulders: 'I don't know what you need this for.' Although his time was short and his knowledge of the Polish language rather rudimentary, Douglas Gill copied out the whole pamphlet and brought it to me in London. It is published here for the first time since its appearance in Poland in 1936.

22 June 1941, is also translated from the Polish. In fact it was the first essay Isaac wrote in his native language after leaving Poland in 1939. It appeared in February 1942, under the pseudonym Ignacy Niemczycki, in the Polish literary weekly *Wiadomosci Polskie*, published in London by a group of Polish refugees of various political tendencies, most of whom supported the Sikorski government-in-exile.

The Nazi invasion of the Soviet Union sent a tremor through the colony of Polish exiles. Their traditional hostility towards the Russians had understandably increased after the debacle of 1939, when they had once again seen their country dismembered by its age-old foes. The sight of Germany and Russia locked in combat provoked a whole range of ambivalent feelings: among many there was a sneaking admiration for the might of the German army, mingled with the suspicion that perhaps more could have been saved by opting for 'the other side'. But there was also hope that Poland might rise again after the two giants had bled each other to death. Thus, by marching into Poland in league with the Nazis in search of security in future struggles, Stalin had trampled under foot all the national sentiments of the Poles. These sentiments now rebounded with a vengeance and weakened Soviet defences. It was indeed in a charged political atmosphere that Isaac's call to rally to the defence of the Soviet Union was read.

✻   ✻   ✻

The essays placed in the second section of the book are addressed directly to the Western audience.

The Ex-Communist's Conscience, a review of *The God that Failed*, was first read at a semi-private gathering of academics at Adams House in Harvard, in the highly charged atmosphere of the Hiss trial, at the height of McCarthyism, in winter 1950. Isaac was precluded from speaking publicly under the terms of his American visa. Among his audience there were quite a few disillusioned former adherents of the Left who listened in respectful, but uncomfortable and hostile silence. They were not much different from our contemporary ex-Trotskyists, ex-Maoists or ex-Castroists, who make of their own disenchantment with a person or an event the pretext for abandoning the cause they once embraced. Because their 'May Days' did not come up to *their* expectations, they are resentful; embarrassed by their former ideal, they now pour scorn on it to the delight of all those against whom they once rebelled.

The critique of Orwell's *1984*, written in December 1954, also places the book in the context of the first Cold War, in which — whatever the intentions of the author — it became 'an ideological superweapon' of the West in its convulsive fear of communism. No other assessment of the novel, so widely discussed and exploited in its eponymous year, has preserved its relevance in the period of the Second Cold War.

Vietnam in Perspective dates from 1965. Isaac was the only non-American invited by the Inter-University Committee to speak at a massive National Teach-in in Washington which demonstrated the growing abhorrence of American policy in Vietnam. Paradoxically enough, this time he had little difficulty in obtaining a visa. And it was a unique kind of visa: the stamp on his passport proclaimed that it had been issued for the express purpose of 'speaking at the National Teach-in against the War'. At the beginning of one of his speeches, Isaac remarked that the Soviet government would not have granted him the freedom to address a mass audience in Moscow, even if he were there to praise Soviet policy. The State Department was more generous. But 'what is the value of freedom if one does not make full use of it?', he exclaimed, and launched into a devastating indictment of the Cold War, of the War in Vietnam and of the whole political philosophy of the United States.

The Tragedy of the Polish Communist Party dates from 1957, when K.S. Karol asked Isaac for a brief outline of the history of Communism in Poland. It might be worth recalling that shortly after the dramatic Twentieth Congress of the Communist Party of the Soviet Union, in February 1956, a communiqué from Moscow announced the 'rehabilitation of the Polish Party and its leaders', who, it was stated, had fallen victim to 'provocations and slanders' during the period of the 'cult of personality'. This short announcement, hardly noticed in the West, was in fact a strange epilogue to one of the greatest tragedies of Communism, in which a whole party had been annihilated. In 1938 the Comintern announced the dissolution of the Polish Party under the pretext that it was corroded by 'Trotskyist and Pilsudskist influences' and had become merely an agency of fascism and the Polish political police. Yet all the members of the Central Committee, threatened by the very same police, escaped from Poland to seek refuge in Moscow. On Stalin's orders they were imprisoned and executed as traitors. Among them were Adolf Warski (Warszawski), the founder of the party and friend of Rosa Luxemburg; Lenski (Leszczynski), a veteran of the October Revolution and a former member of the Executive of the Comintern; Wera Kostrzewa (Koszutska), a most militant woman revolutionary. At the time not much was known about the fate of the victims: Stalin did not bother to stage even a mock trial and at the height of the terror his dealings with the 'fraternal party' were enveloped in murky silence. In Poland the remnants of the illegal party, persecuted by the police, led a precarious existence.

Isaac, himself a former member of the party — he was expelled in 1932 for 'exaggerating the danger of Nazism' and 'sowing panic' in Communist ranks — traced the circumstances of its wholesale destruction. Referring to the interview in a letter to Karol, he wrote that he was fully aware that 'the views expressed here must . . .provoke opposition'. 'I do not pretend,' he continued, 'that what I have to say is a revelation of infallible truth. I would be quite satisfied if my work were to bring new elements into a discussion about the history of the Polish Party and if it helped to a more thorough understanding of its tragic fate.' This wish was fulfilled in a rather unusual manner. The interview, which was recorded, was translated from Polish into French and appeared in *Les Temps Modernes* in March 1958. Soon afterwards the editors of the Warsaw *Polityka*, the official organ of Gomulka's party, planned to reproduce it, but had to abandon the idea after protracted negotiations with the censors. Then the more esoteric theoretical quarterly *Zeszyty Teoretyczno-polityczne* intended to publish it, but did not succeed either. The problem 'to publish or not to publish' came before the Polish Politbureau. There was no clear majority either for or against, so a compromise was reached: it was decided not to publish the text, but to duplicate it and distribute it among party cells. Nicknamed 'Isaac Deutscher's secret speech', it soon became the subject of passionate debate. By 1980–81 the 'secret speech' was largely forgotten, and if it was known to a handful of people of the younger generation, it was in its French, German or English version.

While in 1958 Deutscher's 'Tragedy of the Polish Communist Party' was discussed at the Politbureau and then circulated in a duplicated form, as if it were the rulers' own 'Samizdat', 22 years later the essay was, so to say, *non grata* either with the ruling party or with the opposition. Both sides had their particular reasons for consigning it to oblivion.

There was, of course, great pressure from the intelligentsia for the publication of literature which hitherto, through the fiat of the government, was on the index. Among the books which the opposition wanted to see openly published were those of Gombrowicz, Milosz and Kolakowski. (Solzhenitsyn, in a clandestine edition, sold well in the forecourt of Warsaw University.)

It is true that Polish society is intensely interested in its own past, but it is not eager to learn about the past which it does not consider its own, while the ruling party has no wish to learn about the past which it is still determined to disown. Neither *raison d'état* nor *raison d'opposition* should prevent the independent Left in the West from learning about the tragedy of the Polish Communist Party.

*　　*　　*

Dialogue with Heinrich Brandler is, in a way, introduced by Isaac himself in a lengthy note which he made after their first meeting in xxviii

London. In 1948–49 Brandler was a frequent guest in our home. We used to meet him at the British Museum, bring him back to a hastily prepared supper and talk late into the night. Brandler was a charming and warm-hearted personality, a man of great simplicity and great erudition, though he was not a theoretician. He read in many languages and his interests went far beyond history and politics. The topics of our conversations at the kitchen table ranged widely from the most 'fundamental' issues to lighthearted comment on everyday occurrences, private and public. There was a cordial bond of mutual respect, admiration and affection between the two men: Isaac felt an affinity with the old revolutionary fighter who belonged to the epoch of which he, Isaac, was a historian; Brandler was confident that the story which was part of his life would be well told. He saw Isaac as 'a new Mehring', and that was the highest praise in the estimation of both men.

After Brandler's return to Germany in 1949, they carried on a correspondence in which personal matters, political affairs, memories of the past and contemporary events were discussed in a free and easy manner. In one of his letters Isaac mentioned that he had gone to Oslo to investigate the details of Trotsky's stay in Norway. He had interviewed a number of personalities who had been, in one way or another, involved in that chapter of Trotsky's life. The most valuable material was provided by Trygve Lie who, as Minister of Justice, played a crucial role in expelling Trotsky from Norway. 'I have spent many hours with Trygve Lie,' wrote Isaac, 'and have recorded the conversation which may one day make humorous reading. I also obtained the Notes which Moscow and Oslo exchanged about Trotsky, and other important and interesting material. Alas, only a small part of it can be utilized in my book.' The record of this 'humorous' conversation, published here for the first time, throws a revealing light on the Norwegian politician who in the crucial post-war years occupied the exalted post of the first General Secretary of the United Nations.

*　*　*

The last three contributions to this volume differ in some respect from the others. They are somewhat more 'didactic' and even more explicitly Marxist. They date from 1965–66 and are clearly addressed to the younger generation brought into politics on the unprecedented wave of protest against the armed intervention in Vietnam, against the obsessive clichés of anti-communism and the stultifying Cold

War propaganda. The new generation, said Isaac, was entering the political stage 'without guilty conscience and paralysing misgivings' because it 'has not been degraded by Stalinism, shell-shocked by de-Stalinization or intimidated by McCarthyism'.

The great wave of protest receded; the great opposition foundered. But it proved to be a prologue to a fresh ferment of ideas, to the outburst of a new youthful revolt which found its expression in the exhilarating *événements* — the May Days of 1968 in Paris, Berlin and Rome. More momentous was the 'Prague Spring', cut short by the Soviet invasion of August 1968. On the morrow of the invasion *Pravda*, in a solemn editorial trying to justify the action of the Warsaw Pact countries, listed all the transgressions of which the Czechoslovaks were guilty: among others they had had the temerity to 'open the columns of their newspapers to the writings of such an inveterate enemy of Marxism as Isaac Deutscher'.

Isaac Deutscher did not live to acknowledge this indictment — or should one say, this accolade.

*   *   *

I would like to thank the editorial team of *Verso* for their help, and quite especially Perry Anderson for decisiveness in the face of my unending hesitations as to the content and format of this volume; and Patrick Camiller for his patient work in scrutinizing and adjusting my contribution to it. Fred Halliday, who had edited Isaac Deutscher's *Russia, China, and the West*, made many valuable suggestions and gave me the benefit of his knowledge and experience. Frederic Samson tried, sometimes successfully, to keep up my self-confidence throughout my work of preparing the volume for publication.

Tamara Deutscher, May 1984

Part One
The USSR

1
The Moscow Trial

I

On 22 August the Moscow 'Court' sentenced Zinoviev, Kamenev and others to death. On the night of 23–24 August the sentence was carried out. The intervention of the Socialist and Trade Union Internationals in defence of the accused proved ineffective. Sixteen defendants were shot. But with this the course of events did not come to an end. Another group of old leaders of the Bolshevik Party came under suspicion of having taken part in a terrorist plot and of collaborating with the Gestapo. Bukharin, Rykov, Pyatakov, Radek, Serebryakov, Sokolnikov, Uglanov, and Tomsky became involved in the charges. The Soviet press announced mass arrests among the oppositionists and all those suspected of the slightest contact with them. The trial of Zinoviev and comrades will therefore inescapably be followed — sooner or later — by a new series of 'trials'. Stalin's bloody struggle with his opponents or untrustworthy acolytes is still in progress. The great historical drama has not ended yet. But the August trial in itself has already become a crucial date in the history of the Russian revolution and of the international labour movement.

Stalin's Moscow trial has finally put to death the old Bolshevik party, liquidating its political programme and its ideological tradition. Those whom the GPU has placed in the dock as 'terrorists' and 'Gestapo agents' had been the living embodiment of Marxism and Bolshevism in Russia. During a whole historical epoch they were, in the eyes of the international proletariat, the standard-bearers of socialism.

The main defendant of this 'trial', though absent, was Trotsky, the President of the Executive of the first Soviet in 1905, and in 1917 the leader of October, the organizer of the Red Army, for many years the Commissar for War, one of the main founders of the Comintern, the author of the main programmatic manifestoes and resolutions of the first four congresses of the Communist International — a true leader and hero of the revolution. It was against him that were aimed all the accusations and 'depositions' trumped up at the August trial.

Zinoviev was for years, especially during the world war, the closest disciple and collaborator of Lenin. He was one of the foremost Bolshevik agitators. After the revolution he led the so-called Northern Commune, that is the Leningrad Soviet. He was the head of the Comintern from its foundation in 1919 till 1925.

Kamenev, also one of the foremost propagandists and writers of the Bolshevik movement, was already the head of the Bolshevik faction in the Fourth Tsarist Duma. Next to Zinoviev the closest disciple of Lenin, he led the Moscow Soviet. Until 1926 he was a member of the government as vice-premier, leader of the Supreme Council of Defence and Labour, the Commissar of Industry and Trade, and so on.

Other defendants, like Smirnov (Commissar for Posts), Yevdokimov, Ter–Vaganyan, all belonged to the leading cadre of Bolshevism, as revolutionary fighters during the civil war and then as builders of socialism in peacetime.

There was always a deep difference between the Trotsky and the Zinoviev–Kamenev line. Trotsky pursued an inexorable criticism of Stalinist policies from a Marxist viewpoint, rejecting any ideological compromise with the post-revolutionary bureaucracy. The Zinoviev–Kamenev group entered in 1923 into a struggle against 'Trotskyism' and then, in 1925, passed over to the opposition against Stalin and formed a political bloc with Trotsky. Within this bloc Zinoviev and Kamenev always adopted a conciliatory attitude towards Stalin. After the expulsion of the opposition from the party and the deportation of the leaders, they capitulated before the Stalinist faction. From then on their political activity was one long chain of denunciations of their own views, of self-abasement and degradation. Their 'confessions' at the trial constituted the last link in that chain. With the Stalinist bureaucracy Zinoviev and Kamenev were united by many caste interests and ideological prejudices, and most of all by a common tradition of the struggle against 'Trotskyism'. What separated them from Stalinism was their revolutionary, internationalist tradition of Bolshevism. By sentencing Zinoviev and Kamenev, Stalin sent to death not his declared opponents, but his vacillating allies. This all the more strikingly underlines the real political sense of the trial: the Soviet bureaucracy has pitilessly cut those slight threads which still connected it with the ideology of October.

After the assassination of Zinoviev, Kamenev and other comrades,

Stalin is now preparing a new attack on the leading cadre of the old Bolsheviks. The revolution stands arraigned. Bukharin, member of the Politbureau till 1929, was one of the most eminent theoreticians of the Russian Party and the Comintern. From 1925 to 1928 he was its actual head. As a leader of the right wing he fought together with Stalin against 'Trotskyism' and was the main ideologue of that fight, providing the theoretical arguments against the Left Opposition. In the days of the trial, Bukharin still figured as editor-in-chief of the government paper *Izvestia*. Next to Bukharin as the main spokesmen of the Right Opposition, stood Rykov and Tomsky, both old Bolsheviks, Politbureau members until 1929. Since the revolution, with a few short intervals, Rykov has until now been a member of the Soviet government. After Lenin's death, he occupied Lenin's post for five years as president of the Council of People's Commissars. At the time of the trial he was still the Commissar of Posts and Telegraphs. Tomsky, who saved his honour by his tragic suicide, was the head of the Central Council of Trade Unions. He was, among the Bolsheviks, the most outstanding organizer and leader of the labour movement. Others under suspicion or accusation are also former members of the Left Opposition who, after repeated recantations, were released from prisons and places of exile and nominated to high governmental posts. Eminent economist Sokolnikov was in recent years the Soviet Ambassador in London. Barely a few weeks ago he was still the People's Commissar for Forestry. Pyatakov, highly valued by Lenin who in his will mentioned him as the most remarkable among the young Bolsheviks, till the last days occupied the responsible position of Vice-Commissar for Heavy Industry. Serebryakov, a self-taught worker, was the Secretary of the Party Central Committee, the main 'politruk' of the Red Army during the civil war and a member of the Council of People's Commissars. And Radek — the disciple of Rosa Luxemburg, before the war one of the main leaders of the SDKPiL and of the Left of the German Social Democracy, one of the founders of the Comintern, former oppositionist — was until the last moment a lieutenant of Stalinist diplomacy with special responsibilities and a leading publicist of the Soviet press.

All these people tragically contributed to the strengthening of Stalin's autocracy. They did not flinch from the most servile acts: they confessed to all the likely and unlikely sins, they praised to the sky 'the infallible leader', they defiled their own past and faithfully served the Stalinist bureaucracy. Their misfortune was that their names had once been symbols of the struggle for socialism; and this the Stalinist bureaucracy cannot forgive. It is not satisfied with the fight against 'Trotskyism', which most fully stands for the old ideology of the Russian revolution; it is not satisfied with the fight against its real Marxist opponents. Now it destroys, morally and physically, even its recent allies and disperses its own shadows. The only true crime of these shadows is that once they were the living creative forces of the revolution.

The August trial was an act of bloody vengeance of the political reaction against the revolution, a revenge of the thermidorian bureaucracy on the old party of the October Revolution.

II

The political bureau of the Bolshevik Party after the October victory consisted of Lenin, Zinoviev, Kamenev, Rykov, Tomsky and Stalin. Now Stalin indicts all of them as terrorists and agents of the German political police. All of them except, of course, Lenin, who died before Stalin had time to brand him as a 'Trotskyist' and a 'Gestapo agent'. This fact alone should suffice to demolish the whole criminal accusation. Is it at all possible that all the founders and leaders of the Soviet state suddenly became terrorists, agents of German fascism, the most determined enemies of their own state? No, this fantastic slander could only be the product of political degeneracy. No thinking person would believe it.

In Tsarist times individual terror played an important role in the political life of Russia. Narodnaya Volya and the Social Revolutionaries for decades indulged in the petty-bourgeois romanticism of individual terror. Marxists always fought against this romanticism. They maintained that Tsarist autocracy was the result of Russian class structure and that attempts on the life of individual satraps could do nothing to change the class foundation on which Tsarism was based. Individual attacks are therefore unproductive in their results and only demoralize the revolutionary movement. Only the mass struggle of the proletariat can abolish autocracy. This ABC of Marxism was systematically expounded by all schools of thought in the Russian labour movement in their polemics against the Social Revolutionaries. Trotsky, Zinoviev and Kamenev, among others, wrote innumerable pamphlets and articles along these lines. Who would now believe that these people, in their struggle against Stalin, would use the kind of weapon which they rejected even in the struggle against Nicholas the Bloody?

There is no doubt that terroristic tendencies exist in the Soviet state. The Stalinist regime, throttling every criticism in the ranks of the working class, has created a favourable soil for such tendencies. The new generations of workers, peasants, intelligentsia, are suffocating in the stale atmosphere of absolute barrack-like obedience and the idolatrous cult of Stalin. The new generations have not gone through the school of Marxist consciousness; they know neither the theory nor the practice of the methods of mass struggle. All open political struggle under clear ideological banners has ceased in the Soviet Union since the destruction of the communist opposition. In such conditions individual terror may have some attraction as a political method among some circles of youth. It is possible that from such circles emerged Kirov's assassin. But it is quite certain that none of the old leaders — and especially none of those accused in the trial — could have had anything to do with these utopian and reactionary tendencies of terrorist romanticism. It is enough to compare the 'terrorists' named in the trial with all other types of conspirators known in history in order to realize the absurdity of the accusation. Every method of political struggle almost automatically attracts the people best suited to it: individual terror usually attracts either romantic adventurers, who would stick at nothing, or naive, fanatical dreamers. In the one and the other case the terrorist must possess at least some personal courage and political determination. He must be armed not only with a revolver and a bomb, but also with the conviction of the rightness of his cause. Otherwise he would not be able to withstand the exhausting and dangerous atmosphere of conspiracy. Can one at all imagine a terrorist who would have the courage to lie in wait to take the life of the highest dignitaries of the state and would not have the courage openly to accuse those dignitaries in the course of the trial, to explain the motives which pushed him onto the conspiratorial path, and to present to others the cause in the name of which he had acted? It is true that an individual terrorist may break down, but it is inconceivable that suddenly the whole conspiratorial organization should cover itself in mud, give up its banner and with one voice acknowledge the greatness, the nobility, the probity of those who were to be its 'victims'.

And yet this is the kind of 'conspiratorial organization' that the Moscow trial presented to the world. One after another, these peculiar 'terrorists' devoted themselves to a grim ritual of self-flagellation and to the celebration of the Mass to the glory of Stalin and his Apostles. In nearly identical words they disclosed all the 'secrets' of the alleged plot and immediately showered upon themselves the most abusive insults in the vocabulary of idolatry. The 'terrorist' organization which had been preparing an attempt on Stalin's life was at the same time the temple of the Stalinist cult. The terrorist laboratory producing the *bomb* was at the same time manufacturing the halo of glory for the alleged victim. What a monstrous absurdity!

Here are some samples of the curious language of the terrorists: 'Such was our path and such was the contemptible abyss of treason and baseness into which we have fallen' (Kamenev). 'Who would believe us, who have appeared in court as a counter-revolutionary gang of bandits and murderers, allies of fascism and the Gestapo' (Yevdokimov). 'We are a beastly gang of criminals, an agency of international fascism' [. . . name illegible]. It is impossible to go on quoting these inhuman expressions, which could be uttered by men broken and morally dead, but certainly not by plotters and terrorists.

Zinoviev, Kamenev and others have long given up all political struggle, but Trotsky has not. In innumerable articles and pamphlets Trotsky develops his political platform. He does not conceal his hostility towards the Stalinist regime and openly calls on the advanced elements of the Soviet proletariat to fight that regime. But Trotsky at the same time condemns all thoughts of individual terror as a utopian adventure with counter-revolutionary effects. 'Hypocrisy' — answer the Moscow 'judges' and their hirelings. 'Trotsky condemns individual terror in order all the easier to practise it.' But political hypocrisy, unlike the shamelessness of the GPU, has its natural limits. These limits are determined by the interest of the given political group. For those who want to act politically and to train terrorist cadres, the first indispensable condition must again be the ideological propaganda of terror, which would inculcate into their followers the sense of the rectitude of their cause. It is impossible — politically and psychologically — for any terrorist to recruit followers and prepare them for their task by an open and unambiguous condemnation of terrorism.

The most elementary political reasoning demolishes the whole Stalinist indictment. But it is demolished not only by reasoning. Particular conflicting fragments of the very 'conception' demolish the indictment also. Here is Trotsky, the sophisticated terrorist, the devilish plotter, who receives in Copenhagen the 'terrorist' Berman-Yurin. The prosecution informs us that it is the first time ever that Trotsky has met this his 'agent'. And so this sophisticated conspirator straightaway, in the course of the first conversation with a man completely unknown to him, confides in him his plans, discloses the whole strategy of the 'plot' and entrusts to him personally the carrying out of the most important part of this 'plan' — that is, the attempt on Stalin. More or less the same thing occurred with the defendants Olberg, M. Lurie, and others. But there is more: the crafty leader of the plotters writes to the defendant Dreiser [?] in the USSR a letter in which he simply orders him 'to liquidate Stalin and Voroshilov'. The 'terrorist' Olberg comes to Moscow and, having no personal documents, hides from the authorities. But — lo and behold — after a few weeks he manages to obtain a post as a lecturer in the pedagogical institute, right under the nose of the central authorities in the Moscow suburb of Gorki. This also happens to two other 'Gestapo agents' personally despatched to the USSR by Trotsky: Berman-Yurin and Fritz David. Having returned illegally to the USSR, they soon occupy leading posts in the central state publishing establishments, this time not in the provinces, but in Moscow. To understand this miracle one has to bear in mind that for the last two years the possession of a passport on the territory of the USSR has been strictly mandatory.

The 'agents' sent out by Trotsky were supplied by him with revolvers and ammunition. Yet it is clear that they could have obtained enough weapons in Russia. The indictment informs us that high-ranking officers like Schmidt, the brigade commander, and Kuznetsov, the army chief-of-staff, were also implicated in the plot. A few days after the trial the Soviet press announced the arrest of Putna, the Soviet military attaché in London. The 'plot' must have had its ramification in the higher echelons of the military establishment. Is it conceivable that a brigadier in charge of armed regiments, stores, arsenals, would not have been able to provide the conspirators with a minimum of weapons needed to effect a whole series of assassination attempts. Was it necessary that Trotsky or his son should have helped out? Members of the government — high dignitaries — are involved in the plot. But it transpires that all these highly-placed 'conspirators' have no access to Stalin and Voroshilov. It is only agents from abroad — Olberg, Fritz David — who manage to have access. How sloppily works the imagination of the *metteurs en scène* of the Moscow spectacle.

One could go on multiplying these details ad infinitum if it were not for the physical disgust which overcomes one while wading through this mass of blood and excrement piled up in the columns of the Soviet press. But let us consider one more instance. Some defendants confessed that the terrorist plot had in fact been mounted in 1927.

The official version maintains that the date has been precisely established, and it points to the year 1930 and then to 1932. One way or another, the 'plot' must have lasted at least four years, or at the most nine years. Those who took part were not grey, insignificant figures but widely known political personalities. Moreover, the authorities have not regarded them as above suspicion. All the leaders of the opposition went through the hands of the GPU: they were deported, imprisoned, their names were in the police files. How is it that the plot has been discovered only now? Where, during all these years, was the proverbial 'vigilance' of Stalin's Chekists?

It is known that the Socialist and Trade Union Internationals intervened in favour of the defendants with the Soviet government. The telegram signed by Adler, de Bruckère, Citrine and Schevenels was more than politely phrased. Concretely, it demanded that foreign lawyers should be admitted to the trial. To this Moscow answered with a flood of vulgar abuse. No wonder. The idea was unacceptable to the directors of the show. The mere presence of people who were not in the iron grip of the GPU, who would pose questions and endeavour to throw an objective light on the affair, would have shattered the whole cobweb of the indictment. This the producers could not allow to happen. One should recall that in 1922, during the trial of the Social Revolutionaries who made an attempt on the life of Lenin and Uritsky, the Soviet government admitted as counsels of defence a group of foreign socialist leaders like Vandervelde, Rosenfeld and others. Then, in 1922, the judges had nothing to hide from the public opinion of the world proletariat. They were trying people who really had made an assassination attempt. Now, in 1936, the judges are ordered to made a murderous attempt on the old leaders of the revolution. And therein lies the secret of the reply which — now in the period of the Popular-Frontist idyll — the Moscow authorities gave to the Socialist International.

'But the defendants themselves rejected counsels of defence' — is the perfidious argument which *Pravda* uses in dismissing Adler's and de Brouckère's proposals. Quite unnecessarily, the paper still tries to save scraps of appearance. It could give a much simpler answer: but the defendants themselves asked for the death sentence; how then could anyone dare to say that their lives should be spared? Such an argument would have been much clearer and more in line with the spirit of the Moscow trial.

‡   ‡   ‡

The cunning game which the GPU has played with the defendants is clear for all to see. The defendants were given their parts to play, and they recited them from memory. For acting well they were to be rewarded with mercy. Zinoviev and Kamenev were faced with the alternative: either no confessions, in which case you will face tortures 'on the quiet' and a shot in the head in the cellars of the GPU; or else you play your part in the miserable comedy in open court and you remain alive. The wretched capitulators chose the second course. They hoped that, at the price of the most terrible moral suicide, they would save their physical existence. For the nth time they again believed in Stalin's promises, and for the last time they were deceived. They played their role down to the last detail. They even demanded their own execution, because that was part of the script. They deluded themselves that the whole spectacle would be nothing more than a masquerade. After the performance they took off the masks and asked for the promised 'reward': they handed to their executioners a plea for clemency. But the logic of the trial did not allow the executioners to keep their promise. The GPU could not leave alive the witnesses who had been forced to be partners in crime. They had to be destroyed. All traces of the greatest falsification in history had to be wiped out. Zinoviev, Kamenev, Smirnov and comrades were incapable of dying in dignity. They had not enough strength to repulse Stalin's terrorist blackmail. In their behaviour lies the main mystery of the trial. This mystery can be understood only against the historical background of the factional struggles in the old party. For nearly ten years Stalin had subjected Zinoviev, Kamenev and their comrades to a murderous training in capitulation. By hitting them with the full force of the machinery of terror and blackmail, then appealing to their common tradition and old friendship, and then again playing on the note of 'common concern' about the 'interests' of the Soviet state, he extorted from them one 'self-criticism' and act of contrition after another. Each 'self-criticism' ever more pitilessly deprived the former heroes of every vestige of dignity. Every capitulation pushed the capitulators deeper into the pit of degradation and abasement. For ten years the Stalinist engine for destroying revolutionaries had to work full steam, until the victims were 'ready' for the Moscow trial. It took Stalin ten years to smash Zinoviev's and Kamenev's backbones, so that their shadows could be put in the dock of the 'Moscow Court'.

In these grim days, when Yagoda's beast-like 'justice' reigns in the former revolutionary country, we should bow our head over the fresh grave of Tomsky, one of the best, most faithful sons of the working class, the self-educated worker, the foremost fighter for socialism. Tomsky had nothing to do with so-called Trotskyism. He was an ideological adversary of the Left Opposition against which he fought. But, terrified by the result of that struggle, he was too proud to follow the path of Zinoviev and Kamenev, too helpless to extricate himself from the traps set for him: he announced his political testament with a revolver shot. The tragic protest of Tomsky disturbed the bloody triumphs of the thermidorian reaction and saved the honour of the old banners of Russian socialism.[1]

III

Stalin's St Bartholomew Night closes an era in the evolution of the Soviet state. To understand the August events, one has to be aware of the social and political evolution the Soviet Union has undergone during the last years.

The Soviet state began its existence as a proletarian democracy. The whole power was, in the first period of the revolution, vested in the 'Councils of Workers', Soldiers' and Peasants' Deputies', or Soviets. Members of the Soviets were freely elected by popular vote and controlled by the masses. In the Soviets decisions were taken by majority vote. The minority had the right of criticism and discussion, on condition that in practice it carried out the resolutions of the majority. In this way the Soviets reflected the mood and the will of the working people, assuring them the freedom to influence and determine the most important matters of state. At that time the regime of internal democracy also characterized the trade unions and the Bolshevik Party. In 1920–21 the Menshevik opposition led by Martov was still active in the Soviets, and presented its own political platform at trade-union congresses. Within the ruling Bolshevik Party a plurality of views were debated. Even during the most difficult moments of the civil war the most important economic and political problems were the subject of wide discussions in which even

1. On the morrow of the verdict *Pravda* wrote: 'The most profound satisfaction evoked by the sentence is now added to the feeling of anger and indignation. "A dog's death to the dogs!" — is the enthusiastic answer millions give to the verdict of the court. Millions of working people began their working day in a spirit of joy.' For the scribes of *Pravda* it is not enough to spit on the defendants. They also have to revile the masses by imputing to them their own sadistic perversity.

Lenin remained sometimes in a minority. Nobody had dreamed of the sanctity of the leadership. Of course, a leader of Lenin's stature had enormous authority, but it was not the will of the 'infallible leader' that prevailed, but the democratically expressed wish of the majority. These methods of proletarian democracy in no way hampered the Soviet state in surviving the most difficult period of the civil war, of the blockade and famine. On the contrary, they constituted that state's main strength.

Today no trace remains of such a regime in the state and the party. In recent years the Soviet Union has been the scene of barrack-like obedience and absolute compliance with all the orders of the 'leader'. The working masses have been completely deprived of the right to criticize and discuss, or to take decisions affecting the political life of the country. In the factory, in the trade union, in the Soviet, in the party organization the worker is gagged. Any expression of dissent from the official command has for years been treated as an act of 'wrecking' and 'counterrevolution'. A powerful police apparatus assures obligatory 'enthusiasm' for every official decree. All power over the country is concentrated in the hands of a small clique of dignitaries. All power over these dignitaries is concentrated in the hands of 'The Leader', 'The Father of the Peoples', 'The Radiant Sun' — Stalin.

The political evolution of the Soviet state — from proletarian democracy to Stalinist autocracy — has its deep social reasons. On the foundations of the revolutionary state there came into being a new privileged caste — the post-revolutionary bureaucracy. This caste has been gradually usurping all possible privileges for itself, to the detriment of the proletariat. While the overwhelming majority of Soviet workers — in spite of the economic progress of the Soviet Union — still live in utter poverty, the bureaucracy manages to lead a 'carefree and happy' existence. The salaries of the highest layer of Stalinist officials sometimes reach several thousand roubles, while the wages of the majority are no more than 100, 200, or 300 roubles per month. To obtain its material privileges the bureaucracy had to establish its political absolutism. First of all, it had to free itself from control from below and from inconvenient criticism by the workers. It had to gag all opponents who expressed aspirations inimical to the new layer of parasites. The bureaucracy had to spread the legend of its own infallibility. Stalinism is the ideology of that layer, and Stalin is its representative, its prophet and its God incarnate.

Soviet absolutism is the result of a long-term process connected with various historical circumstances: with the internal class-relationship in post-revolutionary Russia (the conflict between the socialist aspirations of the proletariat and the peasantry's ideas of property, the technical industrial backwardness of the country), as well as with the international pattern of class forces (that is, with defeats of the labour movements in Europe and Asia, defeats which weakened the Soviet proletariat). A more detailed analysis of these circumstances would be out of place here.[2] To understand better the basis of the Soviet bureaucracy's power over the proletariat, one should consider the following: The bureaucracy not only administers the state apparatus, but it also administers directly the enormous productive apparatus of the Soviet Union, its factories, mines, communications network, etc. This allows it to exert an enormous pressure on the working masses dependent on it. It exploits the exceptional position which it occupies in the productive process to silence and stifle any opposition.

The bureaucracy's absolutism bases itself on the social foundations of the revolution. But it is also a thunderous negation of the ideals and traditions of the revolution. This contradiction determines the whole history of Stalinism, with its bizarre twists and turns. To maintain its own power, the bureaucracy has in its own way to preserve the foundations of the social revolution. In order to amass the privileges, to increase and widen them, it must undermine these foundations. To gain authority and to lull the vigilance of the masses, Stalinism had not only to terrorize them but also to dress itself in the garb of the October tradition. It had to introduce the cult of the past, which like all other cults consists of hollow deceitful rituals. There arose the Lenin Mausoleum; vows of faithfulness to the letter of Leninism were proclaimed so as more shamelessly to betray its spirit. But the greater the gulf between the bureaucracy and the proletariat, the more the traditions of the revolution hinder Stalinism. The cult of Leninism on which the bureaucracy has leant for so long is becoming ballast which weighs it down. In recent years these conflicting tendencies between the interests and ideology of Stalinism were contained in a 'peaceful' and 'evolutionary' form. But there comes a moment when the process acquires convulsive and violent forms. The chasm between the ruling hierarchy and the proletariat, between the Stalinist reality and the reality of October, has become so profound that the bureaucracy is forced to launch an assault not only on the living spirit but also on the wandering ghosts of the revolutionary past. The world of Red Marshals, the world of those bureau-

2. See *The Unfinished Revolution*, chapter four, Oxford 1967. Ed. note.

cratic upstarts, with breasts covered in medals, is colliding with everything which was once or still is the hope of the deceived proletariat. Such is the social background of the bloody war declared by Stalin on the whole former leadership of the Soviet state.

In this Stalin has on his side all the reactionary refuse of Soviet society. The chief prosecutor at the trial was Vyshinsky, the old Menshevik who in 1920, after the civil war, joined the Bolsheviks. The whole press campaign against the 'Gestapo agents' is conducted in *Pravda* by the same Zaslavski who, as a Menshevik in 1917, accused Trotsky and Lenin of being agents in the pay of Wilhelm II. One could say that this is a cunning revenge of Menshevism over Bolshevism, if such a concept were not an undeserved slander on genuine Mensheviks. Genuine Mensheviks in exile, like Dan and Abramowich, openly defend their political stand. Whatever one may think of their political views, one could not accuse them of dishonesty. After a lost struggle, they did not, like the Vyshinskys, the Zaslavskis and other careerists (of whom there is a multitude in the ranks of the bureaucracy) rush to the trough of the victors. No, it is not Menshevism but the flotsam and jetsam of Menshevism that has been wreaking revenge on old adversaries.

The Moscow trial is closely linked to the foreign policy of the Soviet bureaucracy. Stalinism tries to protect itself from criticism from outside. This is what *Pravda* wrote on 16 August: 'Against our land . . . [the Trotskyists] . . . are ready to march with anybody, with Whiteguardists, with German fascists, with fascists of other countries. In France the Trotskyists oppose the Popular Front and play into fascist hands. In Germany the Trotskyists are Hitler's agents. In Poland the agents of the Polish police . . . they count mainly on Polish–German intervention. Hence their close and tight union with the espionage organization, the Gestapo.'

The moment chosen for throwing this stink bomb into the ranks of the international labour movement is not accidental. On the day on which Tass announced the Moscow trial, the Paris *Humanité* published an article by Duclos the leader of the French Communist Party, under the title: 'Popular Front or Gleichschaltung?' Duclos tries to explain the new turn of the French Party, which today proclaims the necessity of moving from the united front policy to that of the Popular Front. The leadership of the PCF —instructed by Soviet diplomacy — has decided to harness the French proletariat to the chariot of French imperialism. To that end it calls for a further capitulation of the proletariat before the bourgeoisie and gives up completely any idea of class struggle. Down with the division of

16

French society into contending classes! It is not enough to fraternize with the bourgeois radicals! For fraternization with the extreme right! Any reactionary who opts for the military alliance of France and the USSR is our friend. For this friendship the French proletariat will have to pay with its head. This is the main sense of the slogan of the All French Front . . .[3]

World reaction is triumphant in the aftermath of the Moscow 'trial'. It is bent on persuading the masses that the Russian revolution has proved to be nothing but a bloody nonsense. But this triumph is premature. After the Russian revolution, just like after all the other revolutions in history, there came a period of political reaction. *Political power* passed from the hands of the working classes into the hands of the new privileged stratum. But the basic *social gains* of the revolution remained intact. The socialized means of production work — in spite of the parasitical role of the bureaucracy — not for capitalist profit but for social needs. No force would be capable of returning to the landlords the land which now belongs to the peasants. There is no doubt that the Soviet economy is making considerable progress in many fields. And this is so not thanks to the bureaucracy, but in spite of it, in spite of its blunders, corruption and adventurism. The productive forces of the USSR develop with a revolutionary vigour which has so far remained unbroken by the destructiveness of the bureaucratic system.

The triumph of reaction is therefore premature . . .[4]

Nevertheless, the social gains of the Soviet proletariat are in mortal danger. Liquidating the old revolutionary leadership, Stalin is yet, in the long term, incapable of stabilizing his autocracy. On the contrary. By disarming and atomizing the proletariat, the Stalinist bureaucracy paves the way for a social counterrevolution — that is, for its own annihilation. The methods of Stalin's assault on his opponents, so panicky and so bloody, testify to the tremendous, incalculable tensions in society.

The further destiny of the USSR does not depend, however, exclusively on the internal alignment of its class forces. Now *it depends mainly on the deeds of European workers*. A victory of socialism, if only in one of the West European countries (in France or Spain),

3. There follows a section analysing Stalin's Popular Front policies. Ed. note.
4. Owing to poor typography, the next eight lines are missing from the original text. Ed. note.

would bring back to the Russian working class its old revolutionary vigour, deal a blow to the bureaucratic absolutism and revive Soviet democracy. History still leaves socialism some time to save its burning edifice. Let us not lose faith in our old ideals . . .[5]

1 September 1936.

First published as a pamphlet by the 'Swiatlo' cooperative, price 30 groszy. The stamp of Warsaw University Library bears the date 7 October 1936. Translated by Tamara Deutscher.

5. The last few lines are illegible in the handwritten copy. Ed. note.

2
22 June 1941

Eight months have passed since the fateful date of 22 June 1941 when Hitler began his march on Russia. From that day the two most powerful armies in the world have been locked in epic combat from the Baltic to the Black Sea. Although the German Panzer divisions have in this time conquered a territory no smaller than that of Germany itself, nothing foreshadows the breakdown of the super-human heroism with which the Russian revolution fights for its life and for its banner. Bleeding profusely it finds its greatness anew. The destiny of the world now hangs in the balance across the vast spaces of the USSR. Everywhere — in occupied Europe, in the British Empire, in both Americas — people are listening with the same anxiety and hope to the sounds from the distant battlefields. This does not mean, however, that the conflicting class interests have now been replaced by a peaceful class idyll. But in the present war divergent class interests have become temporarily so interwined that a diehard English conservative, a liberal, a bourgeois democrat, a Polish socialist, a Komsomol youth from a kolkhoz — all link their hopes and fears to the struggle on the Don and the Neva.

There is no need to conceal that in this enormous historical game different sides play for *different* stakes. For English conservatism the Empire is at stake, with all its economic advantages derived from the exploitation of the colonies. Bourgeois democracy knows that the German bombers and tanks are out to destroy not only the Soviet state, but also the whole parliamentary system of democratic freedoms — the system which is the historic product of Western European capitalism. Finally, for socialists it is obvious that on the Neva, the Volga, the Don and the Azov Sea stand perhaps the last bulwarks of defence in the battle so tragically, but temporarily, lost on the Vistula, the Spree, the Danube and the Seine. It is a battle for the very existence of the workers' movement and the freedom of

European peoples — a freedom without which socialism cannot be achieved. Such is the objective logic of historical development. Only the blind or pretenders to the role of quislings fail to understand that logic. In the terse war communiqués we socialists read not only the reports about 'normal' war operations; we are also reading in them the fate of the deadly struggle between revolution and counter-revolution.

Since 22 June 1941 the Russian Revolution has once again begun to forge unbreakable links with the European labour movement. These links are proving stronger than all the opportunistic manoeuvres of Soviet diplomacy in recent years. It was not the Russian Revolution that in September 1939 shared the torn body of Poland with German fascism. In those unhappy September days Russia had not shown her true revolutionary face — no revolution in history has yet taken on the shape of a jackal scrounging the battlefield. The face which was then turned towards the despairing worker and peasant was the totalitarian mask imposed by the post-revolutionary bureaucracy. Now history is stripping off that mask and revealing the Revolution's true countenance: bleeding but dignified, suffering but fighting on. Cruelly, but justly, history is putting an end to all cynical masquerades.

What is left of those congratulatory telegrams in which the Kremlin spoke high-sounding words about 'the Russo–German friendship cemented by blood spilled in common'? How many other castles, built not so much in the air as on the wrongs done to nations, were to be 'cemented' by the wretched Kremlin architects? On the very eve of 22 June, Moscow was still trying to salvage its friendship with the arch-executioner of Europe by recognizing his occupation of Yugoslavia, Greece and Norway. The shadow of total war was already darkening the German–Soviet boundary when communiqués and denials, laboriously produced in the offices of the Narkomindel, tried to prove to an incredulous world that the giant concentration of German troops presented no danger to the Soviet Union, and that nothing had yet clouded the friendship between Berlin and Moscow. Ostriches hatched in eagles' nests were timorously burying their heads in diplomatic sands refusing to admit that a storm was imminent. But an approaching storm does not usually wait for the ostriches to trot out to confront it.

One fundamental truth about the German–Soviet war has to be understood: the heroic resistance of the Russian workers and peasants is proof of the vitality of revolutionary society. Soviet workers and peasants are defending everything which, in spite of various deformations, has remained of the revolution: an economy without capitalists and landlords. They defend what they see as their socialist fatherland — and here the accent is on the adjective no less than on the noun. They defend it not because, but *in spite of* the privileges which the new bureaucracy has usurped for itself; not because, but in spite of the totalitarian regime with its GPU, concentration camps, cult of the leader, and the terrible purges. Whoever has had an opportunity to observe Soviet reality even for a short time knows that the totalitarian regime had not strengthened but weakened the Soviet state. The huge quantity of modern weapons which the Red Army wields in battle could have been produced on a far greater scale and in better quality without the whip that lashes the backs of the Soviet workers. The sword of the revolution would be sharper today if it had been honed by a true democracy among the working masses. Solidarity with Russia does not in any way demand that this truth be concealed.

22 June 1941 also cleared up another confusion endemic in the socialist camp, which found expression in the cliché about the 'solidarity of totalitarian regimes'. Nearly two years of German–Soviet 'friendship' and the policy of annexations which culminated in the first Finno–Soviet War, seemed to confirm the slogan about the solidarity of totalitarianisms. From today's perspective, however, the motives of Soviet policy appear more clearly. That was the period in which the Soviet Union was obsessed with assuring the most advantageous strategic positions for the coming conflict with the Third Reich. At the root of Soviet expansionism there was none of those elements which characterize every genuine imperialism. There was no frantic quest for markets, for raw materials, or for profitable investment of capital. Soviet annexation policy was dictated not by the needs inherent in its socio-economic structure, but by the exigencies of the politico-strategic game. This does not mean, of course, that we should condone or justify Soviet policy. There is a limit beyond which, from a socialist viewpoint, no state should be allowed to proceed even in the struggle for its own existence. The freedom and self-determination of other nations constitutes such a limit. Moreover, it is clear that even from an utterly pragmatic standpoint, the violation of the sovereignty of neighbouring countries has proved to be of doubtful advantage to the Soviet Union.

Since 1939 Soviet diplomacy has treated the problem of defence in purely military terms, neglecting all political and national considerations. A great deal of thought has been given to bases, territories, strategic positions, while the national sentiments of the Poles, Lithuanians, Letts, Estonians, Finns and others have been treated with contempt. In the moments most critical for the survival of the Soviet Union, these aroused nationalist sentiments have rebounded with a vengeance. The defence of Leningrad, for example, was certainly not strengthened by the damaging wound inflicted on the Finnish nation allegedly for the sake of that city's defence. If Hitler's armies have appeared on Finnish soil as avengers of Finnish national pride, if the Finns could watch the bombardment of Leningrad with some *Schadenfreude*, the ground for this ironic state of affairs was prepared by the Soviet assault on Finland in December 1939.

However we evaluate the final balance-sheet of this period, one fact remains obvious: it was not a period of 'solidarity' between 'two totalitarianisms', but one of preparation for a fight to the death between them. The application of a purely political conception — totalitarianism versus democracy — is in this case utterly misleading. In the German–Soviet war the struggle is not simply between two 'totalitarianisms', but between two different ideologies based on totally different socio-economic structures. One can, of course, demonstrate very striking analogies between the two regimes, but these do not take into account the socio-economic elements which for a Marxist remain decisive. The differences can be summed up as follows: The totalitarianism of the Third Reich is designed to impose the most draconic discipline on the working masses and on the German bourgeoisie itself in preparation for the final struggle of German imperialism for domination of the world. Soviet totalitarianism, in contrast, is a product of the combined difficulties of building socialism in a backward, peasant country and of the struggle of the new bureaucratic strata for a privileged position in post-revolutionary society. The fact that the 'solidarity of totalitarianisms' has turned out to be only a short-lived truce, a prologue to their armed conflict, is certainly neither an accident nor a whim of history. Between the two 'twin-like' states there exists, in fact, a vast gulf: the German–Soviet war is the most profound class conflict of our epoch, a conflict on a gigantic scale. In spite of all the crimes committed by the USSR against European socialism, in spite of concentration camps, mass deportations and violations of human dignity in the USSR, this conflict is a *war between socialism and capitalism*.

British workers, guided by a healthy democratic and class instinct, responded to the appeal for tanks for Russia by a record increase in production, although previously during the first Finno–Soviet war they had had nothing but contempt for Soviet diplomacy.

Some socialist writers, just like some ex-communists, have attempted to apply the concept of totalitarian solidarity to the analysis of the Soviet and German economies. The German ex-communist Borkenau, in particular, reached the peak of absurdity when he tried to demonstrate the 'kinship' of the two economic structures. He based his argument on the increased *étatisme* and dictatorial military state planning which he identified with the Soviet state economy. It is obvious that such an argument is theoretically primitive in the extreme. German state economy, in spite of its expansion, constitutes only an adjunct and complement to the capitalist economy of the trusts and cartels. The controls imposed on German capitalists are dictated by the needs of the war economy, and, in the last resort, serve the interests of the German capitalist order. In the Soviet economy, on the other hand, production, with the partial exception of agriculture, is fully nationalized with no room for capitalist profit. The 'quantitative' differences in the development and extent of the state economy in Germany and Russia have decisive importance and determine fundamental, socially 'qualitative', differences. To treat the high salaries of Soviet dignitaries as 'capitalist profit' is an obfuscation which defies every category of political economy.

The problem of the Soviet Union is the contradiction between progressive relations of production tending towards socialism and its totalitarian political regime. The whole tragic development of the Soviet state has been and remains marked by this contradiction. Unless these contradictory dimensions of Soviet reality are clearly distinguished, one cannot correctly understand either the internal development of the Soviet Union or its role in world politics. Communist glorifiers point exclusively to the tendency of the Soviet economy towards socialism and present the transformation as an accomplished fact haloed with rosy legends. The victims of anti-Soviet obsessions, on the other hand, see only the black horror of the political regime and haughtily dismiss the still vital socio-economic currents of the revolution, polluted and defiled as they are. An objective socialist point of view allows us to see the two faces of the Soviet state. The reactionary element of Soviet reality found expression in the nearly two-years-long friendship with the Third Reich, in the division of 'spheres of state interests', and in the trampling on the independence of East European nations. At the same time, however, the progressive element of Soviet reality was bringing that game to an end. The Soviet Union could not *à la longue* play the role of Italy or Japan; Stalin could become neither a will-less tool nor a willing partner of the Axis, in spite of the fact that he was prepared to pay, and has paid, an inordinately high price for evading the inevitable war.

The internal contradiction between the socio-economic and political elements of the Soviet regime has also affected the situation in Eastern Poland during the period of Soviet occupation. The grim state of political affairs prevailing under the occupation has been extensively described in the Polish press and there is no need to recapitulate the facts again. Of course, the very fact of the occupation should be condemned. Even more reprehensible, however, is the way in which it has been implemented: abolition of all local self-government, the cruelty of mass deportations, the banning of independent workers' organizations, and the imposition of the whole byzantine Soviet model upon the country's cultural life. Yet simultaneously a radical social upheaval has taken place, involving the abolition of landed estates and big private capital, whose true extent and importance has been stubbornly left unrecognized. True, this was a revolution brought on the points of bayonets, a revolution achieved by barbarous means in an atmosphere of a bizarre mixture of socialism and Asiatic methods. But a revolution brought on bayonets and carried out by barbaric means is *still* a revolution; and it would be difficult to imagine that Polish socialism would now fight for the restoration of the status quo of 1939 with regard to the property relations on its eastern borders. The changes in social relations brought about by the occupation, if they were to survive the war, would stimulate further changes towards socialism. These are not belated, retrospective conjectures, but the first steps in understanding the progressive and *potentially* socialist element which has not yet disappeared from Soviet reality.

The whole complexity of the Soviet occupation of Poland brings to mind an illuminating historical analogy. Polish history, unfortunately, knows many instances of revolutionary reforms brought from outside 'on the points of bayonets'. Sometimes these were the bayonets of revolution, sometimes those of counter-revolution. Thus feudal relationships in rural Poland were brought to an end in turn by the Austrian Kaiser, the Prussian King, Napoleon, and finally the Russian Tsar. In the formation of the Polish class structure these were progressive measures, but at the same time they reflected the fatal feebleness of this class structure and, particularly, the weakness of our own bourgeois revolution. Our deformed socio-national development was the price we paid for the feebleness of our own revolution and for the debility of our own reformist movements in the past. Our Staszics and Dekerts were not Marats or Dantons, and so the occupying monarchies (or Napoleon, for whom Polish independence was, as for Stalin, merely a pawn in the political game) appeared before our peasant masses as their champions against feudal landlords, while in emigration the democratic dreamers and socialist visionaries were helplessly drafting paper projects of partial and meagre land reform. Unfortunately, history repeats itself — but, contrary to Marx's saying, what once occurred as drama, appears the second time not as farce, but as the most terrible tragedy. Today, as in the nineteenth century, the basis of this deformation remains nearly identical: anachronistic relations of ownership were destroyed from the *outside* because the forces working for their destruction from the *inside* did not possess the necessary courage and energy to cope with the task. The consequences and lessons for the future are all too obvious.

The course of the war may bring the contradiction between the USSR's reactionary political regime and its progressive economic structure to a highly explosive state. The manner in which this contradiction is resolved will determine not only the fate of the Soviet Union, but also the fate of socialism in the world for generations to come. Soviet 'totalitarianism', unlike the German, is being dealt severe blows. According to the opinion of many serious military commentators, Soviet troops entered the military campaign with powerful equipment equal or only slightly inferior to that of the German army. If they have suffered serious defeats, this has been largely due to the debility of the Soviet regime and to the general disorganization which its 'Asiatic' methods have produced. The spirit of sacrifice and the impressive heroism of the people are there for all to see, but sacrifice and equipment are often wasted by the fallibility of 'infallible' governments. Before the eyes of the Soviet people the war is dispelling the legend of the infallibility of totalitarianism, and this must push the Soviet regime on the road of profound internal transformations. The democratization of the Soviet regime would not only prove salutary for the Soviet Union itself, but would also act as a powerful impulse for the development of socialism elsewhere.

What would the alternative, a Soviet defeat, mean for us? It would, in the first instance, discredit the idea of socialism for a long, long time to come. Whether we like it or not, socialism (regardless of its shade and tendency) bears the responsibility, in the eyes of the working class, for the outcome of the Soviet experiment. This truth is unaffected by the fact that the Soviet regime is only the bastard offspring — or prodigal child — of socialism. In the historical perspective of the global contest between capitalism and socialism, the Soviet regime would, if it were defeated, remain only a tragic episode, an 'experiment' like the Paris Commune, in which the proletariat, bleeding in vain for over two decades, was finally crushed despite its heroism, as it was crushed before on the barricades of Paris. After the Paris Commune there followed a period of stagnation in the socialist movement. With the defeat of the Soviet commune we would face not only a period of stagnation, but a long ghastly night of triumphant and barbaric counter-revolution. But as the struggle in the east continues, we can still hope, as Broniewski said in his beautiful poem, that Warsaw will once again rise up on the 'reinforced concrete of socialism' — a socialism without totalitarian admixture.

Reprinted from *New Left Review* 124, November–December 1980.

3

Reflections on the Russian Problem

No events in human history have given rise to such violent controversy as have revolutions. The great disputes of the seventeenth century turned on the Cromwellian revolution. The French revolution dwarfed all other events of the eighteenth century as a centre of intellectual interest. The great ideological disputes of the nineteenth century were in a sense a post-script to the revolution of the preceding age and a prelude to the social convulsions of our own time. The Russian Revolution of 1917 has undoubtedly been the most significant event in our eventful epoch. Like the others, it has found its enthusiastic admirers; and it has aroused boundless hostility. Enthusiasts as well as enemies have vied with each other in wishful thinking and blindness to facts. And, again, the Russian revolution has — like its predecessors — outgrown and outwitted both foe and friend. The historical process has taken its own course — cutting across all the formulae of the politicians and sweeping aside almost all the calculations of the sociologists. The impetus of the drama has grown beyond the powers even of its participants and actors, many of whom have been crushed and destroyed in the process. Only history will tell who will ride the stormy wave of the Russian revolution until the nation's life flows out into the broader and quieter waters of a non-revolutionary epoch.

The controversies around every revolution have sprung from the obvious fact that a revolution destroys the old established interests, ideals, customs and habits and that it undertakes to replace them by a totally new mode of life. This alone would suffice to let loose all the passions and furies of the human mind and heart. But this is merely a commonplace. What keeps the controversy alive and feeds it during many decades is the complexity of the phenomenon, its fantastic many-sidedness which usually escapes the contemporary mind. Political formulae simplify the problems; yet if there is anything that does not lend itself to simplification, it is surely the terrific process by which the whole life of a nation is turned upside down and reduced to a chaos from which it must then painfully struggle to recover. *Grau ist alle Theorie und ewig grün ist der Lebens Baum.* [1]

Historical perspective is essential for a balanced and unbiased judgment. Until men, with their virtues and their vices, their magnificent deeds and their horrifying crimes have been relegated to history, enthusiasts will persist in their admiration for the virtues — genuine and imaginary — while critics will allow the crimes to overshadow the achievements; and this is not only because of narrow motives and prejudices, but because in the one pattern of revolution the virtues are all but fused with the vices.

Every genuine revolution is an orgy of destruction. But no revolution is genuine until it achieves something more, until it shakes a nation for a new upsurge of its creative forces. The era of the English Civil War was full of crime and horror; but some of the roots of the branches and the flowers of English progress are firm in the dirty soil of that era. The guillotine dominated the scene of Jacobin France; its shadow was the more dreadful because it fell on the fresh ruins of the Bastille. Those who fought the French Revolution had their eyes fixed on that monstrosity that grew out of the Cult of Reason. The Cult must have appeared to them as a sanguinary masquerade; and they were certainly right. Yet it was out of the dirt and horror of Jacobin France that French liberalism and French democracy grew. The highest recognition of human rights and liberties was born out of acts in which all human rights and liberties were totally obliterated. The continental sympathizers of the Jacobins outside France behaved as if they were stricken with blindness. They adhered to the great ideals — Liberté, Egalité, Fraternité — proclaimed in Paris. And — to use a modern idiom — the myth of the French Revolution possessed their minds so thoroughly that they mistook the new French tyranny for the reign of liberty. Beethoven was not repelled by the pandemonium of Robespierrre's Terror. Nor was he disillusioned by the cruelties of the Thermidor and the Consulate; it was only the Empire which eventually filled him with disgust. Others of his contemporaries continued to see their liberal dreams embodied in Napoleon's conquests and in Fouché's police-state. The *fata morgana* of the revolution was stronger than the revolution itself.

The judgment of the French historian has — in spite of all that is

1. 'Grey is all theory: ever green is the tree of life.' A shortening of the well-known lines from Goethe's *Faust* of which Lenin was particularly fond. Ed. note.

being said in Vichy-France now — come much nearer to the attitude of the believer of Jacobinism than to that of its implacable foes. And the cry: 'Back to the ideals of the French revolution' has become the battle-cry in France's present struggle for survival. The guillotine and *La Terreur* have assumed much smaller proportions in the historical perspective — they have appeared less essential than that permanent contribution to human progress which was made by revolutionary France.

The Pandora box of the Russian revolution is still open. It still releases its monsters and its fears. It would be foolish and dishonest to deny this. No motives of political expediency can be strong or convincing enough to do away with this aspect of the problem. It would be futile to portray Stalin's Russia as the realm of democracy. It would be an unpardonable stupidity to take the 'freedom-loving' phraseology of the Kremlin at its face value. The Russian version of the guillotine — the firing-squads of the GPU — has not yet disappeared.

> *The same arts that did gain*
> *A power must it maintain —*

This is as true of Russia's Protectorate as of England's.

But Russia is Janus-headed. The other face shows strain, effort, suffering and hope. The revolution has stirred and stimulated a wealth of creative forces hidden underneath the surface of Russian life. It has awakened many dormant energies which could find no outlet under the old regime. This is the fundamental fact without which no understanding of Russia's role in this war is possible. First, there is the record of material achievement: the vast centres of a new industrial civilization which have sprung up, almost overnight, on the borderlands of the Eurasian continent. The weight of Russia's new industries — developed on the Volga, in the Urals, in Siberia, in the taigas of the north and on the plains of the Far East — tells already on the battlefields; and it will tell on the scales of the peace. Here is a new factor which is playing and will play an enormous part in shaping the destinies of the world. The war has revealed its existence and its overwhelming strength which grew unnoticed and ignored in the years before the war. Here is a mass of many, many millions of forsaken human beings who have learned to read and write. The whole achievement might perhaps be dismissed as just another accumulation of lifeless matter, as one heap more of iron and steel destined to be scrapped by the contempt of history, had it not been for the tremendous upsurge of mental powers and moral energies by which it has been accompanied. Those mental and moral energies may still be — as indeed they are — unconscious of their own purpose. But they cannot be conjured out of existence. Nor can their basic soundness be denied. No collective Frankenstein would be able to raise itself to the heights of heroism and sacrifice to which the Russian people rose among the ruins of Sebastopol, Leningrad and Stalingrad. The ruthless will-power of the leaders, the weight of a prodigious military machine, the cleverness of the strategy — all these would not have sufficed to do the job. They can all be found in the armies of the Third Reich, developed to an even higher degree of efficiency and perfection. They were enough to drive forward disciplined human masses intoxicated by unparalleled victories. But they would not have sufficed to sustain and keep together a nation which had drained the cup of defeat almost to the last bitter dregs. The dynamic of post-revolutionary Russia has not been merely material. It must have been anchored in some deep ideals which live in the minds and hearts of the people. Nobody can yet say into what those ideals will ultimately crystallize or towards what purpose they are going to be directed. Russia's dynamic may be used for evil or for good. But hope still lies at the bottom of the Pandora box which has been open since October 1917.

It is a fallacy to treat a revolution *en bloc*. Every revolution goes through a series of metamorphoses. The starting-point is left far behind; and the road of history is a tortuous one. The onlooker tends to fix his eyes on the starting-point and to overlook the zig-zags that follow; and the revolution itself is entangled in its own illusions and myths. At every twist and turn of the course which carries it away from the starting-point, it looks back to its origins and repeats an oath of allegiance to them. At every stage of its evolution, the revolution reasserts its own identity. The illusion is not altogether illusion. The continuity of the revolutionary process is a fact. But continuity itself implies change and the recurrent disruption of continuity.

The starting-point of every social revolution so far has been the promise of full and unqualified equality to the oppressed and the disinherited. What followed was a painful and stormy drift away from Utopia. The oppressed and the disinherited storm the Bastilles and the Winter Palaces, and every revolution appears to them as the Doomsday in which they are the supreme judge. Their anger and their passion are the battering rams which break the old order. The *sansculottes* of the Parisian suburbs and the Red Guards of Viborg and Krasnaya Presnya performed the same function with the same zeal and the same hopes. On the morrow of their victory, the new regime proved unable to fulfil the promise. The claim to equality is the terrific liability on which the new regime is bound to default. The triumphant revolution is entangled in a tragic net from which it can get loose only by chopping off its own limbs. The more it mutilates itself in the process, the more desperately must it look for props and crutches to support its precarious 'balance'. It must also look for new stabilizing factors in the social environment of the post-revolutionary era.

Before Cromwell could firmly base his Protectorate on the merchants of London and on his major-generals, he had to silence John Lilbourne who had persistently voiced the original claims of the revolution. The stage for the Empire of Napoleon was set in the long series of 'purges' which started with Hébert, the leader of the most radical wing of Jacobinism, engulfed Danton and Robespierre and finished with Babeuf, the last epigone of the egalitarian spirit of the revolution. The repetition of the process in Russia looks almost like a plagiarism committed by history on its own previous performance. Yet there are new elements in this plagiarism.

The revolutions of the seventeenth and the eighteenth century drift away from Utopia into the haven of a bourgeois society. It is more difficult to see the port towards which the Russian revolution is sailing through the storms of war. Those social layers which managed to stabilize the life of seventeenth-century England and eighteenth-century France are absent in Russia. The bourgeoisie has been destroyed. The proletariat and the peasantry have been reduced to political silence and harnessed to the planned economy; they are not the ruling or dominant classes of contemporary Russia. The new 'élite' is still in the stage of formation; and its outlook has not yet been clearly defined.

The American sociologist Burnham has coined the phrase the 'managerial revolution'. He forecast a stage in which modern society can be dominated neither by the capitalist nor by the worker and in which the industrial manager becomes the dominant figure. As a sweeping generalization, this is too tempting to be true. Managerial society, technocracy and so on have gained much more ground in the books of some theoreticians than in real life. Yet if any nation on earth has come near the pattern of a managerial society, it is Russia. So far the only 'stabilizing' force which has emerged from the Russian upheaval has been the 'class' of administrative and industrial managers. Their role can in many repects be compared to that played by the City merchants of the Cromwellian era. It is they who have, probably not fully consciously, undertaken the task of taming the 'unruly elements of the revolution'. It is they who have put their stamp on the psychological outlook of the country, on its industrial aspirations and endeavours. It is undoubtedly their 'style of life' which has manifested itself in such unique strokes of economic strategy as the leap-frogging of whole industrial complexes and combines, with their machinery and labour, over hundreds and thousands of miles to Russia's east. The imaginative novelty of that 'economic strategy' corresponds to the 'dynamism' of a young and vigorous social force making its first ambitious appearance in the national arena.

It must not be forgotten that the several hundred thousand technicians and industrial managers who are fighting this war in Russia's mines and factories received their training only some three, five or six years ago. A few figures illustrate the magnitude of the process. Not much more than ten years ago only about twenty thousand engineers were employed in Soviet industry. The programme of industrialization called for hundreds of thousands of technicians. The 'output of industrial officers' became an inseparable part of the successive five-year plans. The number of engineers in Russia increased about thirty times during the pre-war decade. More than 160,000 young Soviet citizens graduated from technical colleges in the course of the second plan. These figures reflect the leaps and bounds by which a new social group has emerged. The new industrial manager has been given a privileged social status. His slogan is 'Away with the *uravnilovka*'[2]; his faith, machine worship, and his ideals, absolute obedience of the workers, ruthless discipline in production and one-man control in factories. The managerial phalanx, itself an offshoot of the revolutionary plebs, has brought to a close the plebeian phase of the revolution.

But the end is not yet. The structure of the Russian Protectorate has itself not taken on any final shape. In a totalitarian state which was arming itself to the teeth the officers' corps reappeared on the stage, rehabilitated and elevated to a peculiar position of social respectability. A rigid military hierarchy was reintroduced at the end of the thirties, and a distinctive *esprit de corps* has taken hold of the commanders of the Red Army. The war has added incalculable momentum to this development. Towards the close of 1942 not less than five hundred officers were promoted to generals in the course of

2. *Uravnilovka:* egalitarian wages policy.

a few weeks. The promotions to the lower ranks of colonels and majors must have been proportionately more numerous. No doubt, promotions on such a scale were dictated by the actual needs of the war. But whatever the immediate reasons, the fact itself could not fail to affect the social outlook. The new officers' corps has evoked the old Imperial military tradition which the revolution was supposed to have renounced 'once and for all'. The historian will probably describe the set of military reforms which were carried out towards the end of 1942 as a concentrated ideological counter-reform. Not only was the political commissar, the errant shadow of the civil war, banished from the army; not only were the new Orders of Suvorov and Kutuzov, the national heroes of old monarchist Russia, placed above the orders of Lenin and the Red Banner; in addition, the officers' corps was ordered to sew on epaulettes, the symbols of the old Imperial army, on the twenty-fifth anniversary of the Red Army; and the Regulations of Peter the Great were recalled to the memory of the Russian soldier as a source of inspiration and as a valid code of behaviour. *Pravda,* the official party paper, honoured the military leaders as the 'sovereigns of the people', a description as flattering as it was 'anti-constitutional'.

The revolution seems to renounce its own origins and its own programme. It seems to abdicate step by step to the new social groups which may be able to stabilize a new social hierarchy. Yet this is only half the truth. The continuity of the revolutionary process is still something more than merely an outward appearance. It is symbolized by Stalin himself, the living link between all the phases of the process. Stalin is the underground leader of the Tsarist days and the member of the Central Committee of October 1917. He carries with him his somewhat obscure legend of the civil war and the prestige of the only authorized successor to Lenin. He is at the same time the tamer of the 'old Bolshevism' of Trotsky, Zinoviev, Kamenev, Bukharin. He has paved the way for the new hierarchy of industrial managers and generals. He has bowed to and endorsed the new hierarchy by assuming, at the age of sixty-two, his first military rank — the rank of Marshal. But he has not only bowed to the new hierarchy, he also keeps it under control. It is he who creates the marshals and it is he who is potent to hurl them down from the Tarpeian rock of the revolution. In the history of revolutions only the Lord Protector was equal to Stalin in embodying the unity of the revolution throughout all its transient metamorphoses. No French Jacobin career is comparable. Stalin is Robespierre and the First Consul in one person.

The new hierarchy is very strong, but is it equally stable? It may still take much time and many a convulsion before the vortex of changes stops swallowing new and new victims. At this point all the analogies with previous revolutions fall short. The problem may briefly be put thus: Cromwell's England and Napoleon's France could bring the revolutionary process to a standstill because the merchants of the City and the French bourgeoisie grew and matured as social forces under the pre-revolutionary regimes. They possessed the social tradition and confidence which were needed for the task of stabilization. The industrial managers and the new marshals of Russia possess no such qualities. Their capacity for 'stablization' is still an unknown quantity. The Russian revolution has uprooted the old order much more radically than any of its predecessors could possibly do. It has irrevocably barred the way to any restoration, and it has not yet firmly paved the way for any new permanent solution. This has, of course, little to do with the stability of Stalin's personal rule, which may survive a number of new phases, provided Stalin's stupendous adaptability does not fail him. But the issue is much wider than the fortunes of Stalin's personal rule.

This, then, is the vicious circle. The Russian revolution is still drifting away from its starting-point, but the haven at which it could cast anchor is not yet in sight. The task of post-revolutionary stabilization has become immensely difficult and complicated in the 'century of the common man', when so many old social hierarchies lose their balance and the new ones seem to totter as soon as they are set up. Any post-revolutionary hierarchy resembles a throne established on the crater of a volcano. The degree of its stability or instability depends on whether the volcano has already disgorged the whole of its lava content or not. Here, the student of history can only put the question-mark without attempting to formulate any reply.

Reprinted from *Political Quarterly*, January–March 1944.

4

Two Revolutions

An eminent French historian once wrote: 'Consider the revolutions of the Renaissance: in them you will find all the passions, all the spirit, and all the language of the French revolution.'[1] With some reservations, one might also say that if one considers the Great French Revolution, one can find in it the passions, the spirit, and the language of the Russian Revolution. This is true to such an extent that it is absolutely necessary for the student of recent Russian history to view it every now and then through the French prism. (The student of the French Revolution, too, may gain new insights if occasionally he analyses his subject in the light of the Russian experience.) Historical analogy by itself is, of course, only one of the many angles from which he ought to approach his subject; and it may be downright misleading if he merely contents himself with assembling the points of formal resemblance between historical situations. 'History is concrete'; and this means, among other things, that every event or situation is unique, regardless of its possible similarity to other events and situations. In drawing any analogy, it is therefore important to know where the analogy ends. I hope that I shall not offend badly against this rule; and I would like to acknowledge my great debt to the eminent French historians whose works on the French Revolution have helped me to gain new insights into the Russian Revolution.

It is well known that the controversy over the 'Russian Thermidor' played in its time a great role in the struggles inside the Bolshevik Party. Trotsky placed his thesis about the Russian Thermidor in the

---

[1] The publication of a French edition of *Stalin: A Political Biography* (English edn. New York and London, Oxford University Press, 1949) has given me an opportunity to comment on one aspect of that book, the analogies between the Russian and the French revolutions. These comments, written in 1950, appear here in substantially the same form as in the introduction to the French edition of *Stalin* (Paris, Gallimard).

very centre of his denunciation of the Stalinist regime. This issue was dealt with only indirectly in my political biography of Stalin. (In my view, the Russian counterparts to the Jacobin, Thermidorian and Bonapartist phases of the revolution have in a curious way overlapped and merged in Stalinism.) A critical examination of this whole problem will be found in my forthcoming *Life of Trotsky*, where it properly belongs. For the present I will concentrate on another perspective on recent Russian history, a perspective somewhat similar to that which was drawn by Albert Sorel in relation to the French Revolution in his monumental *L'Europe et la Révolution Française*. I have in mind the reassertion of national tradition in a revolutionary society.

The Bolshevik revolution of 1917 was in intention a radical break with Russia's past, a break with her old social outlook, with her old methods of government, with her customs, habits and traditions. It was a great and stormy funeral of all the anachronisms inherited from centuries of backwardness, serfdom and tyranny. The three post-revolutionary decades, however, saw a complex and contradictory development: on the one hand, Russia's advance, with gigantic strides, in industrialization and education, and a release of national energies such as only a great revolution can produce; on the other hand, an amazing resurrection of Russia's buried past, and the revenge of that past upon the present. It is as the embodiment of this contradictory development that I wish to consider Stalin. To an almost equal degree, Stalin represents the impetus given to Russia by the revolution and the triumph of the traditions of the *ancien régime* over the original spirit of the revolution. Yet, did not Napoleon I represent a similar phenomenon? Were not the revolutionary and the *Roi Soleil* blended in his personality as much as the Leninist and Ivan the Terrible (or Peter the Great) are blended in Stalin?

Those who are interested mainly in the individual psychology of historical personalities may be outraged by this comparison. Stalin, they may object, has none of the *élan*, the *esprit*, the charm, and nothing of the originality of mind and expression with which nature so richly endowed Bonaparte. This is willingly admitted. But we are concerned here with something else, with the respective functions of the two personalities in the history of their countries; and these ought to be viewed in the light of broader, impersonal factors, of the moving forces, the motives and objectives of the two revolutions, and in the light of their different social backgrounds and national traditions. Incidentally, even the contrast between the individual characteristics of the two men fits in with and can up to a point be explained by the contrast between their national backgrounds and traditions. Napoleon, the Emperor, descended indirectly from an absolute monarchy, the chief representative of which appears, in historical idealization, as the *Roi Soleil.* The Tsar who in a sense is Stalin's political ancestor could earn, even from his apologists, no brighter epithet than *Grozny* — the Awe-inspiring. Napoleon has the clear air, bright colour, and elegance of Versailles and Fontainebleau as his background; while Stalin's figure harmonizes with the grim *ambiance* of the Kremlin. Thus, even the individual temper of the two men seems to reflect something impersonal.

Albert Sorel describes how heavily tradition weighed upon the revolution: 'Events hurled them [the members of the Convention] abruptly into power: if they had had a taste for liberty, they would have had no spare time to serve an apprenticeship in it.'[2] The leaders of the Russian Soviets had just as little spare time in which to serve an apprenticeship in liberty as had the leaders of the Convention. 'At the beginning of the revolution, the minds of men rushed towards the ideal: everything was destroyed, everything was renewed; France was recreated, so to speak, after having been annihilated . . . Disorder, anarchy, civil war ensued. Foreign war was added. The revolution was threatened, France invaded. The Republicans had to defend at one and the same time the independence of the nation, the territory of the homeland, the principles of the Revolution, the supremacy of their party, even their own lives . . . With pure reason confounded, they fell back brutally on empiricism: they turned from instinct to custom, to routine, to precedents: none was for liberty, countless numbers were for despotism. Thus all the processes of government of the *ancien régime* were seen to insinuate themselves, in the name of expedience, into the revolution. Once having regained their place, they remained there as masters. All the theoreticians' art consisted of nothing more than masking and disguising them.'[3] How admirably these words suit the fortunes of the Russian revolution as well!

Yet, while it is right to point to this reassertion of tradition, a reassertion that some may regard as natural and sound and others may view as a distortion of the revolution, it would be wrong to see in the post-revolutionary regime nothing but a prolongation of the *ancien régime.* Under the Empire, French history did not merely

---

[2] Albert Sorel, *L'Europe et la Révolution Française* (third edn. Paris 1893), Part I, p. 224.

[3] Ibid. pp. 224–5.

pick up the threads that had been violently snapped by the Convention; it wove the pattern of a new France and it worked the threads of tradition into that new pattern. The same may be said of Stalinist Russia. She may feel the revenge of the past on herself, but she does not revert to that past. The Bourbon monarchy could never have produced anything like the Napoleonic Code, that legal-philosophical mirror of a bourgeois society. Similarly, planned economy could never have come into existence within the framework of the old Russia. To make it possible, nothing less than the October Revolution was needed; and in it, in the principle and the practice of the planned economy, the October Revolution has survived and developed, despite the insinuation of 'all the processes of government of the *ancien régime*'.

In the case of the Russian revolution, it would be even more unrealistic than in that of the French to deny or overlook what is essentially new and epoch-making in its achievement. There may have been some justification for Sorel's view that if the French revolution had not taken place, the *ancien régime* would, in the course of time, have done some of the work that was accomplished only after its overthrow.[4] The point is that within the shell of France's *ancien régime* the elements of a modern bourgeois society had achieved a relatively high degree of maturity; the revolution merely broke the shell and thereby facilitated and speeded up the organic growth and development of those elements. Even so, historians like Michelet, Jaurès and others, who stressed the essentially new and creative work of the revolution, seem nearer the truth than Sorel, whose emphasis on historical continuity, so original and illuminating in many respects, appears in others to be exaggerated and essentially conservative. In the case of Russia, the limits within which the law of historical continuity operates are undoubtedly much narrower. The elements of the present collectivist society, with its planned economy — let us leave aside whether this society deserves to be called socialist or not — hardly existed under the surface of Russia's *ancien régime*. They are largely the conscious creation of the revolution and of the post-revolutionary government. As a builder of a new economy and a pioneer of new social techniques, Stalin, for all his limitations and vices — the limitations of an empiricist and the vices of a despot — is likely to leave deeper marks on history than any single French revolutionary leader. Here perhaps

---

[4] This idea was, of course, developed before Sorel by Alexis de Tocqueville in *L'Ancien Régime*.

is the point at which the difference in the very nature of the two revolutions tends to make further comparisons misleading.

Let us now try to investigate how far the analogy holds good in a different field — in the French revolution's foreign policy, in its impact on the world and the world's impact on it. Sorel, who surveyed this vast field with the greatest thoroughness and understanding, tells us: 'To come to terms with the French revolution, the old Europe abdicated its principles; to come to terms with the old Europe, the French revolution falsified its own. France had solemnly renounced conquests . . . Victory made the revolution bellicose. The war, begun for the defence of French territory, continued for the invasion of neighbouring territories. After having conquered in order to liberate, France partitioned in order to retain.'[5] Reading this, one cannot help thinking of Yalta and Potsdam, where by acquiescing in the expansion of Stalinist Russia the statesmen of the capitalist West so clearly abdicated their principles, while Stalinist Russia, by insisting on strategic frontiers and on the absorption of most of the neighbouring lands which had once been conquered by the Tsars, so flagrantly falsified her own. Is it really true that history does not repeat itself? Or that in the repetition the original drama becomes a farce? Is it not rather that in its Russian repetition the French tragedy appears magnified and intensified, projected as it is from the European to the global scale and from an epoch preceding the steam engine to the age of atomic energy?

Let us once again compare the original with the repetition: 'Not being able to destroy all the monarchies, she [the revolution] was forced to come to terms with the monarchs. She vanquished her enemies, she pursued them on their own territory, she effected magnificent conquests; but to keep them at peace, it was necessary to treat; to treat, it was necessary to negotiate, and to negotiate was to return to custom. The *ancien régime* and the revolution compromised not on principles which were irreconcilable, but on frontiers which were changeable. There existed only one idea in common on which the old Europe and Republican France could understand each other and come to an agreement: it was *raison d'état*. It ruled their treaties. The territories not having changed their places, and the ambitions of states remaining what they were, all the traditions of the old statecraft were reborn in the negotiations. These traditions accorded only too well with the designs of the revolutionaries —they placed at the service of the victorious revolution the methods of the

[5] Sorel, p. 3.

ancien régime.[6] While from the angle of the internal development of the revolution it may be said that up to a point the phases corresponding to Jacobinism, Thermidorianism, and Bonapartism have merged in Stalinism, in its foreign policy during the Second World War victorious Stalinism simply put to its service the methods of the *ancien régime.* I have described in my book how at Potsdam and Yalta Stalin's 'conduct, aspirations, methods of action, even his gestures and caprices vividly resembled the behaviour, the aspirations and gestures of Tsar Alexander I at the conclusion of the Napoleonic wars.'[7] And what was Stalin's conception of the preponderance of the Great Powers and of the division between them of spheres of influence if not that old *raison d'état,* the only idea which he held in common with Churchill and Roosevelt? That this *raison d'état* agreed, in a way, with a revolutionary design subsequent events were to reveal.

Russia, like France before her, has carried her revolution abroad. It was not, let us note, in the Jacobin and Republican period that Europe caught the revolutionary infection from France. And it was not in the heroic, Leninist period that the Bolshevik revolution spread beyond Russian frontiers. The two revolutions were carried abroad by rulers who had first tamed those revolutions at home. 'The revolution was arrested in France and in a way congealed in military despotism; but, by the very action of that despotism, it continued to propagate itself in Europe. Conquest spread it among the peoples. Although greatly degenerated, it retained enough appeal to excite them.'[8] And again: 'It was in that form that the revolution appeared to have arrested itself and fixed itself in France; it was in that form that Europe understood it and imitated it.'[9] It is in its Stalinist, and not in its Leninist and Trotskyist form that the revolution has come to a halt and has fixed itself in Russia, and it is in this form that it has spread, to the amazement of disillusioned ex-communists who have difficulty understanding how a revolution so 'greatly degenerated' has been able to retain so much appeal.[10]

Like Bonapartist France, Stalinist Russia has created a whole system of satellites. In this Stalin might find a grave warning to himself. It was the revolt of its own satellites that contributed so

[6] Sorel, pp. 544–5.

[7] *Stalin,* p. 530.

[8] Sorel, pp. 4–5.

[9] Ibid, p. 548.

[10] The reader will find a more detailed discussion of this point in *Stalin,* chapters 13 and 14.

signally to the downfall of the Bonapartist empire. Two of these satellites, Prussia and Italy, inflicted on France some of its most severe setbacks. It was an Italian patriot who wrote in 1814 the following significant words: 'It is painful for me to say it, for no one feels more than I the gratitude which we owe Napoleon; no one appreciates better than I the value of each drop of that generous French blood which watered the Italian soil and redeemed it; but I must be permitted to say it, for it is the truth: to see the French depart was an immense, an ineffable joy.' We have heard Tito uttering similar words about the Russians, and who knows how many Eastern European communists would be happy to utter them if they could? To Bonaparte, and many of his compatriots, the behaviour of Italy and Prussia looked like the height of ingratitude. So does the behaviour of Tito to Stalin. But what is it that gives rise to that 'ingratitude'?

Neither of these systems of satellites has lacked redeeming features. 'In the countries which France united with her territory or constituted in her image,' says Sorel, 'she proclaimed her principles, destroyed the feudal system, and introduced her laws. After the inevitable disorders of war and the first excesses of conquest, this revolution constituted an immense benefit to the peoples. This is why the conquests of the Republic could not be confused with the conquests of the *ancien régime*. They differed in the essential characteristic that, despite the abuse of principles and the deviations of ideas, the work of France was accomplished for the nations.'[11] Without repeating here my analysis of our contemporary counter-part to this phenomenon, I shall only say that I do not believe that the verdict of history on the Stalinist system of satellites will in this respect be more severe than it has been on the Bonapartist system.[12] However, the French system of satellites was not saved by its re-deeming features. It would be difficult to find a more brilliant and more convincing explanation of this fact than the one offered by Sorel:

The French republicans believed themselves to be cosmopolitans, but they were that only in their speeches; they felt, they thought, they acted,

[11] Sorel, p. 547.

[12] I was brought up in Poland, one of Napoleon's satellite countries, where even in my day the Napoleonic legend was so strongly alive that, as a schoolboy, I wept bitter tears over Napoleon's downfall, as nearly every Polish child did. And now I live in England, where most school children, I am sure, still rejoice over the story of the defeat of Napoleon, that villain of the English traditionalist historians.

they interpreted their universal ideas and their abstract principles in accordance with the traditions of a conquering monarchy . . . They identified humanity with their homeland, their national cause with the cause of all the nations. Consequently and entirely naturally, they confused the propagation of new doctrines with the extension of French power, the emancipation of humanity with the grandeur of the Republic, the reign of reason with that of France, the liberation of peoples with the conquest of States, the European revolution with the domination of the French revolution in Europe . . . they established subservient and subordinate republics which they held in a sort of tutelage . . . The revolution degenerated into an armed propaganda, then into conquest . . . [13]

In the same way, the Russian Stalinists think of themselves as internationalists, but they feel, think, and act with the tradition of a conquering monarchy behind them; and so they, too, confuse the emancipation of mankind with the grandeur of their republic and the reign of reason with the rule of Russia. No wonder that the reaction of the satellite peoples tends to take a familiar form: 'The peoples easily understood this language [of emancipation spoken by the revolution] . . . What they did not understand at all was that, using this language, . . . she [France] aimed at enslaving them and exploited them. They made no distinction, moreover, between her and the man who governed her; they did not investigate the phases through which the French revolution had passed, and how the Republic had transformed itself into an empire; they knew the revolution only in the form of conquest . . . and it was in that form that, even by virtue of its principles, they came to abhor it. They rose against its domination.'[14] We are not prophesying here a rising of the peoples against Stalinist domination. But there can be little doubt that the peoples of Eastern and Central Europe, who might have understood well the language of social emancipation spoken by Russia, cannot understand why they should become subordinate to Russia; that they, and others, make no distinction now between the Russian revolution and 'the man who governs her'; that they are not interested in the stages by which the Republic of the Workers' and Peasants' Councils has become transformed into something like an empire; and that they know the Russian revolution largely in the form of conquest.

Having indulged in these comparisons, I cannot but point out

[13] Sorel, pp. 541–2.
[14] Ibid. p. 5.

where and why this broad historical analogy ceases to apply. I shall not dwell on the obvious differences — in some respects important, in others irrelevant — between two revolutions, one of which was bourgeois in character and the other proletarian, at least in origin. Nor shall I expatiate on the major differences between the international scene as it looks now and as it looked a century and a half ago. But a few words ought perhaps to be said on one important development — the Chinese revolution — which has come to light only very recently.

The lightning collapse of the Kuomintang and the absolute victory of the communist armies have clearly altered the international balance of power. In the long run, the Chinese revolution must also have its repercussions inside Russia. This revolution obviously deserves to be placed in a different category from the 'revolutions from above' that took place in Eastern and Central Europe in the years 1945–48. The latter were mainly the by-products of Russia's military victory: 'Although the local Communist Parties were its immediate agents and executors, the great party of the revolution, which remained in the background, was the Red Army.'[15] In contrast to this, even though it may have drawn moral inspiration from Russia, Chinese communism can rightly claim that its revolution has been its own work and its own achievement. The very magnitude of the Chinese revolution and its intrinsic momentum have been such that it is ludicrous to consider it as anybody's puppet creation. This is not a satellite of the Russian revolution, but another great upheaval in its own right. For this phenomenon we find no parallel in the epoch of the French revolution. To its very end the French revolution stood alone. One can only think of an imaginary analogy: one may wonder what Europe would look like if, at the turn of the eighteenth and nineteenth centuries, Germany, then disunited and backward, had carried out more or less independently its own version of the French revolution. A combination of a Jacobin or Bonapartist France with a unified, Jacobin Germany might have given history a direction different from that which France alone could impart to it. Perhaps there would have been no Waterloo. Or perhaps the anti-revolutionary forces of Europe would have joined hands much earlier and more resolutely than they did against France alone.

Both Stalinists and anti-Stalinists have recently begun to foster the legend that Stalin has been the actual inspirer of the Chinese revolution. How is this to be reconciled with his role in the events in China

[15] *Stalin*, p. 554.

in 1925–27? How is this to be squared with Stalin's own statement at Potsdam that 'the Kuomintang is the only political force capable of ruling China'?[16] It may be argued that at Potsdam he was ostensibly disavowing the Chinese communists only to trick his Western allies. But this was hardly the case. The version of events which seems much nearer to the truth is that until very late in the day Stalin had a low opinion of the ability of the Communist Party to bring China under its control, and that he went so far as to attempt, even in 1948, to dissuade Mao Tse-tung from launching the series of offensives which was to bring victory to Chinese communism. A letter from Stalin to Mao to this effect was apparently read at the Conference of the Chinese Communist Party that took place shortly before the opening of the offensive; but the Conference rejected Stalin's advice.[17]

In his untimely scepticism about the Chinese revolution, Stalin appears true to character. He made a similar miscalculation in the middle 1920s, before Chiang Kai-shek started his great march to the north. In March 1926, the Russian Politbureau discussed whether it should encourage Chiang (then still Moscow's ally and honorary member of the Executive of the Comintern) in his plans for the conquest of the whole of China. Stalin insisted that Chiang be advised to content himself with the area in the south, where he was in actual control, and to seek a *modus vivendi* with Chang Tso-lin's government which still controlled the north. Chiang disregarded this advice and shortly thereafter established his control over all of China. More than two decades later, Stalin again seems to have overrated the stability of an old and decaying regime and underrated the revolutionary forces opposed to it. With much more justification than Tito, Mao Tse-tung might therefore say that not only was his regime not created by force of Russian arms, but that he secured its triumph against Moscow's explicit advice.

Whatever the truth about Stalin's role in these events, the Chinese

---

[16] For instance, see James F. Byrnes, *Speaking Frankly*, New York 1947, p. 228.

[17] In *The Times*, a special correspondent wrote on his return from Peking: '. . .there is much evidence to suggest that the Kremlin did not anticipate the sweeping victory which Chinese Communism was so soon to gain . . . As late as July 1948 the Russians neither expected nor desired an immediate Communist victory in China. In that month the Chinese Communist Party held a conference to discuss plans for the coming autumn campaign. The advice from Russia was to continue guerrilla warfare for the coming year in order to weaken America, who was expected to continue to pour arms into China in support of the Kuomintang. Russia opposed any plan to end the civil war by taking the large cities. Russian advice was rejected by this conference, the contrary policy was adopted . . .' *The Times*, 27 June 1950. Similar reports have appeared in many other papers.

44

revolution is likely to affect strongly the fortunes of Stalinism. In my book, Stalinism was shown to be primarily the product of the isolation of Russian Bolshevism in a capitalist world and of the mutual assimilation of the isolated revolution with the Russian tradition. The victory of Chinese communism marks the end of that isolation; and it does so much more decisively than did the spread of Stalinism in Eastern Europe. Thus, one major precondition for the emergence of Stalinism now belongs to the past. This should stimulate processes inside Russia, tending to overcome that strange ideology and frame of mind which formed themselves in the period of isolation. Yet we know how often in history effects do outlast causes; and for how long they do so!

While in one of its repercussions the Chinese revolution tends to deprive Stalinism of its *raison d'être*, in another it tends to strengthen and consolidate it. Stalinism has not only been the product of isolated Bolshevism; it has also reflected the ascendancy of the Oriental, semi-Asiatic and Asiatic, over the European element in Russia, and consequently in the revolution. Mao Tse-tung's victory enhances that element and imparts to it immense additional weight. How much more real must his own *Ex Oriente Lux* sound to Stalin himself now than it did in 1918, when he published it! So much indeed has the Oriental element come to predominate in the whole international communist movement that the struggle between communism and anti-communism is more and more becoming identified, not only geographically, with the antagonism between East and West. The fact that communism is in its origin a Western idea *par excellence* and that the West exported it to Russia is almost forgotten. Having conquered the East and absorbed its climate and traditions, communism in its Stalinist form not only fails to understand the West, but itself becomes more and more incomprehensible to the West. In Russia, the Greek Orthodox and Byzantine tradition has refracted itself in the revolution. Will the Confucian tradition now similarly refract itself through Chinese communism?

The political history of Stalin is a tale not lacking in grimness and cruelty, but one ought perhaps to be cautioned against drawing from it a moral of disillusionment or despair, for the story is not yet finished. Nearly every great revolution has destroyed as many hopes as it has fulfilled; every revolution therefore has left behind it an aftermath of frustration and cynicism. As a rule, men have been able to do full justice to the whole experience only from a long perspective of time. 'What do we know, after all?' Louis Blanc once wrote in a similar context. 'In order that progress be realized, perhaps it is necessary that all evil alternatives be exhausted. The life of mankind is very long, and the number of possible solutions very limited. All revolution is useful, in this sense at least, that every revolution takes care of one dangerous alternative. Because from an unfortunate state of affairs societies sometimes tumble into a worse state, let us not hasten to conclude that progress is a chimera.'[18] Let us not hasten to do so.

[18] Louis Blanc, *Histoire de Dix Ans* (10th edn., Paris, n.d.), I, 135.

Part Two

Cold War

1

The Ex-Communist's Conscience

Ignazio Silone relates that he once said jokingly to Togliatti, the Italian Communist leader: 'The final struggle will be between the communists and the ex-communists.' There is a bitter drop of truth in the joke. In the propaganda skirmishes against the USSR and communism, the ex-communist or the ex-fellow traveller is the most active sharpshooter. With the peevishness that distinguishes him from Silone, Arthur Koestler makes a similar point: 'It's the same with all you comfortable, insular, Anglo-Saxon anti-communists. You hate our Cassandra cries and resent us as allies — but, when all is said, we ex-communists are the only people on your side who know what it's all about.'

The ex-communist is the problem child of contemporary politics. He crops up in the oddest places and corners. He buttonholes you in Berlin to tell the story of *his* 'battle of Stalingrad', fought here, in Berlin, against Stalin. You find him in de Gaulle's entourage: none other than André Malraux, the author of *Man's Estate*. In America's strangest political trial the ex-communist has, for months, pointed his finger at Alger Hiss. Another ex-communist, Ruth Fischer, denounces her brother, Gerhart Eisler, and castigates the British for not having handed him back to the United States. An ex-Trotskyite, James Burnham, flays the American businessman for his real or illusory lack of capitalist class consciousness, and sketches a programme of action for nothing less than the world-wide defeat of communism. And now six writers — Koestler, Silone, André Gide, Louis Fischer, Richard Wright and Stephen Spender — get together to expose and destroy 'the god that failed'.

The 'legion' of ex-communists does not march in close formation. It is scattered far and wide. Its members resemble one another very much, but they also differ. They have common traits and individual features. All have left an army and a camp — some as conscientious objectors, some as deserters, and others as marauders. A few stick quietly to their conscientious objections, while others vociferously claim commissions in an army which they had bitterly opposed. All wear threadbare bits and pieces of the old uniform, supplemented by the quaintest new rags. And all carry with them their common resentments and individual reminiscences.

Some joined the party at one time, others at another; the date of joining is relevant to their further experiences. Those, for instance, who joined in the 1920s went into a movement in which there was plenty of scope for revolutionary idealism. The structure of the party was still fluid; it had not yet gone into the totalitarian mould. Intellectual integrity was still valued in a communist; it had not yet been surrendered for good to Moscow's *raison d'état*. Those who joined the party in the 1930s began their experience on a much lower level. Right from the beginning they were manipulated like recruits on the party's barrack squares by the party's sergeant-majors.

This difference bears upon the quality of the ex-communist's reminiscences. Silone, who joined the party in 1921, recalls with real warmth his first contact with it; he conveys fully the intellectual excitement and moral enthusiasm with which communism pulsated in those early days. The reminiscences of Koestler and Spender, who joined in the 1930s, reveal the utter moral and intellectual sterility of the party's first impact on them. Silone and his comrades were intensely concerned with fundamental ideas before and after they became absorbed in the drudgery of day-to-day duty. In Koestler's story, his party 'assignment', right from the first moment, over-shadows all matters of personal conviction and ideal. The communist of the early drafts was a revolutionary before he became, or was expected to become, a puppet. The communist of the later drafts hardly got the chance to breathe the genuine air of revolution.

Nevertheless, the original motives for joining were similar, if not identical, in almost every case: experience of social injustice or degradation; a sense of insecurity bred by slumps and social crises; and the craving for a great ideal or purpose, or for a reliable intellectual guide through the shaky labyrinth of modern society. The newcomer felt the miseries of the old capitalist order to be unbearable; and the glowing light of the Russian revolution illumined those miseries with extraordinary sharpness.

Socialism, classless society, the withering away of the State — all seemed around the corner. Few of the newcomers had any premonition of the blood and sweat and tears to come. To himself, the intellectual convert to communism seemed a new Prometheus —

except that he would not be pinned to the rock by Zeus's wrath. 'Nothing henceforth [so Koestler now recalls his own mood in those days] can disturb the convert's inner peace and serenity — except the occasional fear of losing faith again . . .'

Our ex-communist now bitterly denounces the betrayal of his hopes. This appears to him to have had almost no precedent. Yet as he eloquently describes his early expectations and illusions, we detect a strangely familiar tone. Exactly so did the disillusioned Wordsworth and his contemporaries look back upon their first youthful enthusiasm for the French revolution:

> *Bliss was it in that dawn to be alive,*
> *But to be young was very heaven!*

The intellectual communist who breaks away emotionally from his party can claim some noble ancestry. Beethoven tore to pieces the title page of his *Eroica*, on which he had dedicated the symphony to Napoleon, as soon as he learned that the First Consul was about to ascend a throne. Wordsworth called the crowning of Napoleon 'a sad reverse for all mankind'. All over Europe the enthusiasts of the French revolution were stunned by their discovery that the Corsican liberator of the peoples and enemy of tyrants was himself a tyrant and an oppressor.

In the same way the Wordsworths of our days were shocked at the sight of Stalin fraternizing with Hitler and Ribbentrop. If no new *Eroicas* have been created in our days, at least the dedicatory pages of unwritten symphonies have been torn with great flourishes.

In *The God That Failed*, Louis Fischer tries to explain somewhat remorsefully and not quite convincingly why he adhered to the Stalin cult for so long. He analyses the variety of motives, some working slowly and some rapidly, which determine the moment at which people recover from the infatuation with Stalinism. The force of the European disillusionment with Napoleon was almost equally uneven and capricious. A great Italian poet, Ugo Foscolo, who had been Napoleon's soldier and composed an *Ode to Bonaparte the Liberator*, turned against his idol after the Peace of Campoformio — this must have stunned a 'Jacobin' from Venice as the Nazi-Soviet Pact stunned a Polish communist. But a man like Beethoven remained under the spell of Bonaparte for seven years more, until he saw the despot drop his republican mask. This was an 'eye-opener' comparable to Stalin's purge trials of the 1930s.

There can be no greater tragedy than that of a great revolution's succumbing to the mailed fist that was to defend it from its enemies.

There can be no spectacle as disgusting as that of a post-revolutionary tyranny dressed up in the banners of liberty. The ex-communist is morally as justified as was the ex-Jacobin in revealing and revolting against that spectacle.

But is it true, as Koestler claims, that 'ex-communists are the only people . . . who know what it's all about'? One may risk the assertion that the exact opposite is true: Of all people, the ex-communists know least what it is all about.

At any rate, the pedagogical pretensions of ex-communist men of letters seem grossly exaggerated. Most of them (Silone is a notable exception) have never been inside the real communist movement, in the thick of its clandestine or open organization. As a rule, they moved on the literary or journalistic fringe of the party. Their notions of communist doctrine and ideology usually spring from their own literary intuition, which is sometimes acute but often misleading.

Worse still is the ex-communist's characteristic incapacity for detachment. His emotional reaction against his former environment keeps him in its deadly grip and prevents him from understanding the drama in which he was involved or half-involved. The picture of communism and Stalinism he draws is that of a gigantic chamber of intellectual and moral horrors. Viewing it, the uninitiated are transferred from politics to pure demonology. Sometimes the artistic effect may be strong — horrors and demons do enter into many a poetic masterpiece; but it is politically unreliable and even dangerous. But this is only one of its elements; and even this, the demonic, has to be translated into terms of human motives and interests. The ex-communist does not even attempt the translation.

In a rare flash of genuine self-criticism, Koestler makes this admission:

'As a rule, our memories romanticize the past. But when one has renounced a creed or been betrayed by a friend, the opposite mechanism sets to work. In the light of that later knowledge, the original experience loses its innocence, becomes tainted and rancid in recollection. I have tried in these pages to recapture the mood in which the experiences [in the Communist Party] related were originally lived — and I know that I have failed. Irony, anger, and shame kept intruding; the passions of that time seem transformed into perversions, its inner certitude into the closed universe of the drug addict; the shadow of barbed wire lies across the condemned playground of memory. Those who were caught by the great illusion of our time, and have lived through its moral and intellectual debauch, either give themselves up to a new addiction of the opposite type, or are condemned to pay with a lifelong hangover.'

This need not be true of all ex-communists. Some may still feel that their experience has been free from the morbid overtones described by Koestler. Nevertheless, Koestler has given here a truthful and honest characterization of the type of ex-communist to which he himself belongs. But it is difficult to square this self-portrait with his other claim that the confraternity for which he speaks 'are the only people . . . who know what it's all about'. With equal right a sufferer from traumatic shock might claim that he is the only one who really understands wounds and surgery. The most that the intellectual ex-communist knows, or rather feels, is his own sickness; but he is ignorant of the nature of the external violence that has produced it, let alone the cure.

This irrational emotionalism dominates the evolution of many an ex-communist. 'The logic of opposition at all costs,' says Silone, 'has carried many ex-communists far from their starting-points, in some cases as far as fascism.' What were those starting-points? Nearly every ex-communist broke with his party in the name of communism. Nearly every one set out to defend the ideal of socialism from the abuses of a bureaucracy subservient to Moscow. Nearly every one began by throwing out the dirty water of the Russian revolution to protect the baby bathing in it.

Sooner or later these intentions are forgotten or abandoned. Having broken with a party bureaucracy in the name of communism, the heretic goes on to break with communism itself. He claims to have made the discovery that the root of the evil goes far deeper than he at first imagined, even though his digging for that 'root' may have been very lazy and very shallow. He no longer defends socialism from unscrupulous abuse; he now defends mankind from the fallacy of socialism. He no longer throws out the dirty water of the Russian revolution to protect the baby; he discovers that the baby is a monster which must be strangled. The heretic becomes a renegade.

How far he departs from his starting-point, whether, as Silone says, he becomes a fascist or not, depends on his inclinations and tastes — and stupid Stalinist heresy-hunting often drives the ex-communist to extremes. But, whatever the shades of individual attitudes, as a rule the intellectual ex-communist ceases to oppose capitalism. Often he rallies to its defence, and he brings to this job the lack of scruple, the narrow-mindedness, the disregard for truth, and the intense hatred with which Stalinism has imbued him. He remains a sectarian. He is an inverted Stalinist. He continues to see the world in white and black, but now the colours are differently distributed. As a communist he saw no difference between fascists and social democrats. As an anti-communist he sees no difference between nazism and communism. Once, he accepted the party's claim to infallibility; now he believes himself to be infallible. Having once been caught by the 'greatest illusion', he is now obsessed by the greatest disillusionment of our time.

His former illusion at least implied a positive ideal. His disillusionment is utterly negative. His role is therefore intellectually and politically barren. In this, too, he resembles the embittered ex-Jacobin of the Napoleonic era. Wordsworth and Coleridge were fatally obsessed with the 'Jacobin danger'; their fear dimmed even their poetic genius. It was Coleridge who denounced in the House of Commons a Bill for the prevention of cruelty to animals as the 'strongest instance of legislative Jacobinism'. The ex-Jacobin became the prompter of the anti-Jacobin reaction in England. Directly or indirectly, his influence was behind the Bills Against Seditious Writings and Traitorous Correspondence, the Treasonable Practices Bill, and Seditious Meetings Bill (1792–94), the defeats of parliamentary reform, the suspension of the Habeas Corpus Act, and the postponement of the emancipation of England's religious minorities for the lifetime of a generation. Since the conflict with revolutionary France was 'not a time to make hazardous experiments', the slave trade, too, obtained a lease on life — in the name of liberty.

In quite the same way our ex-communist, for the best of reasons, does the most vicious things. He advances bravely in the front rank of every witch-hunt. His blind hatred of his former ideal is leaven to contemporary conservatism. Not rarely he denounces even the mildest brand of the 'welfare State' as 'legislative Bolshevism'. He contributes heavily to the moral climate in which a modern counterpart to the English anti-Jacobin reaction is hatched.

His grotesque performance reflects the impasse in which he finds himself. The impasse is not merely his — it is part of a blind alley in which an entire generation leads an incoherent and absent-minded life.

The historical parallel drawn here extends to the wider background of two epochs. The world is split between Stalinism and an anti-Stalinist alliance in much the same way as it was split between Napoleonic France and the Holy Alliance. It is a split between a 'degenerated' revolution exploited by a despot and a grouping of predominantly, although not exclusively, conservative interests. In terms of practical politics the choice seems to be now, as it was then, confined to these alternatives. Yet the rights and the wrongs of this controversy are so hopelessly confused that whichever the choice, and whatever its practical motives, it is almost certain to be wrong in the long run and in the broadest historical sense.

An honest and critically minded man could reconcile himself to Napoleon as little as he can now to Stalin. But despite Napoleon's violence and frauds, the message of the French revolution survived to echo powerfully throughout the nineteenth century. The Holy Alliance freed Europe from Napoleon's oppression; and for a moment its victory was hailed by most Europeans. Yet what Castlereach and Metternich and Alexander I had to offer to 'liberated' Europe was merely the preservation of an old, decomposing order. Thus the abuses and the aggressiveness of an empire bred by the revolution gave a new lease on life to European feudalism. This was the ex-Jacobin's most unexpected triumph. But the price he paid for it was that presently he himself, and his anti-Jacobin cause, looked like vicious, ridiculous anachronisms. In the year of Napoleon's defeat, Shelley wrote to Wordsworth:

> *In honoured poverty thy voice did weave*
> *Songs consecrate to truth and liberty —*
> *Deserting these, thou leavest me to grieve,*
> *Thus having been, that thou shouldst cease to be.*

If our ex-communist had any historical sense, he would ponder this lesson.

Some of the ex-Jacobin prompters of the anti-Jacobin reaction had as few scruples about their *volte-face* as have the Burnhams and the Ruth Fischers of our days. Others were remorseful, and pleaded patriotic sentiment, or a philosophy of the lesser evil, or both, to explain why they had sided with old dynasties against an upstart emperor. If they did not deny the vices of the Courts and the governments they had once denounced, they claimed that those governments were more liberal than Napoleon. This was certainly true of Pitt's government, even though in the long run the social and political influence of Napoleonic France on European civilization was more permanent and fruitful than that of Pitt's England, not to speak of Metternich's Austria or Alexander's Russia. 'O grief that Earth's best hopes rest all in thee!' — this was the sigh of resignation with which Wordsworth reconciled himself to Pitt's England. 'Far, far more abject is thy enemy' was his formula of reconciliation.

'Far, far more abject is thy enemy' might have been the text for *The*

God That Failed, and for the philosophy of the lesser evil expounded in its pages. The ardour with which the writers of this book defend the West against Russia and communism is sometimes chilled by uncertainty or residual ideological inhibition. The uncertainty appears between the lines of their confessions, or in curious asides.

Silone, for instance, still describes the pre-Mussolini Italy, against which, as a communist, he had rebelled, as 'pseudo-democratic'. He hardly believes that post-Mussolini Italy is any better, but he sees its Stalinist enemy to be 'far, far more abject'. More than the other co-authors of this book, Silone is surely aware of the price that Europeans of his generation have already paid for the acceptance of lesser-evil philosophies. Louis Fischer advocates the 'double rejection' of communism and capitalism, but his rejection of the latter sounds like a feeble face-saving formula; and his newly found cult of Gandhiism impresses one as merely an awkward escapism. But it is Koestler who, occasionally, in the midst of all his affectation and anti-communist frenzy, reveals a few curious mental reservations: '. . . if we survey history [he says] and compare the lofty aims, in the name of which revolutions were started, and the sorry end to which they came, we see again and again how a *polluted civilization pollutes its own revolutionary offspring*' (my italics). Has Koestler thought out the implications of his own words, or is he merely throwing out a *bon mot*? If the 'revolutionary offspring', communism, has really been 'polluted' by the civilization against which it has rebelled, then no matter how repulsive the offspring may be, the source of the evil is not in it but in that civilization. And this will be so regardless of how zealously Koestler himself may act as the advocate of the 'defenders' of civilization *à la* Chambers.

Even more startling is another thought — or is this perhaps also only a *bon mot*? — with which Koestler unexpectedly ends his confession:

'I served the Communist Party for seven years — the same length of time as Jacob tended Laban's sheep to win Rachel his daughter. When the time was up, the bride was led into his dark tent; only the next morning did he discover that his ardours had been spent not on the lovely Rachel but on the ugly Leah.

'I wonder whether he ever recovered from the shock of having slept with an illusion. I wonder whether afterwards he believed that he had ever believed in it. I wonder whether the happy end of the legend will be repeated; for at the price of another seven years of labour, Jacob was given Rachel too, and the illusion became flesh.

'And the seven years seemed unto him but a few days, for the love he had for her.'

One might think that Jacob-Koestler reflects uneasily whether he has not too hastily ceased tending Laban-Stalin's sheep, instead of waiting patiently till his 'illusion became flesh'.

The words are not meant to blame, let alone to castigate, anybody. Their purpose, let this be repeated, is to throw into relief a confusion of ideas, from which the ex-communist intellectual is not the only sufferer.

In one of his recent articles, Koestler vented his irritation at those good old liberals who were shocked by the excess of anti-communist zeal in the former communist, and viewed him with the disgust with which ordinary people look at 'a defrocked priest taking out a girl to a dance'.

Well, the good old liberals may be right, after all: this peculiar type of anti-communist may appear to them like a defrocked priest 'taking out', not just a girl, but a harlot. The ex-communist's utter confusion of intellect and emotion makes him ill-suited for any political activity. He is haunted by a vague sense that he has betrayed either his former ideals or the ideals of bourgeois society; like Koestler, he may even have an ambivalent notion that he has betrayed both. He then tries to suppress his sense of guilt and uncertainty, or to camouflage it by a show of extraordinary certitude and frantic aggressiveness. He insists that the world should recognize his uneasy conscience as the clearest conscience of all. He may no longer be concerned with any cause except one — self-justification. And this is the most dangerous motive for any political activity.

It seems that the only dignified attitude the intellectual ex-communist can take is to rise *au-dessus de la mêlée*. He cannot join the Stalinist camp or the anti-Stalinist Holy Alliance without doing violence to his better self. So let him stay outside any camp. Let him try to regain critical sense and intellectual detachment. Let him overcome the cheap ambition to have a finger in the political pie. Let him be at peace with his own self at least, if the price he has to pay for a phony peace with the world is self-renunciation and self-denunciation.

This is not to say that the ex-communist man of letters, or intellectual at large, should retire into the ivory tower. (His contempt for the ivory tower lingers in him from his past.) But he may withdraw into a *watch-tower* instead. To watch with detachment and alertness this heaving chaos of a world, to be on a sharp lookout for what is going to emerge from it, and to interpret it *sine ira et studio* — this is now the only honourable service the ex-communist intellectual can render to a generation in which scrupulous observation and honest interpretation have become so sadly rare. (Is it not striking how little observation and interpretation, and how much philosophizing and sermonizing, one finds in the books of the gifted pleiad of ex-communist writers?)

But can the intellectual really now be a detached observer of this world? Even if taking sides makes him identify himself with causes that, in truth, are not his, must he not take sides all the same? Well, we can recall some great 'intellectuals' who, in a similar situation in the past, refused to identify themselves with any established Cause. Their attitude seemed incomprehensible to many of their contemporaries, but history has proved their judgment to have been superior to the phobias and hatreds of their age. Three names may be mentioned here: Jefferson, Goethe and Shelley. All three, each in a different way, were confronted with the choice between the Napoleonic idea and the Holy Alliance. All three, again each in a different manner, refused to choose.

Jefferson was the staunchest friend of the French revolution in its early heroic period. He was willing to forgive even the Terror, but he turned away in disgust from Napoleon's 'military despotism'. Yet he had no truck with Bonaparte's enemies, Europe's 'hypocritical deliverers', as he called them. His detachment was not merely suited to the diplomatic interest of a young and neutral republic; it resulted naturally from his republican conviction and democratic passion.

Unlike Jefferson, Goethe lived right inside the storm centre. Napoleon's troops and Alexander's soldiers, in turn, took up quarters in his Weimar. As the Minister of his Prince, Goethe opportunistically bowed to every invader. But as a thinker and a man, he remained noncommittal and aloof. He was aware of the grandeur of the French revolution and was shocked by its horrors. He greeted the sound of French guns at Valmy as the opening of a new and better epoch, and he saw through Napoleon's follies. He acclaimed the liberation of Germany from Napoleon, and he was acutely aware of the misery of that 'liberation'. His aloofness, in these as in other matters, gained him the reputation of 'the Olympian'; and the label was not always meant to be flattering. But his Olympian appearance was due least of all to an inner indifference to the fate of his contemporaries. It veiled his drama: his incapacity and reluctance to identify himself with causes, each an inextricable tangle of right and wrong.

Finally, Shelley watched the clash of the two worlds with all the burning passion, anger and hope of which his great young soul was capable: he surely was no Olympian. Yet, not for a single moment did he accept the self-righteous claims and pretensions of any of the belligerents. Unlike the ex-Jacobins, who were older than he, he was true to the Jacobin republican idea. It was as a republican, and not as a patriot of the England of George III, that he greeted the fall of Napoleon, that 'most unambitious slave' who did 'dance and revel on the grave of Liberty'. But as a republican he knew also that 'virtue owns a more eternal foe' than Bonapartist force and fraud — 'old Custom, legal Crime and bloody Faith' embodied in the Holy Alliance.

All three — Jefferson, Goethe and Shelley — were in a sense outsiders to the great conflict of their time, and because of this they interpreted their time with more truthfulness and penetration than did the fearful — the hate-ridden partisans on either side.

What a pity and what a shame it is that most ex-communist intellectuals are inclined to follow the tradition of Wordsworth and Coleridge rather than that of Goethe and Shelley.

This essay first appeared as a review of *The God that Failed* in *The Reporter* (New York), April 1950.

2

'1984'–The Mysticism of Cruelty

Few novels written in this generation have obtained a popularity as great as that of George Orwell's *1984*. Few, if any, have made a similar impact on politics. The title of Orwell's book is a political by-word. The terms coined by him — 'Newspeak', 'Oldspeak', 'Mutability of the Past', 'Big Brother', 'Ministry of Truth', 'Thought Police', 'Crimethink', 'Doublethink', 'Hate-week', etc — have entered the political vocabulary; they occur in most newspaper articles and speeches denouncing Russia and communism. Television and the cinema have familiarized many millions of viewers on both sides of the Atlantic with the menacing face of Big Brother and the nightmare of a supposedly communist Oceania. The novel has served as a sort of ideological super-weapon in the cold war. As in no other book or document, the convulsive fear of communism, which has swept the West since the end of the Second World War, has been reflected and focused in *1984*.

The cold war has created a 'social demand' for such an ideological weapon, just as it creates the demand for physical super-weapons. But the super-weapons are genuine feats of technology; and there can be no discrepancy between the uses to which they may be put and the intention of their producers: they are meant to spread death or at least to threaten utter destruction. A book like *1984* may be used without much regard for the author's intention. Some of its features may be torn out of their context, while others, which do not suit the political purpose which the book is made to serve, are ignored or virtually suppressed. Nor need a book like *1984* be a literary masterpiece or even an important and original work to make its impact. Indeed, a work of great literary merit is usually too rich in its texture and too subtle in thought and form to lend itself to adventitious exploitation. As a rule, its symbols cannot easily be transformed into hypnotizing bogies, or its ideas turned into slogans. The words of a great poet when they enter the political vocabulary do so by a process of slow, almost imperceptible infiltration, not by a frantic incursion. The literary masterpiece influences the political mind by fertilizing and enriching it from the inside, not by stunning it.

1984 is the work of an intense and concentrated, but also fear-ridden and restricted imagination. A hostile critic has dismissed it as a 'political horror-comic'. This is not a fair description: there are in Orwell's novel certain layers of thought and feeling which raise it well above that level. But it is a fact that the symbolism of 1984 is crude; that its chief symbol, Big Brother, resembles the bogy-man of a rather inartistic nursery tale; and that Orwell's story unfolds like the plot of a science-fiction film of the cheaper variety, with mechanical horror piling up upon mechanical horror so much that, in the end, Orwell's subtler ideas, his pity for his characters, and his satire on the society of his own days (not of 1984) may fail to communicate themselves to the reader. 1984 does not seem to justify the description of Orwell as the modern Swift, a description for which *Animal Farm* provides some justification. Orwell lacks the richness and subtlety of thought and the philosophical detachment of the great satirist. His imagination is ferocious and at times penetrating, but it lacks width, suppleness and originality.

The lack of originality is illustrated by the fact that Orwell borrowed the idea of 1984, the plot, the chief characters, the symbols, and the whole climate of his story from a Russian writer who has remained almost unknown in the West. That writer is Evgenii Zamyatin, and the title of the book which served Orwell as the model is *We*. Like 1984, *We* is an 'anti-Utopia', a nightmare vision of the shape of things to come, and a Cassandra cry. Orwell's work is a thoroughly English variation on Zamyatin's theme; and it is perhaps only the thoroughness of Orwell's English approach that gives to his work the originality that it possesses.

A few words about Zamyatin may not be out of place here: there are some points of resemblance in the life stories of the two writers. Zamyatin belonged to an older generation: he was born in 1884 and died in 1937. His early writings, like some of Orwell's, were realistic descriptions of the lower middle class. In his experience the Russian revolution of 1905 played approximately the same role that the Spanish civil war played in Orwell's. He participated in the revolutionary movement, was a member of the Russian Social Democratic Party (to which Bolsheviks and Mensheviks then still belonged), and was persecuted by the Tsarist police. At the ebb of the revolution, he succumbed to a mood of 'cosmic pessimism'; and he severed his connection with the Socialist Party, a thing which Orwell, less consistent and to the end influenced by a lingering loyalty to socialism, did not do. In 1917 Zamyatin viewed the new revolution with cold and disillusioned eyes, convinced that nothing good would come out of it. After a brief imprisonment, he was allowed by the Bolshevik government to go abroad; and it was as an émigré in Paris that he wrote *We* in the early 1920s.

The assertion that Orwell borrowed the main elements of *1984* from Zamyatin is not the guess of a critic with a foible for tracing literary influences. Orwell knew Zamyatin's novel and was fascinated by it. He wrote an essay about it, which appeared in the left-socialist *Tribune,* of which Orwell was literary editor, on 4 January 1946, just after the publication of *Animal Farm* and before he began writing *1984.* The essay is remarkable not only as a conclusive piece of evidence, supplied by Orwell himself, on the origin of *1984,* but also as a commentary on the idea underlying both *We* and *1984.*

The essay begins with Orwell saying that after having for years looked in vain for Zamyatin's novel, he had at last obtained it in a French edition (under the title *Nous Autres*), and that he was surprised that it had not been published in England, although an American edition had appeared without arousing much interest. 'So far as I can judge,' Orwell went on, 'it is not a book of the first order, but it is certainly an unusual one, and it is astonishing that no English publisher has been enterprising enough to re-issue it.' (He concluded the essay with the words: 'This is a book to look out for when an English version appears.')

Orwell noticed that Aldous Huxley's *Brave New World* 'must be partly derived' from Zamyatin's novel and wondered why this had 'never been pointed out'. Zamyatin's book was, in his view, much superior and more 'relevant to our own situation' than Huxley's. It dealt 'with the rebellion of the primitive human spirit against a rationalized, mechanized, painless world'.

'Painless' is not the right adjective: the world of Zamyatin's vision is as full of horrors as is that of *1984.* Orwell himself produced in his essay a succinct catalogue of those horrors so that his essay reads now like a synopsis of *1984.* The members of the society described by Zamyatin, says Orwell, 'have so completely lost their individuality as to be known only by numbers. They live in glass houses . . .which enables the political police, known as the "Guardians", to supervise them more easily. They all wear identical uniforms, and a human being is commonly referred to either as "a number" or a "unif" (uniform).' Orwell remarks in parenthesis that Zamyatin wrote 'before television was invented'. In *1984* this technological refinement is brought in as well as the helicopters from which the police supervise the homes of the citizens of Oceania in the opening passages of the novel. The 'unifs' suggest the 'Proles'. In Zamyatin's society of the future as in *1984* love is forbidden: sexual intercourse is strictly rationed and permitted only as an unemotional act. 'The Single State is ruled over by a person known as the Benefactor', the obvious prototype of Big Brother.

'The guiding principle of the State is that happiness and freedom are incompatible . . . the Single State has restored his [man's] happiness by removing his freedom.' Orwell describes Zamyatin's chief character as 'a sort of Utopian Billy Brown of London town' who is 'constantly horrified by the atavistic impulses which seize upon him'. In Orwell's novel that Utopian Billy Brown is christened Winston Smith, and his problem is the same.

For the main *motif* of his plot Orwell is similarly indebted to the Russian writer. This is how Orwell defines it: 'In spite of education and the vigilance of the Guardians, many of the ancient human instincts are still there.' Zamyatin's chief character 'falls in love (this is a crime, of course) with a certain I-330', just as Winston Smith commits the crime of falling in love with Julia. In Zamyatin's as in Orwell's story the love affair is mixed up with the hero's participation in an 'underground resistance movement'. Zamyatin's rebels 'apart from plotting the overthrow of the State, even indulge, at the moment when their curtains are down, in such vices as smoking cigarettes and drinking alcohol'; Winston Smith and Julia indulge in drinking 'real coffee with real sugar' in their hideout over Mr Charrington's shop. In both novels the crime and the conspiracy are, of course, discovered by the Guardians or the Thought Police; and in both the hero 'is ultimately saved from the consequences of his own folly'.

The combination of 'cure' and torture by which Zamyatin's and Orwell's rebels are 'freed' from the atavistic impulses, until they begin to love Benefactor or Big Brother, are very much the same. In Zamyatin: 'The authorities announce that they have discovered the cause of the recent disorders: it is that some human beings suffer from a disease called imagination. The nerve centre responsible for imagination has now been located, and the disease can be cured by X-ray treatment. D-503 undergoes the operation, after which it is easy for him to do what he has known all along that he ought to do — that is, betray his confederates to the police.' In both novels the act of confession and the betrayal of the woman the hero loves are the curative shocks.

Orwell quotes the following scene of torture from Zamyatin:

'She looked at me, her hands clasping the arms of the chair, until her eyes were completely shut. They took her out, brought her to herself by means of an electric shock, and put her under the bell again. This operation was repeated three times, and not a word issued from her lips.'

In Orwell's scenes of torture the 'electric shocks' and the 'arms of the chair' recur quite often, but Orwell is far more intense, masochistic-sadistic, in his descriptions of cruelty and pain. For instance:

'Without any warning except a slight movement of O'Brien's hand, a wave of pain flooded his body. It was a frightening pain, because he could not see what was happening, and he had the feeling that some mortal injury was being done to him. He did not know whether the thing was really happening, or whether the effect was electrically produced; but his body had been wrenched out of shape, the joints were being slowly torn apart. Although the pain had brought the sweat out on his forehead, the worst of all was the fear that his backbone was about to snap. He set his teeth and breathed hard through his nose, trying to keep silent as long as possible.'

The list of Orwell's borrowings is far from complete; but let us now turn from the plot of the two novels to their underlying idea. Taking up the comparison between Zamyatin and Huxley, Orwell says: 'It is this intuitive grasp of the irrational side of totalitarianism — human sacrifice, cruelty as an end in itself, the worship of a Leader who is credited with divine attributes — that makes Zamyatin's book superior to Huxley's.' It is this, we may add, that made of it Orwell's model. Criticizing Huxley, Orwell writes that he could find no clear reason why the society of *Brave New World* should be so rigidly and elaborately stratified: 'The aim is not economic exploitation . . . *There is no power-hunger, no sadism, no hardness of any kind.* Those at the top have no strong motive for staying on the top, and though everyone is happy in a vacuous way, life has become so pointless that it is difficult to believe that such a society could endure.' (My italics.) In contrast, the society of Zamyatin's anti-Utopia could endure, in Orwell's view, because in it the supreme motive of action and the reason for social stratification are not economic exploitation, for which there is no need, but precisely the 'power-hunger, sadism and hardness' of those who 'stay at the top'. It is easy to recognize in this the *leitmotif of 1984*.

In Oceania technological development has reached so high a level that society could well satisfy all its material needs and establish equality in its midst. But inequality and poverty are maintained in order to keep Big Brother in power. In the past, says Orwell, dictatorship safeguarded inequality, now inequality safeguards dictatorship. But what purpose does the dictatorship itself serve? 'The party seeks power entirely for its own sake . . . Power is not a means, it is an end. One does not establish a dictatorship in order to safeguard a revolution; one makes the revolution in order to establish the dictatorship. The object of a persecution is persecution . . . The object of power is power.'

Orwell wondered whether Zamyatin did 'intend the Soviet regime to be the special target of his satire'. He was not sure of this: 'What Zamyatin seems to be aiming at is not any particular country but the implied aims of the industrial civilization . . . It is evident from *We* that he had a strong leaning towards primitivism . . . *We* is in effect a study of the Machine, the genie that man has thoughtlessly let out of its bottle and cannot put back again.' The same ambiguity of the author's aim is evident in *1984*.

Orwell's guess about Zamyatin was correct. Though Zamyatin was opposed to the Soviet regime, it was not exclusively, or even mainly, that regime which he satirized. As Orwell rightly remarked, the early Soviet Russia had few features in common with the super-mechanized State of Zamyatin's anti-Utopia. That writer's leaning towards primitivism was in line with a Russian tradition, with Slavophilism and hostility towards the bourgeois West, with the glorification of the *muzhik* and of the old patriarchal Russia, with Tolstoy and Dostoevsky. Even as an émigré, Zamyatin was disillusioned with the West in the characteristically Russian fashion. At times he seemed half-reconciled with the Soviet regime when it was already producing its Benefactor in the person of Stalin. In so far as he directed the darts of his satire against Bolshevism, he did so on the ground that Bolshevism was bent on replacing the old primitive Russia by the modern, mechanized society. Curiously enough, he set his story in the year 2600; and he seemed to say to the Bolsheviks: this is what Russia will look like if you succeed in giving to your regime the background of Western technology. In Zamyatin, as in some other Russian intellectuals disillusioned with socialism, the hankering after the primitive modes of thought and life was natural in so far as primitivism was still strongly alive in the Russian background.

In Orwell there was and there could be no such authentic nostalgia after the pre-industrial society. Primitivism had no part in his experience and background, except during his stay in Burma, when he was hardly attracted by it. But he was terrified of the uses to which technology might be put by men determined to enslave society; and so he, too, came to question and satirize 'the implied aims of industrial civilization'.

Although his satire is more recognizably aimed at Soviet Russia than Zamyatin's, Orwell saw elements of Oceania in the England of his own days as well, not to speak of the United States. Indeed, the society of *1984* embodies all that he hated and disliked in his own surroundings: the drabness and monotony of the English industrial suburb, the 'filthy and grimy and smelly' ugliness of which he tried to match in his naturalistic, repetitive and oppressive style; the food rationing and the government controls which he knew in war-time Britain; the 'rubbishy newspapers containing almost nothing except sport, crime and astrology, sensational five-cent novelettes, films oozing with sex'; and so on. Orwell knew well that newspapers of this sort did not exist in Stalinist Russia, and that the faults of the Stalinist Press were of an altogether different kind. 'Newspeak' is much less a satire on the Stalinist idiom than on Anglo-American journalistic 'cablese', which he loathed and with which, as a working journalist, he was well familiar.

It is easy to tell which features of the party of *1984* satirize the British Labour Party rather than the Soviet Communist Party. Big Brother and his followers make no attempt to indoctrinate the working class, an omission Orwell would have been the last to ascribe to Stalinism. His Proles 'vegetate': 'heavy work, petty quarrels, films, gambling . . . fill their mental horizon.' Like the rubbishy newspapers and the films oozing with sex, so gambling, the new opium of the people, does not belong to the Russian scene. The Ministry of Truth is a transparent caricature of London's war-time Ministry of Information. The monster of Orwell's vision is, like every nightmare, made up of all sorts of faces and features and shapes, familiar and unfamiliar. Orwell's talent and originality are evident in the domestic aspect of his satire. But in the vogue which *1984* has enjoyed that aspect has rarely been noticed.

1984 is a document of dark disillusionment not only with Stalinism but with every form and shade of socialism. It is a cry from the abyss of despair. What plunged Orwell into that abyss? It was without any doubt the spectacle of the Stalinist Great Purges of 1936–38, the repercussions of which he experienced in Catalonia. As a man of sensitivity and integrity, he could not react to the purges otherwise than with anger and horror. His conscience could not be soothed by the Stalinist justifications and sophisms which at the time did soothe the conscience of, for instance, Arthur Koestler, a writer of greater brilliance and sophistication but of less moral resolution. The Stalinist justifications and sophisms were both *beneath* and *above* Orwell's level of reasoning — they were beneath and above the common sense and the stubborn empiricism of Billy Brown of London town, with whom Orwell identified himself even in his most rebellious or revolutionary moments. He was outraged, shocked, and shaken in his beliefs. He had never been a member of the Communist Party. But, as an adherent of the semi-Trotskyist POUM, he had, despite all his reservations, tacitly assumed a certain community of purpose and solidarity with the Soviet regime through all its vicissitudes and transformations, which were to him somewhat obscure and exotic.

The purges and their Spanish repercussions not only destroyed that community of purpose. Not only did he see the gulf between Stalinists and anti-Stalinists opening suddenly inside embattled Republican Spain. This, the immediate effect of the purges, was overshadowed by 'the irrational side of totalitarianism — human sacrifice, cruelty as an end in itself, the worship of a Leader', and 'the colour of the sinister slave-civilizations of the ancient world' spreading over contemporary society.

Like most British socialists, Orwell had never been a Marxist. The dialectical-materialist philosophy had always been too abstruse for him. From instinct rather than consciousness he had been a staunch rationalist. The distinction between the Marxist and the rationalist is of some importance. Contrary to an opinion widespread in Anglo-Saxon countries, Marxism is not at all rationalist in its philosophy: it does not assume that human beings are, as a rule, guided by rational motives and that they can be argued into socialism by reason. Marx himself begins *Das Kapital* with the elaborate philosophical and historical inquiry into the 'fetishistic' modes of thought and behaviour rooted in 'commodity production' — that is, in man's work for, and dependence on, a market. The class struggle, as Marx describes it, is anything but a rational process. This does not prevent the rationalists of socialism describing themselves sometimes as Marxists. But the authentic Marxist may claim to be mentally better prepared than the rationalist is for the manifestations of irrationality in human affairs, even for such manifestations as Stalin's Great Purges. He may feel upset or mortified by them, but he need not feel shaken in his *Weltanschauung*, while the rationalist is lost and helpless when the irrationality of the human existence suddenly stares him in the face. If he clings to his rationalism, reality eludes him. If he pursues reality and tries to grasp it, he must part with his rationalism.

Orwell pursued reality and found himself bereft of his conscious and unconscious assumptions about life. In his thoughts he could not henceforth get away from the Purges. Directly and indirectly, they supplied the subject matter for nearly all that he wrote after his Spanish experience. This was an honourable obsession, the obsession of a mind not inclined to cheat itself comfortably and to stop grappling with an alarming moral problem. But grappling with the Purges, his mind became infected by their irrationality. He found himself incapable of explaining what was happening in terms which were familiar to him, the terms of empirical common sense. Abandoning rationalism, he increasingly viewed reality through the dark glasses of a quasi-mystical pessimism.

It has been said that *1984* is the figment of the imagination of a dying man. There is some truth in this, but not the whole truth. It was indeed with the last feverish flicker of life in him that Orwell wrote this book. Hence the extraordinary, gloomy intensity of his vision and language, and the almost physical immediacy with which he suffered the tortures which his creative imagination was inflicting on his chief character. He identified his own withering physical existence with the decayed and shrunken body of Winston Smith, to whom he imparted and in whom he invested, as it were, his own dying pangs. He projected the last spasms of his own suffering into the last pages of his last book. But the main explanation of the inner logic of Orwell's disillusionment and pessimism lies not in the writer's death agonies, but in the experience and the thought of the living man in his convulsive reaction from his defeated rationalism.

'I understand HOW: I do not understand WHY' is the refrain of *1984*. Winston Smith knows how Oceania functions and how its elaborate mechanism of tyranny works, but he does not know what is its ultimate cause and ultimate purpose. He turns for the answer to the pages of '*the* book', the mysterious classic of 'crimethink', the authorship of which is attributed to Emmanuel Goldstein, the inspirer of the conspiratorial Brotherhood. But he manages to read through only those chapters of '*the* book' which deal with the HOW. The Thought Police descends upon him just when he is about to begin reading the chapters which promise to explain WHY; and so the question remains unanswered.

This was Orwell's own predicament. He asked the Why not so much about the Oceania of his vision as about Stalinism and the Great Purges. At one point he certainly turned for the answer to

Trotsky: it was from Trotsky-Bronstein that he took the few sketchy biographical data and even the physiognomy and the Jewish name for Emmanuel Goldstein; and the fragments of 'the book', which take up so many pages in 1984, are an obvious, though not very successful, paraphrase of Trotsky's The Revolution Betrayed. Orwell was impressed by Trotsky's moral grandeur and at the same time he partly distrusted it and partly doubted its authenticity. The ambivalence of his view of Trotsky finds its counterpart in Winston Smith's attitude towards Goldstein. To the end Smith cannot find out whether Goldstein and the Brotherhood have ever existed in reality, and whether 'the book' was not concocted by the Thought Police. The barrier between Trotsky's thought and himself, a barrier which Orwell could never break down, was Marxism and dialectical materialism. He found in Trotsky the answer to How, not to Why.

But Orwell could not content himself with historical agnosticism. He was anything but a sceptic. His mental make-up was rather that of the fanatic, determined to get an answer, a quick and a plain answer, to his question. He was now tense with distrust and suspicion and on the look-out for the dark conspiracies hatched by them against the decencies of Billy Brown of London town. They were the Nazis, the Stalinists, and — Churchill and Roosevelt, and ultimately all who had any raison d'état to defend, for at heart Orwell was a simple-minded anarchist and, in his eyes, any political movement forfeited its raison d'être the moment it acquired a raison d'état. To analyse a complicated social background, to try and unravel tangles of political motives, calculations, fears and suspicions, and to discern the compulsion of circumstances behind their action was beyond him. Generalizations about social forces, social trends and historic inevitabilities made him bristle with suspicion. Yet, without some such generalizations, properly and sparingly used, no realistic answer could be given to the question which preoccupied Orwell. His gaze was fixed on the trees, or rather on a single tree, in front of him, and he was almost blind to the wood. Yet his distrust of historical generalizations led him in the end to adopt and to cling to the oldest, the most banal, the most abstract, the most metaphysical, and the most barren of all generalizations: all their conspiracies and plots and purges and diplomatic deals had one source and one source only — 'sadistic power-hunger'. Thus he made his jump from workaday, rationalistic common sense to the mysticism of cruelty which inspires 1984.[1]

[1]This opinion is based on personal reminiscences as well as on an analysis of

In *1984* man's mastery over the machine has reached so high a level that society is in a position to produce plenty for everybody and to put an end to inequality. But poverty and inequality are maintained only to satisfy the sadistic urges of Big Brother. Yet we do not even know whether Big Brother really exists — he may be only a myth. It is the collective cruelty of the party (not necessarily of its individual members, who may be intelligent and well-meaning people) that torments Oceania. Totalitarian society is ruled by a disembodied sadism. Orwell imagined that he had 'transcended' the familiar and, as he thought, increasingly irrelevant concepts of social class and class interest. But in these Marxist generalizations, the interest of a social class bears at least some specific relation to the individual interests and the social position of its members, even if the class interest does not represent a simple sum of the individual interests. In Orwell's party the whole bears no relation to the parts. The party is not a social body actuated by any interest or purpose. It is a phantom-like emanation of all that is foul in human nature. It is the metaphysical, mad and triumphant, Ghost of Evil.

Of course, Orwell intended *1984* as a warning. But the warning defeats itself because of its underlying boundless despair. Orwell saw totalitarianism as bringing history to a standstill. Big Brother is invincible: 'If you want a picture of the future, imagine a boot stamping on a human face — for ever.' He projected the spectacle of the Great Purges on to the future, and he saw it fixed there for ever,

---

Orwell's work. During the last war Orwell seemed attracted by the critical, then somewhat unusual, tenor of my commentaries on Russia which appeared in *The Economist*, *The Observer* and *Tribune*. (Later we were both *Observer* correspondents in Germany and occasionally shared a room in a Press camp.) However, it took me little time to become aware of the differences of approach behind our seeming agreement. I remember that I was taken aback by the stubbornness with which Orwell dwelt on 'conspiracies', and that his political reasoning struck me as a Freudian sublimation of persecution mania. He was, for instance, unshakably convinced that Stalin, Churchill and Roosevelt consciously plotted to divide the world, and to divide it for good, among themselves, and to subjugate it in common. (I can trace the idea of Oceania, Eastasia and Eurasia back to that time.) '*They* are all power-hungry,' he used to repeat. When once I pointed out to him that underneath the apparent solidarity of the Big Three one could discern clearly the conflict between them, already coming to the surface, Orwell was so startled and incredulous that he at once related our conversation in his column in *Tribune*, and added that he saw no sign of the approach of the conflict of which I spoke. This was by the time of the Yalta conference, or shortly thereafter, when not much foresight was needed to see what was coming. What struck me in Orwell was his lack of historical sense and of psychological insight into political life coupled with an acute, though narrow, penetration into some aspects of politics and with an incorruptible firmness of conviction.

because he was not capable of grasping the events realistically, in their complex historical context. To be sure, the events were highly 'irrational'; but he who because of this treats them irrationally is very much like the psychiatrist whose mind becomes unhinged by dwelling too closely with insanity. *1984* is in effect not so much a warning as a piercing shriek announcing the advent of the Black Millennium, the millennium of damnation.

The shriek, amplified by all the 'mass media' of our time, has frightened millions of people. But it has not helped them to see more clearly the issues with which the world is grappling; it has not advanced their understanding. It has only increased and intensified the waves of panic and hate that run through the world and obfuscate innocent minds. *1984* has taught millions to look at the conflict between East and West in terms of black and white, and it has shown them a monster bogy and a monster scapegoat for all the ills that plague mankind.

At the onset of the atomic age, the world is living in a mood of Apocalyptic horror. That is why millions of people respond so passionately to the Apocalyptic vision of a novelist. The Apocalyptic atomic and hydrogen monsters, however, have not been let loose by Big Brother. The chief predicament of contemporary society is that it has not yet succeeded in adjusting its way of life and its social and political institutions to the prodigious advance of its technological knowledge. We do not know what has been the impact of the atomic and hydrogen bombs on the thoughts of millions in the East, where anguish and fear may be hidden behind the façade of a facile (or perhaps embarrassed?) official optimism. But it would be dangerous to blind ourselves to the fact that in the West millions of people may be inclined, in their anguish and fear, to flee from their own responsibility for mankind's destiny and to vent their anger and despair on the giant Bogy-cum-Scapegoat which Orwell's *1984* has done so much to place before their eyes.

'Have you read this book? You must read it, sir. Then you will know why we must drop the atom bomb on the Bolshies!' With these words a blind, miserable news-vendor recommended to me *1984* in New York, a few weeks before Orwell's death.

Poor Orwell, could he ever have imagined that his own book would become so prominent an item in the programme of Hateweek?

3

The Cold War in Perspective

I

'Was this war necessary?' is a question often asked by historians of every major armed conflict. Historians and critics of the Cold War are also beginning to ask it. I am not proposing to do this. As a historian I am always conscious that it is far more difficult to understand what has actually happened and what is happening in human history, than to speculate on what might have happened; and as a Marxist I am not at all inclined to think that the Cold War, global in scope and now nearly two decades old, has been merely a regrettable misunderstanding or an incident which could be deleted from our affairs, an incident caused only by someone's ill-will or imbecility.

I accept the fact that from whichever angle you look at it, the Cold War has to some extent been unavoidable. It developed directly from the tensions which underlay the Grand Alliance in which the United States, Great Britain and the Soviet Union were united in the Second World War. These tensions had been deeper and graver than those that can be found in any wartime coalition. But even if this had not been so, it was not to be expected that the Grand Alliance should survive its victory over Nazi Germany. The victory was too huge for the victors to digest. The spoils were too vast; the unsettlement too frightening; and the disequilibrium of social and political power in the world too acute. Often in history, wars far milder than the world wars of our age were followed by reversals of alliances, when one power or group of powers was frightened by the new strength which their former ally or allies drew from the ruin of a common enemy. In the traditional terms of power politics and diplomacy nothing, therefore, was more natural than the reversal of alliances which our generation witnessed between 1945 and 1950.

We cannot account for the origins and the course of the Cold War merely in the conventional terms of power politics and diplomacy. Both technologically and ideologically history has transcended those terms. Mankind has reached the brink of the nuclear abyss and it has been torn internally as never before, divided over all the great issues of its social and moral existence. Who knows, if the dangers and risks confronting us had been less frightful, we might not have been able to celebrate the twentieth anniversary of the cease-fire in the relative peace in which we have celebrated it.

Not daring to wage a war and unable to make peace, governments and peoples of the world seemed to have resigned themselves to the prospect of an interminable cold war. Yet the danger is only too obvious that this cold war may terminate in total nuclear war, and even if it does not, it has already inflicted and it is still inflicting on mankind devastation and wounds which are all the more terrifying because they are, for the most part, hidden from our eyes.

For what is the cold war; what are its targets and what are its weapons? While still holding the threat of the physical holocaust over our heads, it delivers us immediately to the moral holocaust; it aims immediately at the destruction and mutilation not of our bodies but of our minds; its weapons are the myths and the legends of propaganda. It has often been said that in war truth is the first victim. In cold war, the truth without which men cannot lead any purposeful and fruitful existence is the main and the total victim as it has never been before. And the weapons designed to crush and reduce to ashes the human mind are as potent as any of the weapons designed for physical destruction. And in yet another decisive respect the cold war has already given us the foretaste of the fully-fledged nuclear war: its fall-out cannot be confined to enemy territory; it hits our own lands, it even hits *primarily* our own lands and our own people, it contaminates the moral texture, it destroys and warps the thinking processes of the popular masses in our countries, in all the countries engaged in waging the cold war.

How did this tragedy begin? It is a commonplace of contemporary historians that from the Second World War the United States and the Soviet Union emerged as the two victorious colossi, staring at each other across a power vacuum. This suggestive image, though partly true, seems to me to offer an erroneous *a priori* interpretation of the origins of the cold war and of its course. It puts the two colossi on a plane of equality, as it were, investing each of them with the same power, the same ability to harm the other, and the same threatening looks and gestures. I propose to show briefly what each of these two colossi looked like just before their clash and during it.

There could be no doubt about the power, the vigour, the health and the self-confidence of one of the colossi, the American. The

United States had during the Second World War more than doubled its wealth, its productive apparatus and its annual income. And it held the monopoly of atomic energy. It is no reflection on the bravery and ingenuity of American soldiers, airmen and sailors to say that this nation, the wealthiest of the world, had also the good fortune of having bought its victory at the cheapest price. Not a single bomb had fallen on American soil, and the loss of life the American armed forces had suffered was very small indeed. The American colossus, it might be said, returned from the battlefield with barely a scratch on his skin. And yet there was weakness in him as well, but it lay where he least suspected it — in his own bewilderment with his size and power, and, unfortunately also, in his complacency, self-righteousness and arrogance.

What a different picture the Russian colossus presented! After all his battles and triumphs, he was more than half prostrate, bleeding profusely from his many wounds. The most densely populated, the wealthiest, the most civilized parts of the Soviet Union had been laid waste. At the end of the war 25 million people in those provinces had been rendered homeless and lived in dug-outs and mud huts. The list of casualties amounted to at least 20 million dead! When the first post-war population census was carried out in the USSR in the year 1959, it showed that in all age groups older than 32 years, there were only 31 million men compared with 52 million women. Think what these figures imply. Can you imagine the dreadful shadow they cast upon every aspect of Russian life and policy? For many, many years after the war only old men, cripples, women and children could be seen on the fields of Russia tilling the land. Elderly women had to clear with their bare hands thousands upon thousands of acres of rubble from their native cities. And do you visualize what this deficit of 21 million men, what this lost Russian generation, has meant to the sexual life of the nation, to its family relationships, to its nerves and to its morale? I am speaking about this not in order to enlist here any belated sympathy with Russia's ordeal, but to demonstrate to you how misleading are some of the images and assumptions which have become customary to popular thinking in the cold war.

Yes, at the beginning of the cold war the two colossi confronted each other, but one was full-blooded, vigorous and erect, and the other prostrate and bled white. This is the incontrovertible truth of the matter. And yet shortly after the end of the war the image of the Russian colossus, of a malignant colossus, bent on world conquest and world domination, haunted the popular mind of the West and not only the popular mind. In his famous Fulton Speech of March 1946, the speech that rallied the West for the cold war, Winston Churchill declared that nobody knew 'what Soviet Russia and its communist international organization intends to do in the future, or what are the limits, if any, to their expansive and proselytizing tendencies.' He spoke of the growing Soviet challenge and peril to civilization, of the dark ages that may return, and he exclaimed: 'Beware, I say, time may be short. Do not let us take the course of letting events drift along until it is too late.'

A year later President Truman's Message to Congress, the text of the so-called Truman Doctrine, resounded with the same urgency in proclaiming America's duty to resist communist subversion all over the world and in particular in Eastern Europe. The following year President Truman, already preparing the North Atlantic Alliance, spoke again of the Soviet Union's 'designs to subjugate the free community of Europe', and the text of the Atlantic Alliance, signed on 4 April 1949, provided that 'an armed attack' against any member of the Alliance 'in Europe or North America shall be considered an attack against them all'.

Thus the leaders of the West in the most solemn and formal manner warned the whole world about the reality of the military threat from Russia. This threat served as the justification for the formal reversal of the alliances and the beginning of the rearmament of Western Germany. Yet, if one thing was or should have been clear, it was this: Russia, with 20 million of her people killed and uncounted millions crippled, for many years to come would not be able to wage any major war. She might perhaps fight for her survival if forced, but she was certainly in no physical or moral condition to undertake any large-scale invasion of foreign countries.

Any intelligent demographic expert might have calculated the number of years — fifteen or twenty — which it would take her to fill the gaps in her manpower. Let me also add that between 1945 and 1948, demobilization in Russia proceeded at such a pace that the Soviet armed forces were reduced from nearly 11½ million men to less than 3 million. Only a year after the proclamation of the Truman doctrine did Stalin decide to re-start mobilization; then, in the course of three or four years, after NATO had been formed, after the rearmament of Germany had begun, he raised the number of his men under arms to 5 million. More than once in history had major powers formed alliances and even opened hostilities with the help of false scares. But never before had responsible statesmen raised a scare as gigantic and as unreal as was the alarm about Russia's design for world conquest and world domination, the alarm amid which the North Atlantic Alliance came into being.

But what about Russia's fifth columns? The various Communist parties subservient to Stalin? I would be the last to deny or excuse that subservience for I have exposed and opposed it for nearly thirty-five years, first as a member of the Communist Party and then as a Marxist belonging to no party. But it is one of the shoddiest myths of our time that Stalin and his minions have used the Communist parties to promote world revolution. It is true that anti-communists as well as communists of the Stalinist persuasion have purveyed that myth. But this does not make it more credible. In truth Stalin more often than not used the subservient Communist parties to slow down, to hamper, and even to sabotage the growth of world revolution. He had emasculated them as organs of revolutionary struggle and turned them into the auxiliaries of his diplomacy. He had trained them to extol his tyranny, to praise his 1939 pact with Hitler, to justify his Teheran and Yalta bargains with Churchill and Roosevelt, and to damp down the revolutionary spirit of the Western European working classes in the aftermath of the Second World War.

In the first few years after the war the French Stalinists served gladly in General de Gaulle's governments as junior and meek members, disarming the fighters of the communist Resistance and urging moderation on the workers. The Italian Stalinists, led by Palmiro Togliatti, did the same. It is indeed doubtful whether the bourgeois order would have survived in Western Europe, or rather whether it would have been possible to restore it in the years 1944–45 if the Communist Parties had not, under Stalin's inspiration, so willingly and zealously assisted in this. It is possible to argue that in the post-war revolutionary turmoil, Stalin did more to save Western Europe from communism than the American Administration did or could do; that he had saved France and Italy from communism even before President Truman proclaimed his doctrine. We know now in the teeth of what obstruction from Stalin the Yugoslav communists, led by Tito, accomplished revolution in their country. And we know also how cynically Stalin abandoned the embattled Greek Communists to their fate when they were crushed by British armed intervention.

The key to Soviet policy lay not in any design for world conquest, but in the so-called gentlemen's agreement which Stalin concluded with Churchill in October 1944, on the division of spheres of influence in Europe. Under that agreement, later shame-facedly endorsed by Roosevelt, Russia was to exercise 90 per cent of influence in Eastern Europe and in the Balkans, while 10 per cent was reserved for all other powers. Britain was to exercise 90 per cent of influence in Greece, and in Yugoslavia the division was to be fifty-fifty. To this grotesque gentlemen's agreement Stalin adhered to the letter. Having granted the British a 90 per cent predominance in Greece, he denied the Greek Communists any help and he did not utter even a murmur of protest when they were being put down by force of British arms.

But, naturally enough, he felt entitled to exercise his own preponderance in his own zone of influence in a like manner. He began to impose the Stalinist regime on Eastern Europe. Yet more cunning than Churchill and working in a different social and political medium, he did not have to send out his armoured divisions to crush popular uprisings. He obtained control over his so-called sphere of influence by means of a method which was half-conquest and half-revolution. Yet, up to the moment when the Truman Doctrine was proclaimed, and even for some time later, he still acted slowly and prudently so as to avoid offending his wartime allies. In 1947 the leaders of the anti-communist parties still sat in the governments of Eastern Europe, just as the communists did in Western Europe, in more or less subordinate positions.

It was only after the communists had been ejected from the French and Italian governments — and it was an open secret in Paris and Rome how much the American ambassadors in those capitals had exerted themselves to bring this about — it was only after this that Stalin began to eject the anti-communists from the Eastern European governments and to establish the single party system. Then in June 1947 came the challenge of the Marshall Plan, under which the United States offered on certain terms its economic assistance to all nations of Europe including the USSR. This was a dangerous challenge to Stalin's government and it would probably have been dangerous to any other Soviet Government. For American economic superiority over Russia was at that time so overwhelming, that from the Soviet viewpoint the Marshall Plan represented a threat of an irresistible penetration of American capital into Russia and Eastern Europe.

Stalin not only rejected and forced all Eastern European governments to reject Marshall Aid but, with the communist *coup* in Czechoslovakia in February 1948, he carried the Stalinization of Eastern Europe to its logical conclusion. And he finally pulled down the Iron Curtain over the whole of his zone of influence so as to render impossible any penetration of American or other Western influences. It goes without saying that his actions and the ruthlessness and brutality with which he clamped down a regime of terror on the whole of Eastern Europe provided in Western eyes a justification, one might say a *post factum* justification, for the Truman Doctrine and for the other measures of cold war.

In examining any international conflict it is usually an arid intellectual exercise to ask the simple question: Who started it all? And I do not propose to dwell on this issue or to apportion the blame for unleashing the cold war. As we look back upon the scene of the late 1940s it is, I think, quite clear that two of the major assumptions underlying the Western strategy in the cold war were unreal: the assumption of a more or less imminent military threat from Russia, and the assumption that the motive of Stalin's policy was an international revolutionary aspiration, indeed, a boundless subversive ambition.

I urge you to consider this central paradox of Stalin's rule, a paradox which has had its effect upon the cold war up till now. In his dealings with his own people Stalin was a most ruthless, unscrupulous and bloody tyrant; in his dealings especially with the members of his own party and with communists at large, he was a fraudulent and treacherous manipulator; he had no compunction in extracting from the Russian workers and peasants their sweat and their blood. His great purges, his mammoth concentration camps and his insane GPU stand in history as black monuments to his infamy. Yet this treacherous tyrant was also in his way strangely strict and almost scrupulous in his dealings with bourgeois diplomatic partners. In these dealings he adhered always to the letter of his obligations with a certain Byzantine legalistic punctiliousness. From that letter he would snatch whatever advantage he could by processes of tortuous interpretation, but he rarely if ever permitted himself an open violation of the letter. Even in Stalinizing Eastern Europe he still acted within the letter of his war-time agreements with Churchill and Roosevelt as he interpreted them.

And it may be held that he acted even within the spirit of those agreements. Had not Churchill granted him 90 per cent of control over Eastern Europe and the Balkans? And were Churchill and Roosevelt really so innocent as not to know or guess the manner in which Stalin would exercise that 90 per cent control? Even if they were, was this Stalin's fault or the fault of his government? He stuck to his bargain, got the most out of it in Eastern Europe and did not allow Western European communism to raise its head in the days of its strength and influence. It is now well established that in the years 1948 and 1949 Stalin was to the last opposed to Mao Tse-tung's plans for the seizure of power by the communist armies in the whole of China (although he was not even obliged under any of his wartime diplomatic agreements to exercise a moderating influence in China).

If the purpose of Western cold war strategy was to contain communism, then the historic irony of the situation consisted in this: that no one contained communism more effectively and no one could contain it more effectively than Stalin himself did.

We are confronted here with one of the great puzzles in contemporary history. When the leaders of the West spoke in those early phases of the cold war about the threat from Russia, were they themselves seeing visions and nightmares, or were they conjuring up dangers in which they themselves did not believe?

It is difficult to give a clear-cut answer to this question. In all probability our leaders and cold war strategists themselves partly believed in the dangers they conjured up. Nightmare and reality have mingled and are still mingling in Western cold war thinking. The Second World War, like the first, had produced a genuine revolutionary aftermath of which our possessing and ruling classes had every reason to be afraid. But they failed to understand the phenomenon which inspired them with fear. They saw the social turmoil in which much of Europe was engulfed after the collapse of the Third Reich; they saw the dissolution of the old empires in Asia and Africa; they saw the rising of countless colonial and semi-colonial peoples; yet they could not believe, or they preferred not to believe, that this revolutionary turmoil had a dynamic force of its own, that it had sprung from all past history, that it was anchored in the aspirations of the peoples themselves, and that it was not and could not be anyone's puppet creation.

The conservative mind sees in revolution, as a rule, the malignant intrigue of instigators and agitators, and never the outcome of any legitimate struggle. And so Churchill and Truman, and their associates, came to suspect or half-suspect that the great instigator and agitator behind the revolutionary ferment of the post-war years was none other than Stalin himself, their wartime ally. True, during the war Churchill had more than once expressed his appreciation of the essentially conservative quality of Stalin's statesmanship. 'I know of no government,' Churchill said in the last months of the war, 'which stands to its obligation, even in its own despite, more solidly than the Russian Soviet government. I decline absolutely to embark here on a discussion about Russian good faith.' Yet, only a year later Churchill was already denouncing Stalin in terms in which he had denounced Hitler.

In truth, Stalin's policy was ambiguous. As leader of the new privileged groups in Soviet society, of the bureaucracy and of the managerial elements, he was primarily interested in preserving the social *status quo* within the USSR and without. This accounts for the essentially conservative character of his international policy and diplomacy. He was almost as much afraid of the revolutionary turmoil in the world as were the leaders of the West. He viewed with distrust and even with outright hostility the aspirations of the exploited and oppressed peoples, and yet as the inheritor of the Russian revolution, as Lenin's successor and as the head of the communist movement which even in its degenerated condition still professed its Marxist orthodoxy, he had to present himself as the friend and promoter of every revolutionary interest in the world.

Wherever any revolutionary movement came to the top despite his obstruction, he had to assume the posture of its inspirer and protector. This was the posture he had first assumed towards the Yugoslav revolution, this was the posture he maintained throughout towards the Chinese revolution. Moreover, his kind of revolution, revolution from above, was indeed his answer in Eastern Europe to the Truman Doctrine and the Marshall Plan. Stalin confronted the leaders of the West as a Janus-like opponent: one face conservative, the other revolutionary. And the leaders of the West reacted bitterly and resentfully, because their own political consciences were troubled. They had allied themselves with communism against Nazism and the necessities of this alliance led them to yield up Eastern Europe to Stalin. From the viewpoint of their class interest and class psychology the leaders of the American and British bourgeoisie had acted a most paradoxical and self-contradictory rôle; they had yielded ground to their class enemy; they then sought to regain that ground.

Churchill and Truman tried to wrest from Russia the zone of influence that Churchill and Roosevelt had yielded to her at Teheran and Yalta. They sought to contain Stalin's power at the frontiers of the USSR. This was the first programme of the so-called containment policy, its maximum programme of the years 1946–48. It failed at once and it failed utterly. It speeded up the disaster it was designed to prevent. It provoked Soviet power to erupt all the more violently, to cover hermetically the whole of the Soviet zone of influence, and to grip remorselessly the whole of Eastern Europe.

This first and almost instantaneous defeat of the containment policy was followed by another, by a defeat incomparably more vast and more momentous, the defeat in China in 1949. Here was a gigantic demonstration of the unreality of the major assumptions of Western cold war strategy. No Russian designs against the West and no Russian subversion had brought about or could bring about the explosion of the Chinese volcano. Both Stalin and Truman had worked, each in his own different way, to contain the Chinese revolution, and the volcano had exploded over the heads of both. But while Stalin quickly came to himself, and not only bowed to reality but assumed the posture of the friend and protector of the revolution that had won despite him, our Western cold war strategists refused and are still refusing to face reality.

Shutting their eyes to the inherent momentum, to the innate dynamic force of the Chinese revolution, they treated it as a result of an ignoble intrigue and as a Russian puppet. The vital lesson of the Chinese revolution was that when any great nation struggles to re-cast the very foundations of its social and political existence nothing can stop it, and that the most clever containment policy is and will ever be impotent against the genuine element of revolution. If our statesmen believe that arms and diplomacy can stop mankind in its search for new forms and for a new content of its social existence they are only reactionary utopians; they can delay the process of world-wide change, they can make it more painful and spasmodic, but they cannot halt it.

II

Let me now consider another erroneous cold war assumption. While Western strategists overlooked Russia's real weakness in the early phases of the cold war, when Russia was exhausted and bled white, they also strikingly underrated her potential strength. In the early phases, the cold war was fought on the assumption that Russia would not be able to break the American monopoly of atomic energy for a very long time to come. In those years we were told that Russia lacked the raw materials, the uranium ore, the engineering capacity, and the know-how needed for the production of nuclear energy and for the building up of a nuclear arsenal. Later we were told that even though the Russians had managed to split the atom, they would not be able to pile up a substantial stock of atomic bombs.

Later still we were assured that though she may have a large number of atomic bombs, she would certainly not be able to manufacture H-bombs. And when this proved wrong, the experts maintained that although the Russians had the warheads they did not and would not have the means of delivery that would allow them to strike at the American continent. Intercontinental ballistic missiles were supposed to be beyond the reach of Russian technology. For over twelve years, until the first Russian Sputnik broke into outer space in 1957, the cold war was waged on the assumption of an absolute and unchallengeable American superiority in all fields of technology.

How could so much wishful thinking blind Western statesmen and experts? They sincerely believed in the unchallengeable superiority of the social system which they administered, the capitalist system, and they looked down with genuine contempt on the new economic system with the help of which Russia, in the worst of circumstances, was trying to raise herself from her age-old poverty and backwardness. They did not believe that that system could work. They dismissed all data about Russia's difficult, uneven and yet tremendous economic and social progress as so much bluff and Red propaganda. Only with the great shock of the Sputniks and Luniks came the reluctant realization of the fact that the cold war had reached a stalemate, and that peace rested on a shaky and explosive balance of deterrents.

Yet again and again the assumption of Western and more specifically of American technological and military superiority recurs in Western strategic thinking until it is disproved by some new facts; and then it gives place to panic and fear. In fact, arrogance and panic seem to drive the policy-makers around in a vicious circle.

But let us turn back to the more political presuppositions and notions of the cold war. We have seen how unreal was the notion of a Russian colossus bent on subversion and world domination. During the greater part of the cold war, indeed until quite recently, Western strategic thinking assumed also that the Soviet colossus was a monolith, that the Soviet Union and China and all their allies and satellites formed a single bloc. We were told that Soviet power derived its malignant and threatening character precisely from this, its monolithic quality. Again, this notion had some limited basis in reality. Stalinism had pressed all its subjects into a single totalitarian mould and had imposed an absolute, dogmatic, though unprincipled, uniformity upon the entire Communist movement.

As a historian I remain convinced that Stalinism would have never succeeded in that, as it did, if the Soviet Union had not been exposed to constant hostile and war-like pressures from outside. Those pressures enabled Stalin to blackmail the Soviet people (and foreign communists too) into total obedience. Without the very real threat from Hitler, without the need to counter that threat with a desperate arms race, the people of the Soviet Union would not have submitted to Stalinist terroristic exactions as meekly as they did submit in the 1930s and in the years of the war. They might have refused to accept his dictates after the war if Russia had not had to rebuild her ruins amid new and dangerous pressures from the outside.

Our cold war strategists thus helped to cement the Stalinist monolith. Yet the idea that the Stalinist monolith needed to expand, because expansion fortified and consolidated it, was completely wrong. On the contrary, as it expanded, the Stalinist monolith began to crack and to break up. Tito's 1948 revolt against Stalin foreshadowed this development. By the time of Stalin's death social changes and discontents inside Russia and dissensions between Russia and the other Communist countries worked against the Stalinist monolith. An epoch of change was opening in the communist camp. A few of us here in the West, and we were very, very few indeed, saw the coming change and analysed its first symptoms. We were decried as wishful thinkers and false prophets; our cold war propagandists and our Congresses for Cultural Freedom assumed that the Stalinist monolith was immutable and that it was going to survive Stalin for a long, long time to come.

Among Western statesmen only Winston Churchill, who was again Britain's Prime Minister, kept his eyes and ears open. Shortly after Stalin's death he sought to turn the attention of the Western governments and peoples to the 'wind of change and the new movement of feeling in Russia', and he urged his colleagues in NATO to see whether they could not come to some terms with Stalin's successors. But Churchill, the proud prompter and inspirer of the cold war, was now disavowed by the White House and by his own Foreign Office and his insight was ridiculed. We shall never know what opportunities to halt or abate the cold war and the arms race were missed then. Suffice it to say that these were years when the Soviet Presidium was deeply divided between the faction that was determined to hold on to Berlin, and another faction favouring a Soviet withdrawal from Germany.

Those determined to hold on won the day, not without some assistance, one may assume, from Western irreconcilability. The notion of a Soviet monolith, the notion in which Stalinism itself had gloried, continued to dominate Western strategic thinking. And it did so even when the deep breach between Khrushchev's Russia and

Mao's China became quite apparent to those who could read the signs. The first accounts of this breach — I myself was publishing them in the American press as early as in 1958 — were dismissed by official American spokesmen as utterly groundless. As late as 1961 official Washington was still declaring that those who talked about a Russo-China controversy were dupes of Soviet propaganda. Until the early 1960s the cold war strategy still rested on the assumption of the Russo-Chinese monolith.

When this assumption, too, at last collapsed, the cold war strategists swung abruptly to the opposite extreme and began grossly to exaggerate the extent of the Russo-Chinese controversy, and to exploit it. A new image of Russia began to make its appearance in the West, the image of an emerging bourgeois Russia which must be terrified of the growing power of China, the new dangerous colossus rising across her frontiers. All the malignant character that the cold war ideologists had for so long attributed to the Soviet Union was now transferred to China.

Peking rather than Moscow was now seen as the fount of world-wide subversion, as the threat to world peace. Of course, the Maoists spoke to the West in an idiom more militant and defiant than that used by the Khrushchevites. Of course, their resentment against the West, especially against the United States, was and is very sharp. And the ostracism under which the United States has kept Communist China makes the resentment more and more acute. But all this does not add up to a Chinese menace to the West; and those who speak of that menace do so in order to justify the obsessive hostility towards Communist China shown by all successive American administrations. And so in the last few years Chinese communism became the chief villain; and to drive a wedge between Russia and China was gradually becoming the declared new purpose of Western strategy. There is, of course, nothing reprehensible in the attempt of any power to benefit from the internecine quarrels of its opponents: it has been the loudly proclaimed purpose of communist policy to benefit from the internal contradictions in the capitalist imperialist camp. There would be nothing inherently wicked in the American attempt to drive a wedge between Russia and China, if the wedge were not recklessly driven through the living body of the people of Vietnam and if it did not threaten the peace of Asia and, indeed, of the world. The American administration, I suggest, is dangerously overplaying its hand in Vietnam because it underrates the necessity for Russia to maintain some solidarity with China in the face of armed American pressure on South-East Asia.

Underlying the Russo-Chinese controversy over strategy, tactics and ideology there is still the basic solidarity between the anti-capitalist regimes of the two countries. They can afford to quarrel only when the full blast of Western hostility towards the one and the other has abated somewhat. When that hostility mounts again and hits one of them, they must draw together. Last summer's American armed forays in the Gulf of Tonkin caused the gravest alarm in Moscow. Two months later Khrushchev, the advocate of a Russian *rapprochement* with America, and Mao Tse-tung's chief antagonist, was overthrown. Whatever may have been the domestic reasons for that *coup*, the White House, the Pentagon and the State Department contributed to Khrushchev's fall. Khrushchev's successors set out to mend Russia's disturbed relations with China; and although they have not healed the breach, they have stopped its continuous aggravation.

Whereas Khrushchev spoke of a Russian withdrawal from South-East Asia, his successors insist on Russia's presence there. They are sending arms to Vietnam and talk of sending volunteers. Against the American intervention Peking and Moscow are speaking with almost the same voice no matter how much they actually differ. The clumsy and reckless wedge is achieving the opposite of what it was intended to achieve: instead of driving the Communist powers apart, it imposes on them a measure of unity. As at so many earlier stages, the cold war strategy defeats itself.

From what I have said, it is, I think, quite clear that all the characteristic misconceptions and delusions of the cold war are reproduced in Vietnam. Once again American policy is based on opposition to a genuine native revolutionary force. The Vietcong is backed in its struggle by an overwhelming majority of the Vietnamese peasantry, otherwise it would not have been able to hold its ground and extend its control over three-quarters of the country. No foreign power, no matter how formidable its weapons, can in the long run prevail against this kind of a revolutionary element.

The French have repeatedly found this both in Indo-China and in Algeria; and the British have found it in so many of their former colonies and dependencies. Unwilling to see this, the White House and the State Department are telling the world that the real culprit is once again a foreign Communist power — North Vietnam, and, behind it, the malignant Chinese colossus. The logic of this argument requires, of course, that military blows be inflicted on North Vietnam and, at a further remove, on China. And once again provocation breeds counter-provocation. North Vietnam and China and perhaps even Russia may all be drawn into the fighting in South Vietnam.

Escalation works both ways. And the world listens with dismay to wild talk that the United States ought to use this opportunity in order to destroy the embryo of the Chinese nuclear industry. Can we take it for granted that this wild talk exercises no influence on official American policy? And that the American leaders understand that Russia cannot afford to watch passively any massive American attack on any of the vital centres of China? And that a Soviet government that would try to remain passive might be overthrown within twenty-four hours?

In Vietnam not only American policy has reached an impasse. The whole Western cold war strategy, having for nearly two decades moved in a maze of misconceptions and miscalculations and amid the wreckage of so many illusions, now stands helplessly before the blind Vietnamese wall. It is perhaps time now to draw the balance of this long and terrible venture, to count its material, political and moral costs, and to assess the risks. I am not setting my hopes too high. I do not see the approach of the great cease-fire that would end the cold war.

To some extent, as I have said at the beginning, this has been and is an unavoidable war. The antagonisms and the tensions between the powers cannot be suddenly conjured out of existence. The conflict between capitalism and communism, which some prefer to describe as a conflict between democracy and communism, is not nearing any solution. The hostility between colonialism or neocolonialism and the peoples of Asia, Africa and Latin America will not soon die down. But if the stark realities of these multiple conflicts are likely to remain with us, it may yet be possible for all the forces involved to behave more rationally than they have behaved so far, to lift from these conflicts the hysteria and insanity of the cold war, the fog of myths and legends, and the suicidal intensity of the contest.

I still believe that class struggle is the motive force of history and that only a socialist world — one socialist world — can cope with the problems of modern society. But in our time class struggle has sunk into a bloody morass of power politics. On both sides of the great divide a few ruthless and half-witted oligarchies, capitalist oligarchies here, bureaucratic oligarchies there, are not only holding in their hands all the power of their nations; they have also obfuscated the minds and throttled the wills of their nations, and usurped for themselves the rôles of the chief protagonists in social and ideological conflicts. The class struggles of our time have degenerated into the unscrupulous contests of the ruling oligarchies.

Official Washington speaks for the world's Freedom. Official Moscow speaks for Socialism. 'Save me from my friends!' — Freedom might say. 'Save me from my friends!' — Socialism must say. On both sides of the great divide the peoples have been silent for too long and have for too long identified themselves with their governments and their policies. The world has come very close, dangerously close, to a division between revolutionary and counter-revolutionary nations. This to my mind has been perhaps the most alarming result of the cold war.

Fortunately things are changing in the Soviet part of the world, especially in Russia where the people have been shaking off the old discipline and the old conformism and have been regaining an independent mind and a critical attitude towards their rulers. Things are, I hope, changing here, in the United States too. I see a significant sign of the change in the determination of so many Americans to scrutinize and to argue out the assumptions of their government's policy, assumptions which America has so long accepted without scrutiny and in virtual unanimity.

We may not be able to get away from the severe conflicts of our age and we need not get away from them. But we may perhaps lift those conflicts above the morass into which they have been forced. The divisions may once again run within nations, rather than between nations. We may give back to class struggle its old dignity. We may and we must restore meaning to the great ideas by which mankind is still living, the ideas of liberalism, democracy and communism.

Part Three

Europe

The Tragedy of the Polish Communist Party

Would you throw some light on the key problems of the history of the Polish Communist Party, which I am at present studying? I am particularly interested in the ideological and political currents within the Party, in the background to the formation of its various factions, in the Party's policy during the critical periods of the two interwar decades, and, finally, in its tragic end.

Let us begin with some general reflections and with a remark of a personal nature. When you ask me to speak of the history of the Polish Communist Party you are surely aware of the particular point of view from which I reply. In June 1957, exactly twenty-five years will have elapsed since I was expelled from the Party as an oppositionist. I shall not analyse now the reasons for my expulsion: they have been stated clearly although tendentiously — and with the passage of time their very bias becomes more and more self-condemnatory — in the documents and statements published at the time by the Party leadership dealing with the 'Krakowski affair'. (Krakowski was one of the pseudonyms which I was then using.) From 1932 until its dissolution I was in sharp conflict with the Polish Communist Party. Nevertheless, at the time of the dissolution and of the accusations made against its leaders, I stigmatized these actions as an unparalleled crime committed against the working class of Poland and of the whole world. The opposition group to which I belonged was in fact the only group of members or former members of the Polish CP which denounced this crime then and protested against it vehemently.[1]

---

[1] It is said that at one of the meetings of the Central Committee which took place after October 1956, when Gomulka was relating the story of the Party's dissolution and of the slanders made against its leaders, he was asked whether at that time, in 1938,

It was unquestionably the Polish Communist Party which had the greatest influence on my intellectual and political development. I never doubted that it would be 'rehabilitated' — though even the term 'rehabilitation' is out of place here. It was a great and heroic party, the only party in Poland which represented the interests of the proletarian revolution, the great Marxist tradition, and a true and living internationalism. In this respect no other Polish party could be compared with it. Unfortunately, up to this day the history of the Polish Communist Party still remains a closed and sealed book. The most recent publications which I have had an opportunity to read are on the whole rather pitiable. They note the Party's rehabilitation, but do nothing more. There is no real attempt to depict the great periods in the Party's existence — the high flights and decline. What is striking is a tendency — the result of habits acquired in the course of many years — to be satisfied with clichés and writings in the manner of *Lives of Saints*. The only party in Poland which was worthy of bearing the name of a proletarian and Marxist party deserves to have its record studied in a serious, realistic and critical manner. The Polish CP was once buried under a pile of outrageous slanders. Let us not bury it again, wrapped in shrouds of golden legends to the accompaniment of senseless hymns.

I should like to add a remark of a general methodological character. In order to understand the history of the Polish Communist Party, every important phase of it must be considered from a double point of view: from the angle of the class struggle within Poland itself, and from that of the processes which were taking place within the Communist International and the Soviet Union. These two groups of factors acted upon each other continuously. An investigator who restricts himself to an analysis of only one of these will be unable to grasp the essence of the story. As years went by, the processes occurring in the Soviet Union played a more and more important role and weighed more and more disastrously on the fate of the Polish Party. Therefore to see clearly the policy of the Party and its ideological tendencies and also to understand the factional struggle, we must be continuously aware of the class relationship

---

he himself believed them. Gomulka answered: 'No.' Why, then, had he not protested? he was asked. 'I was not brave enough to do so, or I had not enough self-confidence,' he is said to have replied, 'but if Lenin had been living in Poland, he would certainly have protested in such circumstances.' We must acknowledge Gomulka's sincerity and modesty. Nevertheless, it was not necessary to be a Lenin in order to dare to protest. I knew ordinary workers who had no ambitions towards leadership and who understood that their duty was to protest, and acted accordingly.

within Poland and of the processes of development taking place within the Russian Revolution.

What were the main internal divisions in the Polish Communist Party at the time it was founded, that is to say, at the end of 1918 and the beginning of 1919?

These divisions followed from the fact that the Polish CP was born from the fusion of two parties: the Social-Democratic Party of the Kingdom of Poland and Lithuania (Rosa Luxemburg's party, the SDKPiL) and the Polish Left Socialist Party (the PPS Lewica).[2] Each of these two parties had its own traditions. The Social-Democratic Party grew in opposition to the nationalism and patriotism of the Polish nobility, harking back to the insurrectionist romanticism of the nineteenth century, and placed its main emphasis on proletarian internationalism. The Left Socialist Party had at first adhered to the patriotic-insurgent tradition, and the restoration of Poland's independence had occupied a central place in its programme; but later on it came closer to the internationalist attitude of the Luxemburgist Party. The Left Socialist Party had its affinities with the Left Mensheviks; only under the influence of the October Revolution did it move closer to Bolshevism. The Social-Democratic Party adopted — as the proceedings of its Sixth Congress show —an attitude very close to that of Trotsky, remaining independent both of the Mensheviks and the Bolsheviks. At the time of the revolution, the Luxemburgist Party — again like Trotsky — identified itself with Bolshevism. Here we must take note of the differences within the Party between adherents of the Party's official leaders (Rosa Luxemburg, Marchlewski, Jogiches) and the so-called 'splitters' (Dzerzhinski, Radek, Unszlicht). This was, however, a discord, not a genuine split. The 'splitters' represented a certain opposition to the centralism of the Executive Committee, which operated from abroad. Furthermore, they were somewhat closer to the Bolsheviks. In the Polish Communist Party the SDKPiL tradition was predominant from the beginning. Nevertheless the importance of these differences should not be exaggerated. They were in actual fact

---

[2]The Social-Democratic Party of the Kingdom of Poland was formed in 1893 as a Polish party; the Lithuanian Social-Democrats attached themselves in 1900. From the beginning this party was led by Julian Marchlewski, Leo Jogiches-Tyszka and Rosa Luxemburg. The Left Socialist Party was formed in November 1906, as a result of a split in the Polish Socialist Party (PPS) and of an opposition, stimulated by the 1905 revolution, to Pilsudski's reformist, terroristic and nationalist leadership.

restrained and even obliterated by the real unity of the newly founded Party and the conviction of its members that the old divisions were a matter of the past. The Party's ranks were further united by a sharp awareness of their common and unyielding opposition to the nationalist and reformist Poland, to the Poland of the landlords and petty nobility.[3]

Is it not true that the Communist Party began its political life in independent Poland with a certain moral disadvantage arising from its Luxemburgist tradition, which was opposed in principle to the struggle for national independence?

There is a little truth and a great deal of exaggeration in that. The proof that this is so is seen, for example, in the relative strength of the different parties within the Soviets of Workers' Deputies which were set up, at the end of 1918, in Warsaw, in Lodz, and in the Dabrowa coalfields. In Warsaw the forces of the Communist Party and of the Socialists were equally balanced and, if I am not mistaken, the Bund tipped the scales[4]. There was a similar situation in Lodz, although there the Communists had a certain superiority. In the Dabrowa mining district the Communist Party was incomparably stronger than the Socialist Party, and with this is connected the episode of the Red Republic of Dabrowa. One could say that on the eve of independence, the influence of the Polish CP over the working classes in the main industrial centres was certainly not smaller than that of the reformist and 'patriotic' PPS — it was probably larger.

The situation was complicated. On the one hand, events had *to a certain degree* refuted the assumptions on which Rosa Luxemburg and her comrades had dissented from the 'struggle for national independence'. On the other hand, however, Luxemburg and her followers had been alone in placing their hopes on revolutions in Russia, Germany and Austria, the three empires that had subjugated Poland, rather than on an unending repetition of Polish nineteenth-century insurrections. Pilsudskism — and the Polish Socialist Party

[3] It is a curious fact that the 'splitters' and particularly Dzerzhinski and Radek should have made almost the same criticism of Rosa Luxemburg as the latter made of Lenin during the division of the Party into Mensheviks and Bolsheviks. They accused her of applying a policy of ultra-centralism in the Party, of enforcing too much discipline, etc. In fact, Rosa Luxemburg's Party was led in a manner very similar to that in which Lenin led the Bolshevik Party. This was due essentially to the fact that both parties were operating illegally.

[4] The Bund was the Jewish socialist party, which then maintained an intermediate position between socialist reformism and communism.

which in 1918 was almost inseparable from Pilsudskism — had above all proclaimed its scepticism and distrust of the reality of revolution in these empires. Events had given the lie to this scepticism and distrust. Contrary to Rosa Luxemburg's expectations, Poland had regained her independence; but contrary to the expectations of her opponents, Poland had received it mainly from the hands of the Russian and German revolutions. History showed itself to be more cunning than all the parties; and that is why I do not believe that, in comparison with other parties, the Communist Party entered the phase of independence with any particular 'moral handicap'. Moreover, while the 'Luxemburgists' were rotting in Tsarist prisons and in exile, the Polish bourgeois parties (especially the 'national democrats', who opposed all movements for national independence, but also Pilsudski and the Socialist 'patriots') placed themselves at the service of the occupying powers and collaborated with them; after the fall of these powers, this did not prevent the bourgeois parties from adopting hypocritical, ultranationalist attitudes and from seizing power.

After the foundation of the Polish Communist Party did the old controversy over Poland's independence go on within the Party?

Only at the beginning, and to an insignificant degree; later it stopped altogether. The Party was concerned with other problems — its position in the configuration of social forces; the elaboration of its political line; and, of course, the problem of the Russian Revolution and the prospects of world revolution.

Did not the question of boycotting the Constituent Assembly of 1919 mark the appearance of a new division within the Party?

Unless I am mistaken, this question did not give rise to much discussion. On this matter the Polish and the German parties took similar stands, considering elections to the Constituent Assembly as a diversion which had as its aim the liquidation of the Soviets of Workers' Deputies. The Polish *Seym* and the Weimar Constituent Assembly were regarded as the foundations of a bourgeois parliamentary republic, erected on the ruins of the workers' Soviets — the potential organs of the socialist revolution. Undoubtedly, the two parties made a mistake in proclaiming the boycott of the bourgeois parliament, and in both cases this mistake was a result of the ultraleft mood of the period.

How did the Communist Party react to the Polish–Soviet War of 1920?

The Polish Party treated this war — as it had every reason to do —as a war of the Polish possessing classes (or of their decisive elements) against the Russian Revolution, and as an integral part of the capitalist powers' intervention in Russia. The Party felt it was at one with the Russian Revolution and obliged to defend it. The situation became complicated after Pilsudski's retreat from Kiev and at the time of the Red Army's march on Warsaw. The state of siege and the existence of military tribunals reduced to a minimum the Party's open activities; and it was difficult for both leaders and rank and file to express the various nuances of Communist opinion. Nevertheless I should like to draw attention to characteristic differences which appeared among the numerous groups of Polish Communists living in Moscow. When the question of the march on Warsaw came up, this group split in a rather paradoxical manner. On the one hand, the old 'Luxemburgists', the 'opponents of independence', Radek and Marchlewski,[5] spared no efforts to convince Lenin and the Russian Politburo that the march on Warsaw should not be undertaken, but that peace should be proposed to Poland as soon as Pilsudski's armies had been chased out of the Ukraine. (They succeeded in winning to their point of view only Trotsky, who was then the People's Commissar for War.) On the other hand, the old supporters of independence, former PPS men like Feliks Kon and Lapinski,[6] favoured the Red Army's march on Warsaw; they maintained that the Polish proletariat was in a state of the utmost revolutionary ferment and would welcome the Red Army as its liberator. I should like to report yet another episode: in 1920 the paper *Rote Fahne*, the organ of the German Communist Party, published a protest against the march on Warsaw signed by Domski, one of the most eminent 'Luxemburgist' members of the Central Committee of the Polish Party. By the way, under the conditions of internal democracy, which existed at that time in the Party, the right of a member of the Central Committee to

[5]Julian Marchlewski, one of the closest friends of Rosa Luxemburg, was an eminent writer and Marxist theoretician who played an important part in the German socialist left and in the Polish movement. After the October Revolution he stayed in Russia.

[6]Feliks Kon, a veteran of Polish patriotic socialism, was one of the founders of the Communist Party and with Marchlewski and Dzerzhinski was a member of the 'Provisional Communist Government', set up during the Red Army's march on Warsaw. Lapinski belonged to the same group as Feliks Kon, and in the twenties he played an important role in the Comintern.

publish such a protest was considered as something quite natural. Domski remained a member of the Central Committee and played a leading role in it for many more years, until 1925 precisely.

You asked whether the Luxemburgist tradition was not a moral embarrassment for Polish communism. I have no intention of defending *post factum* Rosa Luxemburg's ideas about national independence. I shall simply say that the Red Army's march on Warsaw was a much more serious and more damaging moral handicap for the Polish CP than had been all of Rosa Luxemburg's real or imaginary mistakes taken together; about these mistakes both her bourgeois opponents as well as Stalin (the latter misusing, in his characteristic manner, quotations from Lenin) have made an enormous amount of noise. However, the mistake made by Lenin in 1920 — let us call things by their proper name — was a real tragedy for the Polish CP, because in effect it pushed the Polish proletarian masses towards anti-Sovietism and anti-communism.

Nevertheless, after 1920 the Party rapidly regained its strength — didn't it?

Yes, to a certain extent. That does not alter the fact that the march on Warsaw also had certain permanent effects: it undermined the trust of the Polish working masses in the Russian Revolution. However, after 1920 the workers recovered fairly quickly from their first enthusiasm for Polish national sovereignty, and from the illusions that went with it. In the relatively freer atmosphere which followed the war, the working class had the opportunity to view the events more calmly. It became known that Lenin's government had done everything possible to avoid war between Poland and Russia and that without Pilsudski's march on Kiev there would probably never have been any Soviet march on Warsaw. The Polish working class came to understand that Pilsudski, in 1920, was fighting not so much for Polish independence as for the estates of the big Polish landowners in the Ukraine, and also to satisfy his own dreams of grandeur. The early years of the twenties marked another increase in the influence of the Polish Communist Party, an influence which reached its peak in 1923, particularly in November, at the time of the general strike and the rising of the Cracow workers.

This was the time of the 'three W's' leadership, wasn't it?

It was. One of them, Warski, was a former Luxemburgist, and the two others, Walecki and Wera (Kostrzewa), were former Left Socialists. Nevertheless, they formed a united leadership which proved that the old divisions within the Party had been overcome. Now, however, we are approaching a particularly critical period, when the development of the class struggle in Poland was complicated once more, and to a certain extent distorted, by the influence of events taking place in the Soviet Union. For many years, I personally believed that in Poland, as well as in Germany, the year 1923 was one of a 'missed revolution'. Now, after an interval of thirty-five years, I can no longer be so sure that the historical evidence bears out the correctness of this point of view. In any case, we certainly had many elements of a revolutionary situation: a general strike, the rising of the Cracow workers, the army going over to the side of the working class, and more generally, the country in a state of utter ferment. The only factor, it seemed, which was lacking was the initiative of a revolutionary party which might have led the revolution to success. The Polish CP did not show that initiative. In accordance with the resolutions of the International, the Party was then following a policy of united front with the socialists. Up to a certain moment, this policy had produced excellent results, enabling the Party to widen its influence, and introducing more vigour into the class struggle. But at the same time, the Party leadership left the political initiative to the Socialists; and in the critical days of November 1923, this produced unfortunate consequences. The rank and file felt that the Party had allowed a revolutionary situation to pass by without taking any advantage; and they reacted, not without bitterness, against the 'opportunism' and the lack of revolutionary initiative of the 'three W's'.

As I have said, the situation became even more complicated because of events taking place in the USSR. At that time the struggle between the so-called triumvirate (Stalin, Zinoviev and Kamenev) and Trotsky broke into the open. At once it took on extremely violent forms unknown hitherto in the movement. The European Communist parties were deeply disturbed, all the more so as until then Trotsky, like Lenin, had been the International's inspirer and greatest moral authority. In the autumn of 1923 the Central Committees of the Polish, French and German parties protested, in one form or another, to the Central Committee of the Soviet Party against the violence of the attacks on Trotsky. Those who protested had no intention of associating themselves with Trotsky's specific policies. They were simply warning the Soviet leaders of the harm which the campaign against Trotsky was doing to the Communist movement, and they appealed to them to settle their differences in a manner worthy of Communists. This incident had serious consequences. Stalin never forgot or forgave this protest. Zinoviev, who was then president of the International, viewed it as a vote of no confidence in himself. Immediately, the Communist parties of Poland, France and Germany became involved in the internal Soviet conflict. The leadership of the International — in other words, Zinoviev and Stalin — dismissed from their posts the principal leaders of the three parties who had dared 'to come to Trotsky's defence'. A pretext was provided by the mistakes committed by these leaders, notably by the group of the 'three W's' in November 1923; they were expelled for 'opportunism, right deviation, and failure to exploit a revolutionary situation'.

Does it not follow from your account that those who criticized the 'three W's' were justified?

Even if they were justified, that did not authorize the leadership of the International in Moscow to intervene in such a drastic manner in the internal affairs of the Polish Party. I must add that the leadership of the German and French parties was changed in the same way.[7] In all these cases the changes were brought about as a result of orders from above, and not as a result of decisions taken by the members of the Party in a way corresponding to the principles of internal democracy. This was the first dangerous attack on the autonomy of the Communist Party, the first act, as it turned out, of 'Stalinization', although this was done not only by Stalin, but by Zinoviev also. Both played demagogically on the feeling of disillusionment which existed among the rank and file of the Polish and German parties. This feeling was understandable and it turned violently against the 'three W's' in Poland (as it did against Brandler in Germany). It is possible that if the Party had been free to decide for itself, it might have changed its leadership. Nevertheless, more important than the fact of the change itself was the manner in which it was carried out: the way was opened to further unscrupulous interference by Stalin in the affairs of the Polish Communist Party, an interference which was to end in the Party's assassination.

How did the Party react to this first act of deliberate interference?

[7] In France, Monatte, Rosmer and Souvarine were dismissed from the leadership of the Communist Party.

Passively, unfortunately. Many of its members were more or less in favour of the 'three W's' being replaced. And even those who weren't did not oppose it. The operation was mild in comparison with the expulsions, purges and forced recantations which were to follow. Stalinism was only in its formative period, and could not yet show its claws. The attack on the displaced leaders was carried on with relative moderation and correctness of form — and this facilitated its acceptance. What was decisive, however, was the Party's psychological attitude — its misguided conception of solidarity with the Russian Revolution, its belief that any conflict with Moscow must be avoided, no matter at what cost. The moral authority of the Soviet Party, the only one which had led a proletarian revolution to victory, was so great that the Polish Communists accepted Moscow's decisions even when Moscow abused its revolutionary authority. Stalinism was indeed a continuous succession of abuses of this kind, a systematic exploitation of the moral credit of the revolution for purposes which often had nothing to do with the interests of communism but served only to consolidate the bureaucratic regime of the USSR. During the years 1923–24 it was vital for Stalin to attack Trotskyism in the whole International. Warski and Kostrzewa tried to safeguard their own position by dissociating themselves from their own protest against Moscow's anti-Trotsky campaign. Their motives were understandable. In Moscow the majority of the Politburo and of the Central Committee had come out against Trotsky. In view of this, Warski and Kostrzewa decided that they could not support the minority in the Soviet Party and thus expose themselves to the charge of interfering in the internal affairs of the Party. That did not, however, protect the Polish Party from Soviet interference. Thus, although the 'three W's' had some sympathy with the views of the Trotskyist opposition, they came, in fact, to support Stalin and Zinoviev and to proclaim their loyalty to them. For this moment of weakness they had to pay dearly later on.

What was the change in the Party's policy after 1923?

What was called 'the left' took over the leadership: Domski, Zofia Unszlicht, and Lenski. Both in the International as a whole and also in the Polish Party the new policy presented a sharp reaction from the orientation of the preceding period. This was, in fact, the time of an 'ultra-leftist' policy. If in 1923 the Party did not show enough revolutionary vigour, its policy during the years 1924 and 1925 was marked by a false excess of that vigour. This was all the more harmful because after the crisis of November 1923 the objective possibilities of revolutionary action had decreased. During this period the Polish CP rejected the united front tactic completely and dispersed its efforts in futile adventures. The result? It lost its influence and cut itself off from the working masses.

It is worth recalling that, at the beginning of 1924, in local elections, the Polish CP was still stronger than the Socialist Party. This success, however, was no more than a delayed echo of the radicalization of the masses which had taken place in 1923, and it did not foreshadow the rise of a new revolutionary wave. In the following year the Communist Party's influence declined drastically. The Party was unable to lead any mass action. This was not only a Polish phenomenon. The same fluctuations could be seen in all the Communist parties of Europe — all were, in fact, pursuing the same ultra-leftist policy with similar results. This was the time of the Fifth Congress of the Comintern; it was called the 'Bolshevization Congress', but actually it was the 'Stalinization Congress'. Henceforth, all parties were subjected to the same treatment; all followed the same 'line'; all had recourse to the same tactical tricks; all launched the same slogans without taking into account differences in the class relationships of different countries, in the level and form of class struggle, etc. The movement had reached the stage of bureaucratic uniformity. The Polish Party was affected by this even more painfully than were other European parties because its revolutionary tradition had been deeper and stronger, and it operated in conditions of complete illegality,[x] appealing continuously to the spirit of revolutionary self-sacrifice and to the heroism of its members, which never failed. Bureaucratic uniformity and revolutionary enthusiasm are a contradiction in terms.

Nevertheless, at the end of 1925, Warski, Walecki and Kostrzewa returned to the leadership of the Party, didn't they?

Yes. The ultra-leftist policy was soon discredited in the eyes of the Party, and that of the 'three W's' was almost automatically vindicated. Whatever might be said against Warski and Kostrzewa, they had the gift of feeling the moods of the working class and the ability to strengthen and widen contacts between the Party and the masses. The periods when they led the Party were, in general, those when the

---

[x] The Polish CP was made illegal at the beginning of 1919, only a few weeks after the proclamation of Polish independence. It remained illegal until 1944.

Party expanded and conducted its activity on a grand scale, although it frequently lacked — how shall I put it? — a revolutionary edge. The return of Warski and Kostrzewa to the leadership of the Polish Communist Party was, again, due more to what was then happening in Russia than to the change of climate in the Polish Party.

In Russia, a new political situation had developed. The triumvirate had broken up. Zinoviev and Kamenev had turned against Stalin, and shortly afterwards they were to ally themselves with Trotsky. Stalin formed a bloc with Bukharin and Rykov and followed what has been called 'a rightist line' in the Soviet Party and in the International. What was called the 'Polish right', the 'three W's', came back into favour for the time being because they had lent support to Stalin and Bukharin. On the other hand, a part of the ultra-leftist leadership, Zofia Unszlicht and Domski, sided with Zinoviev; it was for this reason, more than for any mistake they had committed in Poland, that they were removed.[9] Once more, calculations connected with the struggle in the Soviet Party were decisive. Lenski, in spite of his ultra-left policy, remained in the leadership, sharing influence with the 'three W's'; Lenski, unlike Domski and Unszlicht, had come out against the Zinovievist opposition. More than this, he became the leader of the Stalinist nucleus within the Polish CP, whereas Warski and Kostrzewa, although completely loyal to Stalin, maintained a certain reserve towards him and were closer to Bukharin's group. Later this division within the Polish Party was to be crystallized in the formation of a 'minority' faction led by Lenski and a 'majority' led by Warski and Kostrzewa. At the beginning of 1926 these two factions shared the leadership and both were responsible for policy, in particular for the 'May mistake', that is, the support the Polish CP gave to Pilsudski at the time of his coup d'état of May 1926.

Could you say something more about the 'May mistake' and explain its background? Among old Party militants I often find the following thesis: at the time of the coup the Party could not avoid supporting Pilsudski, who had the confidence of the Polish Socialist Party and of the entire left, and whose 'putsch' was directed against the so-called Chjeno-Piast government (a coalition of the right-centre). The Party, they say, considered that the coup constituted in a certain measure the beginning of a bourgeois revolution, and as such was relatively progressive, because during the previous period only the semi-feudal

[9] At that time, too, Treint was eliminated from the leadership of the French Communist Party, of which he had been general secretary.

landed proprietors had held power, to the exclusion even of the bourgeoisie.

The 'May mistake' is clearly of fundamental importance in the history of Polish communism. I cannot attempt to give you here a detailed explanation of its background. This would require an analysis of the most complicated class relationships and political forces.[10] Therefore, I shall simply try to sketch in certain broad historical outlines. Again, it is essential to examine the situation on two levels: on the level of the class struggle in Poland, and on that of the internal development of the Soviet Party and the Comintern.

Let us begin with the purely Polish aspect. Poland was going through a crisis of the parliamentary regime. No stable government could be formed on a parliamentary basis, and this reflected the breakdown of the social and political equilibrium outside parliament. All the possibilities of parliamentary alliances had been exhausted. The masses were utterly disillusioned with the regime, which proved incapable of providing employment and of protecting workers from the catastrophic results of the currency devaluation, which had deceived the peasants' expectation of land reform, which had condemned the national minorities to oppression and despair. On the other hand, the propertied classes were equally opposed to parliament and to the 'omnipotence of the Diet'. They were afraid that the feeble Polish parliamentarianism, unable to ensure stable, let alone 'strong' government, might expose the existing social system to the danger of violent attack and revolution. Objectively, the situation was ripe for the overthrow of the parliamentary regime. Theoretically, there were three possibilities. The parliamentary regime might have been overthrown by a fascist mass movement, similar to Nazism or the Italian prototype. This, however, was not the actual prospect. For reasons which I shall not examine here, all attempts to launch such a movement in Poland, attempts repeated more than once both before and after 1926, failed. Our native varieties of fascism or Nazism were little more than comic-opera creations.

The second theoretical possibility consisted in the overthrow of the bourgeois-parliamentary regime by proletarian revolution — for this, one might have thought, the Polish CP should have been preparing. However, during the months preceding the May coup the CP had been preparing for almost everything except revolution. Up to a

[10]Shortly before the war I wrote a large-scale study of the history of working-class movements and class struggles in Poland; unfortunately this manuscript was lost.

point, this fact reflected the ebb of the militant mood among the working class, the shock the 1923 disaster had inflicted on them, and, finally, the exhaustion of the movement by the pseudo-revolutionary, sterile 'activities' of 1924-25. The Communist movement lacked self-confidence; and when there was little self-assurance in the vanguard, there was, naturally, even less of it in the working class as a whole. Not believing in its own strength, the working class was inclined to place its hope in external forces and to calculate the benefits which it might obtain for itself through the activities of other classes or social groups. Such was the objective political background to the 'May mistake'.

A remark in passing — the Polish Communist Party's 'May mistake' began even before 1926. If my memory does not mislead me, it was Warski who, on behalf of the Communist group, offered an emergency motion in the Diet in the autumn of 1925 on 'the dangers threatening the independence of Poland'. The motion was as unexpected as it was amazing. It was astonishing that a friend of Rosa Luxemburg should suddenly raise an alarm about the 'dangers threatening Poland's independence'. In the situation of 1925 it was difficult to see what justified the alarm. The conclusion of this emergency motion was even more amazing. In it, Warski — to meet the 'threat to independence' — demanded the immediate return of Pilsudski to the post of commander-in-chief of the armed forces (this at a time when Pilsudski had left the army and was sulking in his retreat in Sulejowek).

The spectacle was tragi-comic indeed! Hardly five years had elapsed since Pilsudski had marched on Kiev, mainly in order to return the Ukrainian estates to their landowners, and the Communist Party was now calling back this man of destiny to head the army in order to safeguard national independence. It is enough merely to describe the situation in these terms — and these are the only realistic (though grotesque) terms — to dispose of the theory according to which the comeback of Pilsudski was supposed to mark the beginning of the bourgeois revolution in Poland. How could the defender of the feudal estates of the *szlachta* (nobility and gentry) have become transformed suddenly into the inspirer of the bourgeois revolution, the main task of which is usually to destroy feudalism, or what is left of it?

I have mentioned three possible solutions to the crisis of the parliamentary regime in Poland. The third solution consisted in the setting-up of a military dictatorship. Pilsudski was clearly the candidate, the pretender. He had this advantage over other generals: he enjoyed a high reputation. A legend surrounded him as a fighter for national independence, as former chief of the Polish Socialist Party, as the anti-Tsarist terrorist of 1905, and as the founder of the Polish legions in 1914. By clamouring for his return, the Polish CP blindly and in spite of itself wove a few of its own purple threads into the fabric of this rather phony legend. The Party helped to create illusions in the working masses about the 'Grandad' (*Dziadek*), as Pilsudski was called familiarly, and so to prepare the way for the May coup d'état. How much more correctly did Adolf Nowaczynski, the talented clown of the National-Democratic petty bourgeoisie, grasp Pilsudski's role when he nicknamed him 'Napoleon IV, the very smallest'! How much more appropriate it would have been for Marxists, who should have learned the art of political analysis from Marx's *18th Brumaire*, to take this view of Pilsudski!

It is, nevertheless, true that Pilsudski was opposing a centre-right government, presided over by Witos, which represented the interests of the petty nobility and gentry. Is it not true that it was precisely this government which had abolished parliamentary liberties and begun to set up a fascist regime? Do not these facts — independently of what happened in 1920 — indicate that the Party was right to a certain extent to support Pilsudski?

It is undeniable that this is how the situation appeared to very many communists — and even more so to socialists. Nevertheless these were optical illusions; and their spell was broken only when it was too late. In any case one could not, without simplifying things too much, define the Witos government as one representing the interests of the large landowners. Witos represented a compromise between the interests of the landed gentry and those of the rich peasantry, a compromise that had been reached at the expense of the poor peasants, robbing the latter of the benefits of an agrarian reform. This compromise was clearly the result of the aspirations of the landlords and the kulaks. Moreover, it was not true that the danger of fascism came from this government. The government coalition represented the most reactionary combination of interests and forces that was possible *within the framework* of the parliamentary regime, but it worked precisely within that framework. Outside parliament it did not possess a political force strong enough to be set against the 'omnipotence of the Diet'. This was the insoluble dilemma of the Polish propertied classes and their traditional parties; they were incapable of maintaining their class domination either by a stabilization of the parliamentary regime under their own auspices or by overthrowing that regime. As in Marx's description of the 18th Brumaire, only the executive, the state machine, could solve this dilemma, at least for a time. Throughout the twenty years between the two wars, the objective conditions favourable to the rise of a real fascist dictatorship did not exist in Poland, if by 'fascist' we understand a totalitarian dictatorship based on a strong and clearly counter-revolutionary mass movement. There was no lack of candidates for the role of Hitler or of Mussolini, but in Poland the counter-revolution never succeeded in setting such a mass movement in motion. The counter-revolution could only offer a 'dictatorship of the sword'. And once again, as in Marx's classic description, we were witnessing the quarrels and the coarse rows between our own pseudo-Napoleon and our own Changarnier, quarrels over whose sword was to rule the nation — Pilsudski's or Haller's.[11] (There are probably few in Poland today who realize that Haller was at one time Pilsudski's most important rival.) And because of the role that the 'independence mythology' played in our political life and also in our political thinking, the choice of the sword depended on the sheath. Only Pilsudski's sword, sheathed in the legends of the struggle for independence, was considered worthy of exercising power over the people and capable of beheading the feeble body of Polish parliamentarianism.

In other words, Pilsudski expropriated the Polish landlords and bourgeoisie *politically* in order to preserve their *social* domination over the proletariat and the peasantry. When, in May 1926, we saw President Witos, with his trousers half-buttoned, scuttling through the courtyard of the Belvedere Palace in Warsaw, pursued by detachments of Pilsudski's forces, we were witnessing, in fact, an act of political expropriation. To the working class and to its parties this looked like the beginning of economic and social expropriation. But Pilsudski saved the Polish propertied classes in spite of themselves and in spite of their traditional representatives; and he did this with the help of the workers' parties.[12]

[11] General Josef Haller, commander of the Polish divisions in France during the First World War, was the hero of the extreme right in Poland, and was Pilsudski's antagonist during the 1920s.

[12] The western reader will see clearly the analogy between this attitude of the Polish Communists and socialists and the illusions which Proudhon, for example, entertained for a time with regard to the person of Napoleon III, or Lassalle with regard to Bismarck. Polish Marxists — especially Rosa Luxemburg's followers — had adopted a very critical attitude towards the traditions and methods of Proudhonism and Lassallism.

All of this does not yet explain fully the origin of the 'May mistake'. Even before the May coup, the leaders of the Polish Communist Party had a premonition that Pilsudski was getting ready to seize power and that this augured nothing good for the working classes. Warski, it seems, said so publicly. Indeed, even some of the leaders of the Polish Socialist Party had few illusions on this score. I remember how, as a novice journalist of nineteen, on the first night of the putsch I found myself by chance in Warecka Street, in the office of Feliks Perl, editor of *Robotnik*,[13] the historian of the Polish Socialist Party, and one of its most eminent leaders. Perl was very worried and indignant. Every few minutes he grabbed the telephone and demanded to be put through to Pilsudski's headquarters, to General Tokarzewski, if I am not mistaken, and with a sweet-and-sour look on his face asked: 'Any news on *our* front, comrade general? How are *our* troops getting on?' Replacing the receiver, he paced nervously up and down, and forgetting that I was there, grumbled to himself: 'This adventurer has landed us in the soup ['adventurer' applied to Pilsudski]. If he fails, things will go badly, but if he wins, he'll thrash us.' This scene repeated itself several times during the night. Meanwhile, the presses in the *Robotnik* printing shop were turning out an appeal 'to the toiling people of the capital' in which the 'adventurer' was hailed as a firm friend of the working class and of socialism.

But let us come back to the Polish Communist Party. Its leaders were too good Marxists to be, in normal circumstances, taken in so easily by optical illusions, even when these illusions originated in the peculiar class relationships in the country. There was another and perhaps a weightier reason for the 'May mistake', and it should be sought in the ideological atmosphere and in the policy of the Soviet Communist Party and the Comintern. The Polish Party was not alone in making such a 'mistake': a similar one on a gigantic scale, which was to have tragic consequences, was committed by the Chinese Communist Party when it blindly supported Chiang Kaishek and the Kuomintang. And in nearby Romania, almost at the same time — I think this was also in May 1926 — the extremely weak Communist Party supported a similar military putsch carried out by General Antonescu.

This was, we remember, the time of the Stalin–Bukharin bloc. Trotskyism had already been routed; the bitter struggle between the Stalin–Bukharin group and the so-called Leningrad opposition led

[13] *Robotnik* was the main newspaper of the Polish Socialist Party.

by Zinoviev and Kamenev was in full swing. Bukharin for reasons of principle, and Stalin for tactical reasons, had both declared themselves the defenders of small peasant property and of the peasantry in general, which was supposedly threatened by the Leningrad opposition. The actual disagreements were over domestic, economic and social policies but, as usual, Stalin transformed a discussion on specific policies into a great dogmatic battle in which the issue at stake was allegedly the fundamental attitude towards the 'middle strata' — the peasantry and the petty bourgeoisie. Stalin and Bukharin accused the Leningrad opposition of hostility towards the 'middle strata' and of failing to understand the importance for the proletariat of the alliance with these strata. This discussion formed a sequel to the anti-Trotskyist campaign of 1923–25, during which the most serious accusation made against Trotsky had been that in his theory of the permanent revolution he too had not 'appreciated at their true value' the importance of the middle strata, their progressive role, and the need to form alliances with them. Trotsky, it was said, had not understood in 1905 the necessity for a bourgeois revolution in Russia (and in the other backward countries) or had underestimated it; that was why he had proclaimed that in the twentieth century the bourgeois-democratic revolution and the socialist revolution would merge into a single one ('permanent revolution') to be accomplished under the leadership of the proletariat throughout. To try and 'skip' the bourgeois stage of the revolution, so the argument ran, was the characteristic aberration of Trotskyism.

I cannot enter here into an analysis of these extremely complex problems; I am concerned now with their repercussions in Poland. The Comintern was just then busy eradicating the Trotskyist and Zinovievist heresies. The distinctive marks of these heresies were defined as an 'ultra-leftist' and negative attitude towards 'alliances with the middle strata', a fundamental unwillingness to make such alliances, and an unwillingness to recognize that bourgeois revolution, especially in the underdeveloped countries, formed a separate stage of historical development, in which the bourgeoisie played a progressive and even a revolutionary role. The Comintern was as if seized with an obsessional cult of 'alliances'. Any sign of scepticism with regard to this cult was stigmatized as Trotskyism. The cult of alliances served a double purpose: within the Soviet Union it justified the 'rightist' line of Bukharin and Stalin; internationally it justified Soviet policy in China, which subordinated the Chinese CP to the Kuomintang and placed it under Chiang Kai-shek's orders. The principles and the methods of this policy were soon applied, automatically and bureaucratically, to all the parties of the International, and among them obviously to the Polish Party. Translated into the terms of Polish politics, this line implied an 'alliance' with Pilsudski as the representative of the 'progressive' forces of the 'bourgeois' revolution. Pilsudski suddenly appeared almost as the ideal ally — and only the Trotskyists and the Zinovievists could spurn the ideal.

At this time were there any Trotskyist or Zinovievist groups within the Polish Communist Party?

As I have already mentioned, Domski and Zofia Unszlicht had ideas which brought them close to the Zinovievist opposition. However, by that time, they had been removed from any activity in the Polish Party. Nevertheless, the Party leadership was fully aware of the practical and political questions as well as of the doctrinal issues which had been raised; and it worked under the pressure of the ideological conflicts in Moscow. At this time Warski and Kostrzewa showed a quite extraordinary docility towards Stalin. They cherished the illusion that by paying the price of submissiveness they would buy for themselves freedom of action in their own Party. Handicapped as they were by their double 'mistake' of 1923 (their intervention in Trotsky's favour and their 'opportunist' policy in Poland), they were anxious to provide every possible proof of their conversion to the new 'Bolshevism' that spoke of two *distinct* stages in the revolution, the bourgeois and the socialist, the 'Bolshevism' that attached so much importance to its alliance with 'progressive bourgeois' elements. The whole Party propaganda was carried out in this spirit; and it created certain conditioned political reflexes within the Party which definitely contributed to the 'May mistake'.

In addition we must examine the effect on the Party's state of mind of the campaign which was carried out with the aim of liquidating what was called the 'Luxemburgist heritage'. This, by the way, is a problem which so far has not received the attention it deserves in Poland, probably because those who study the Party's history have not been equipped sufficiently to tackle the problem — they lack both method and factual knowledge. The most extraordinary myths have multiplied around the 'Luxemburgist heritage'. I do not want this statement to give rise to misunderstandings: I do not claim that Rosa Luxemburg was infallible, and I am not a Luxemburgist. Undoubtedly, she made some mistakes, but they were no more serious than those committed by Lenin or even by Marx, and in any case they were in quite a different category from Stalin's 'errors'. It was, and still is, necessary to analyse these mistakes rigorously and objectively, and to see them in their true proportions. This, however, was not the kind of analysis in which Stalin was interested; nor was Zinoviev in the years 1923–24, when, in the name of the 'Bolshevization' of the Polish CP, they declared a holy war on Luxemburgism — that is, on the main ideological tradition of Polish communism. In order to realize what really mattered to Stalin it would be enough to re-read his notorious 1931 letter to the editor of *Proletarskaya Revolutsiya*. Instinctively, Stalin detected Rosa Luxemburg's affinity with Trotsky. And, even though there had been no Trotskyist opposition within the Polish Party during the 1920s, that party reeked to him of 'Trotskyism'; Stalin considered Luxemburgism as the Polish variety of Trotskyism. This provoked the *furor theologicus* with which the Comintern set out to crush the Luxemburgist heritage.

It is undeniable that this heritage was not above criticism. Lenin's attitude on the question of national independence, or rather of the self-determination of oppressed peoples, was more realistic than that of Rosa Luxemburg. As far as the agrarian question was concerned, Rosa Luxemburg and her disciples did not go beyond advocating the socialization of farming, without understanding the necessity, in Russia and Poland, to share out the land of the semi-feudal latifundia among the peasants. This attitude did not allow Polish communism to exercise revolutionary influence over the peasantry in 1920, particularly in the eastern marches. At the time of the anti-Luxemburgist campaign, however, it was not enough to analyse these mistakes critically. The whole way of thinking, which belonged both to Luxemburgism and to Marxism — the traditions of true internationalism, the Party's specifically proletarian and socialist orientation, its healthy suspicion of the leaders (genuine or self-appointed) of the so-called middle strata — had to be rooted out. Thus the Polish CP began to atone for the Luxemburgist 'sins' against national independence by belated and absurd demonstrations of its reverence for the fetishes of patriotism; and it began to pay undeserved homage to the 'Legends of Independence'. From this there resulted the paradoxical spectacle, which I described above, when, in 1925, Warski sent out a cry of alarm at the dangers which faced national independence and demanded the return of Pilsudski to the post of commander-in-chief. On the one hand Warski was prey to the qualms of his own political conscience, and on the other hand he echoed the anti-Luxemburgist exorcisms that came from Moscow. As if to expiate the 'anti-patriotic' sins of his youth, Warski — and in his person Polish Marxism at large — went to Canossa. On this pilgrimage the Party was once more torn and tormented by bitter misgivings: it paid homage to the would-be dictator, of whom Rosa Luxemburg had said, at the beginning of the century, that his whole 'patriotic' ideology was but the sublimation of the dream of a déclassé petty nobleman who, even under tsardom, saw himself as the future gendarme-in-chief of his 'own' independent Polish state. Rosa may have been mistaken about the chances of bourgeois Poland regaining independence, but she was not wrong about Pilsudski's ambitions and the nature of Pilsudskism.

Finally, Luxemburgism, like Trotskyism, was charged with the mortal sin of failing to understand the Party's tasks in a bourgeois revolution. In their enthusiasm to fight and defeat the Luxemburgist tradition, the Party leaders suddenly discovered that in Poland history had put on the agenda the bourgeois-democratic revolution, and not, as they had thought hitherto, the socialist revolution, which would complete our overdue and unfinished bourgeois revolution. But if the bourgeois revolution was on the agenda, who could be its chief and its leader? Neither in its youth nor in its maturity had the Polish bourgeoisie produced a Danton or a Robespierre. How could it produce one in its old age? But an offshoot of our petty gentry, our 'frontiersman-gentry',[14] could still produce our own parish-pump edition of the 18th Brumaire. It was in him, then, that our Marxists, misled and hopelessly confused by Stalinism, discovered the hero of the bourgeois stage of the revolution. The situation was grotesque precisely because this *bourgeois* revolution was designed to overthrow a government presided over by Witos, the leader of the kulaks, backed by the largest section — the peasant section — of the Polish bourgeoisie. And in retrospect the vicious circle in which the Polish CP moved under Stalinist guidance can be seen even more clearly: in 1926 the Party saw in Pilsudski an ally against the 'fascism' of Witos; and a few years later, in the Popular Front period, it greeted in Witos a fighter and an ally in the struggle against Pilsudski's 'fascism'. Incidentally, without any Stalinist promptings, the Polish Socialist Party was floundering in the same vicious circle.

You have recalled the analogy between the Polish CP's 'May mistake' and the support the Chinese CP was giving to Chiang Kai-shek at the same time. Did the Polish CP give its support to Pilsudski on definite

---

[14] Pilsudski came from the eastern borderlands of the old Poland, famous for the fanfaronades and feuds of its Falstaffian gentry.

orders from Moscow in the same way as the Chinese supported Chiang Kai-shek?

No. Not at all. Stalin's and Bukharin's attitude towards Pilsudski was different from that towards Chiang Kai-shek. In Chiang Kai-shek, then an honorary member of the executive of the International, they saw an ally of the Soviet Union and of Communism. In Pilsudski they saw the enemy of the 1920 war. Not only had Moscow not advised the Communists to support Pilsudski, they immediately took an unfavourable view of the CP's stand in the May coup d'état. Moreover, when the Communist group in the Diet decided to vote in the presidential election for Pilsudski, it was prevented from doing so by the veto of the executive of the Communist International. It was not 'orders from Moscow', which were responsible for the 'May mistake', but rather a certain political fetishism which spread from Moscow and which was inseparable from that stage of the Stalinization and bureaucratization of the Comintern. Stalin did not prompt Warski to report to Pilsudski's headquarters during the May coup. Yet Stalinism was responsible for the 'May mistake', because it had confused the Polish CP, as it had confused other Communist parties, because it had made it impossible for the Party to analyse situations and problems in the Marxist manner, because it had terrorized the Party leaders with cults that did not allow them to work out policies in accordance with the demands of our class struggle and our ideological tradition. One may say what one likes against 'Luxemburgism', but within the framework of this 'ism' there was certainly no place for anything even remotely resembling the 'May mistake'. Can anyone imagine Rosa Luxemburg reporting docilely at Pilsudski's GHQ and declaring her Party's support for his coup? It took a luckless disciple of hers, a disciple whose backbone was already hopelessly deformed by Stalinism, to perform the feat.

How long did the Party maintain this policy?

For a very short time. On the day following the coup d'état or very shortly afterwards as far as I can remember, Communist Party proclamations were circulating in Moscow, branding Pilsudski as a fascist dictator. Pilsudski himself did not allow the Party to cherish any illusions; he refused straightaway to grant an amnesty to the thousands of imprisoned Communists, he boasted loudly of the 'strong-arm' government he was going to set up, he repudiated all 'social experiments' and reforms, and he sought at once to come to terms with the big landowners.

There are some mistakes which are committed in a few days or even hours, but which cannot be repaired in decades. The 'May mistake' was of this kind. In fairness to the Communist Party leaders it must be said that despite Pilsudski's reactionary and dictatorial manners, the Polish Socialist Party backed him for two years or more, while the Communists recovered quickly from their May 'intoxication' and began at once to wage an active struggle against Pilsudski, continuing to do so until the end. Disoriented and knocked off balance as it was, the Communist Party was still the only one to defend the cause of democratic liberties, while the declared upholders of democracy — the socialists — helped Pilsudski to strengthen his position and to undermine all democratic institutions. Warski tried as best he could to make good the 'May mistake'. On this occasion he showed great dignity, militancy and personal courage. In the name of the Party, he hurled accusations in Pilsudski's face and for this, on the dictator's orders and in the dictator's presence, he was dragged out of the National Assembly by Pilsudski's guards. In order to realize the effect that Warski's cry, 'Down with the dictator' had, one must bear in mind the cult which surrounded Pilsudski at that time. Pilsudski himself was as if taken aback by this cry: this was the first attack on his legend, the first attempt to tear it to shreds. I also remember the image of Warski at the Theatre Square on 1 May, 1928. He was marching in the forefront of our huge and illegal demonstration, through the hail of machine-gun fire and rifle shots with which we were greeted by the Socialist Party militia;[15] while tens and hundreds of wounded were falling in our ranks, he held up his white-grey head, a high and easy target visible from afar; unyielding and unmoved, he addressed the crowd. This was the image of him I had in my mind when, some years later, it was announced from Moscow that he was a traitor, a spy, and a Pilsudski agent.

What responsibility had the different 'majority' and 'minority' factions for the 'May mistake'? Did this split exist even before 1926?

As far as I know these divisions did not exist before 1926. It was, in

[15]Shortly afterwards this militia was to break with the Socialist Party and enter Pilsudski's service.

fact, the 'May mistake' which brought them into being; if my memory does not betray me, these two factions first came to the fore at the plenary session of the Central Committee in September 1926. And, as it happens, the new split was traced back to previous dissensions. Lenski, the leader of the minority, belonged in 1924–25, after the 'three W's' had been dismissed, to what was called the 'left'. Most of those who had belonged to it were now indeed on the side of the minority; and many of those who had belonged to the 'right' were now on the side of the majority. Even older antagonisms played a role, for two of the leaders of the majority, Kostrzewa and Walecki, had come from the Left Socialist Party; as for the opposition between Warski and Lenski, an attempt was made to trace it back to the conflicts within the Social-Democratic Party (the Luxemburgists) before the First World War. Nevertheless, it seems to me that these were artificial genealogical trees, and that they were dragged in quite gratuitously. Their irrelevance to the situation of 1926 is proved by the fact that both factions, the majority as well as the minority, were responsible for the 'May mistake'. At the critical juncture both behaved in exactly the same way. Both supported Pilsudski. Both equally recognized their responsibility for the blunder — the question they quarrelled about was which of the factions had contributed more and which had contributed less to the 'May mistake'.

The majority was particularly identified with the theory of the 'two distinct stages of the revolution' and the tactic of the united front, in which the Communist Party marched, or limped, behind the Socialist Party. It was a little more difficult to define the attitude of the leaders of the minority, who themselves did not go to the trouble of defining it. To a large extent they represented a mood of 'radicalism' in the Party rather than any precise theoretical concepts. In no instance did they fight against the fetishes which were being imposed on the Polish Party by the Comintern, and which had contributed to the 'Bolshevization', or in other words to the bureaucratization of the Polish CP. To that extent they contributed in a greater measure, perhaps, to the moral disarming of the movement. Both factions shared responsibility and each tried, not very effectively, to shift the blame to the other. This was a difficult period. The Party was split from top to bottom and indulged in mutual and sterile recriminations.

The recriminations were sterile because neither of the two factions was in a position to reveal the true sources of the mistake; neither was capable even *post factum* of making a Marxist analysis of the May putsch and of the regime which came out of it. Each faction sought in its adversary the cause for the Party's moral-political disaster; neither dared to look for the cause in the Comintern; neither had the courage to attack the fetishes of Stalinism; neither had the courage to challenge the false 'Bolshevization' of the Party. Neither dared to submit to a critical analysis the methods by which the 'Luxemburgist heritage' had been fought; neither had the nerve to try to save what had been and still was great and valid in this heritage. Let us hope that the Polish working class will now rediscover this heritage at last. It will find there its own past and its own forgotten greatness. However, it is quite possible that habits of thought, formed not just in these last years but for a good thirty years, will make it difficult for the young as well as for the old generation of Polish Marxists to find a key to that heritage. I should like to add that this cannot be a question of using, for some tactical purposes, a few isolated fragments of Rosa's thinking, such as, for example, her initial doubts about 1917 — there is no lack of such attempts to 'use' Rosa Luxemburg in present-day Poland. No, the task of Polish Marxists is to assimilate the sum and substance of the ideas of our greatest revolutionary, the ideas which are in full harmony with the enduring achievement of Lenin.

But let us come back to the Polish CP. The Party was then searching exclusively within itself for the causes of its political errors. The leaders hoped to remain at the helm with the support of the ruling circles in the Soviet Union. Warski and Kostrzewa relied more, perhaps, on the support of Bukharin, who was then the moving spirit in the International. As for Lenski, he staked his future on Stalin. The two factions were desperately afraid of the possibility of a conflict with the Russians; they feared that this would amount to a break with the revolution and with the international Communist movement. I am not making here any indictment of the men who led the Polish Party. They had their reasons for behaving as they did. I know from my own experience, as the former member of an opposition which was not afraid of conflict with the Soviet Party and which undertook the struggle in 1932 with full knowledge of what was involved — I know from my own bitter experience that in fact all the groups which did not recoil from this conflict condemned themselves to isolation and political impotence. But the fact that the leaders of the Polish Party had submitted to Stalin did not save them from political impotence either. And it did not save them from leading the working class into a blind alley; it condemned them to intellectual and moral sterility, and the Party — to death.

The conflict between the majority and the minority already presented a sad spectacle of that sterility. It was like a quarrel of damned souls imprisoned within the enchanted circle of Stalinism. There was no endeavour to find an explanation of the situation and to investigate the mistakes made and the tasks ahead; all were merely anxious to display Stalinist orthodoxy and loyalty to the bosses of the Comintern. Each faction used the latest orthodox formula to whiten itself and blacken its adversary. Any student who would now immerse himself in the Party literature of this period would be struck by the scholastic methods of this controversy, by the obsessive repetition of some magic formulas, and by the queer violence of a debate, the object of which remains altogether elusive.

Did you yourself belong to the majority or to the minority?

I did not belong to either, probably because when I joined the Party, at the age of nineteen, the dividing line had already been drawn and I did not really understand what it was all about. However, I remember clearly that in 1926–27 I had a very sharp sense of the futility of the dispute. It seemed to me that the majority carried the burden of a certain opportunism, and that the minority had the more revolutionary dynamic. What disturbed me about the latter was its intellectual crudity and inclination towards sectarianism. It seemed to me that the majority represented a more serious school of thought and a deeper Marxist tradition. This was the predominant view among the group of comrades with whom I mixed, young Communist as I then was. This may have induced me to keep aloof from both factions and to search in a different direction for a way out of the impasse. I am convinced that the history of the Polish Party must be tackled afresh; to approach it from the angle either of the old minority or of the old majority would lead nowhere and would bring no positive result, intellectually or politically.

Which of the factions was dominant in the Party after May 1926?

At the time of the coup d'état the two factions shared the leadership, and this state of affairs lasted almost until the end of 1928. At the beginning of this period, Warski's and Kostrzewa's ascendancy was more marked, if only because the Bukharinist line still predominated in the Comintern. As usual, their influence showed itself in a more 'organic' activity of the Party, in a closer link between the Party and the masses, in a greater realism of its agitation, and in its stronger pull on the left elements in the Socialist Party, and also on the rural population and on the national minorities. In spite of the mutual recriminations which weakened it, the Party had in certain respects recovered quickly from its 'May mistake'. The working class had 'forgiven' that mistake. Hadn't the Communists admitted their error sincerely and unambiguously? After all, they all shared the same illusions. The Party was now gaining strength. This was proved, for example, by the results of the municipal elections in Warsaw, where, in 1927, more votes were cast for the CP's illegal list than for the list of any other party. The electors knew that their pro-Communist votes were lost, that none of our candidates would get into the municipal council, but they nevertheless demonstratively voted Communist. This was again a period when in the main industrial centres — Warsaw, Lodz, the Dabrowa coalfields — the CP was stronger than the Socialist Party, in spite of severe police persecution and wasteful interfactional struggle. In 1928 the Communist Party really was leading the working class in its struggle against the Pilsudski dictatorship. The fear which seized the Pilsudskists and a section of the Socialist Party explains the bloody repression of May 1, of which I spoke earlier. (The illegal Communist demonstrations were very often larger than the demonstrations of the Socialist Party, which marched under the double protection of the police and their own armed militia.) In spite of all the handicaps and difficulties, the Party had some chance of going over to the offensive again. Just at this moment, however, it suffered a new blow, which knocked it off its relative balance and rendered it powerless.

Are you referring to the change in the leadership and to the elimination of Warski and Kostrzewa?

Yes. And once again it was not *what* happened that mattered so much as *how* it happened. Whether Warski and Kostrzewa or Lenski was at the helm was less important than the fact that the change was brought about solely from 'above', that it bore no relation to the logic of the class struggle in Poland. Once again, the Russian Party and the International weighed on the fate of Polish Communists and the Polish working classes.

At the Sixth Congress of the International, in the summer of 1928, the struggle between Stalin and Bukharin, previously confined within the Soviet Politburo, had burst into the open. Acting under the pressure of the USSR's internal crisis, Stalin was reviving his policy towards the peasantry and preparing the wholesale collectivization. A huge social drama was being enacted in the Soviet Union, and it entailed another drama, less obvious but in its consequences equally grave, for European Communism. Having broken with Bukharin on domestic issues, Stalin set out to eradicate all Bukharinist influence in the Comintern and to change international Communist policy. Automatically, this involved the condemnation of the 'majority' in the Polish CP. Warski and Kostrzewa were deprived of all influence. The steering wheel was violently turned 'left'. In 1929 Molotov put forward the ill-fated conception of a 'third period' which, briefly, consisted in this: the capitalist world was entering a directly revolutionary situation, and consequently the Communist movement must go over to an offensive struggle for power; social-democracy, otherwise 'social-fascism', was Communism's main and most dangerous enemy; moreover, the left wing of the social-democratic parties was more dangerous than the right wing; the Communists should direct their main fire against that enemy; they were forbidden to enter into any agreements with Socialists, they should set up their own Red Trade Unions (breaking away from the general trade unions) and, with their help, organize general strikes and armed insurrections. The policy of the 'third period' was in force from 1929 to 1934. This was the time when Nazism was growing like an avalanche in Germany, and in the face of this threat, to which the Social-Democrats were surrendering anyhow, the Communist Party found itself disarmed. When the Party was told that its main enemy was not Hitler but 'social-fascism', and that it had no right to ally itself with social-democracy against Nazism, German Communism, tied hand and foot, was delivered over to the heroes of the swastika.

In Poland the *direct* results of this policy were not yet quite as tragic, but they were grim enough. The simmering conflict between Pilsudski on the one hand, and the Socialist Party and the peasant movement on the other, was nearing the boiling point. These were the years of the Left-Centre opposition. Pilsudski seized the leaders of this opposition and had them imprisoned and tortured in the fortress of Brzesc. The anti-Communist terror, too, had grown more intense and reached a climax with the tortures inflicted on Ukrainian Communists imprisoned in Luck. In these conditions the policy and the slogans of the 'third period', diligently translated into Polish by Lenski, had all the characteristics of a malignant political diversion. The Party member had to 'concentrate the fire' on the victims of Brzesc and not on their executioners; he had to believe that the Party's gravest sin would be to support the struggle of the Left-Centre against Pilsudski, or to turn this struggle into a fierce revolutionary contest, which the leaders of the Left-Centre neither could nor wished to do.

In conditions incomparably more serious, the Polish CP repeated the whole series of ultra-left mistakes which it had committed in 1924–25. It indulged once more in ultra-revolutionary acrobatics, which consisted in launching revolutionary activities with great energy into an empty space — activities the aims of which became less and less real. Loud and big words were not followed by deeds. The Party operated exclusively within its own ranks — and these were melting away. It cut itself off from the working and peasant masses who had been first aroused and then confounded by the half-hearted struggle of the Left-Centre. It lost common language with the mass of workers and found itself driven more and more towards the fringe of politics, towards radical but politically impotent déclassé petty-bourgeois elements (mostly Jewish). The leaders did not, and would not, see the vacuum around the Party and the moral ravages in the rank and file. In the long run a revolutionary party cannot tolerate with impunity a divorce between word and deed; nor can it turn its back on reality and feed on the conventional fictions of a pseudo-revolutionary 'line' without having one day to pay for all this with the distortion of its own character. This indeed was the price the whole Comintern paid for the policy of the 'third period'. The Polish Party, in addition, laboured under the dictatorship of a faction which — following Stalin's example — dragged its inner-party opponents in the mud, gagged them, and thus stopped all the processes of opinion-formation within the party. These characteristics of the Stalinist inner-party regime, with which Poland was to become so thoroughly acquainted in the 1940s and 1950s, existed by the end of the twenties and had become fully developed in 1932–33. The phenomenon was all the more paradoxical because it did not result from the 'corruption of power', which to some degree may be expected in a ruling party, nor did it come about through the growth of a bureaucracy jealous of its social and political privileges. The Polish Communist Party remained the party of the oppressed and the persecuted. Its members and followers continued to crowd Pilsudski's and Rydz-Smigly's prisons. The dream of proletarian revolution and socialism still animated them. It was this dream precisely that made them inclined to accept blindly everything which came from the Soviet Union — the fatherland of the proletariat. Instead of being true to itself, the Party was becoming false to itself. Guided by its devotion to the cause of revolution, it was losing itself as the party of revolution.

In the middle 1930s there took place in the Party a turn in favour of the Popular Front. How did this influence the Party?

At this time, I was already out of the Party. Cut off from it, I could judge the facts from the outside only. Whatever else may be said about it, the policy of the Popular Front undoubtedly rejuvenated and refreshed the Party, which came into contact with reality. This brought new elements within the Party's sphere of influence. The intellectuals, who were then attracted by the Polish Party, now play, it seems to me, an important role in Poland's political life. That is why to the young generation they present this period as idealized and enveloped in a beautifying mist. Nevertheless, we must examine it coolly and objectively.

The Popular Front was the extreme opposite of the policy of the 'third period'. Yesterday's 'social-fascists' turned out to be anti-fascist fighters. Even the right-wing leaders of the peasant movement, like Witos, were recognized as knights-errant of democracy and progress. By comparison with the moderation of the Party's new tactical line, the 'opportunism' of Warski and Kostrzewa looked like exuberant ultra-radicalism. Yet the slogans of the Popular Front were, in 1935 and 1936, launched by the same leaders (Lenski and Henrykowski) who in the previous years had directed their main fire against the 'social-fascists' and who had considered 'united front from below' as the only admissible policy, and who had expelled hundreds of militants simply because they had dared to doubt whether social-fascism was really 'the main and most serious danger'. Once again, what is important is not so much *what* policy was applied as *how* it was applied. No inner-party discussion had preceded this violent change of line, which only followed the change of line of the Comintern, a line based in its turn on the calculations of Stalin's foreign policy. The effect which the reversal of policy had on the Party itself was therefore full of contradictions. On the one hand, the break with the 'third period' had a stimulating and reviving influence on the Party, and allowed it to escape from its vacuum. On the other hand, the mechanical character of this turn, coming entirely from 'above', increased still further the atrophy of political thinking among the cadres of old militants, who had already become accustomed to replace one set of political rituals by another at a single word of command and to consider all political notions and all watchwords as so many conventional phrases with no living content. Cynicism and ideological apathy made serious inroads. The young, who began their political life under the banner of the Popular Front, greeted the new slogans much more seriously and threw themselves with enthusiasm into the thick of anti-fascist activity. Nevertheless this period was not conducive to the formation of Marxist consciousness in the young; they absorbed only very little of the Party's specifically Communist tradition. The Party propaganda, disseminating the vaguest of 'democratic' and anti-fascist slogans and the most insipid 'let's all get together' proclamations, was jettisoning all the criteria of proletarian interest and class struggle. It hardly differed from the routine propaganda of right-wing socialists, except that it markedly lacked any genuineness. Ideological shallowness and a patriotic-democratic vulgarity characterized the Party which once drew its inspiration from Rosa Luxemburg's flaming thought.

I am dwelling on this not in order to tear open old wounds or revive lapsed controversies, but in order to show the state of spiritual weakness in which the Party found itself on the eve of its assassination, and so to explain the passivity and the silence with which in 1938 it received its own death sentence and endured the unparalleled slaughter of its leaders.

A picture presenting the Polish CP as a flourishing, intellectually healthy body, brimming over with strength, which suddenly fell a victim to Yezhov's provocation, would be false and unhistorical. There is no need to resort to such a myth in order to rehabilitate the Party. Moreover, this would transform the very act of rehabilitation into a magic ritual. How did it happen, we must ask, that a Party which had to its credit decades of underground struggle and a long (seventy years long!) and proud Marxist tradition submitted meekly to this horrible outrage — without a protest, without making any attempt to defend its martyred leaders and fighters, without even trying to vindicate its honour, and without declaring that in spite of the death sentence Stalin had passed on it, it would live on and fight on? How could this happen? We must be fully aware of the moral corrosion to which Stalinism had for so many years exposed Polish Communism in order to understand its complete collapse under the blow.

At the time of its dissolution, the Polish CP was charged with being 'infected' with Trotskyism and of being an agency of the Polish political police. What in fact was the influence of Trotskyism on the Party?

The Trotskyist opposition in the Party was formed in the years 1931–32. It grouped comrades who had formerly belonged both to the minority and to the majority, and others who had not been connected with either faction. The opposition did not *a priori* take up a Trotskyist stand. It was formed on the basis of a critical view of the policy of the 'third period', the slogans about 'social-fascism', the 'united front only from below', etc., and also of the bureaucratic inner-party regime. Demanding the right of self-determination for the Polish Party, the opposition adopted a critical attitude towards the regime that was prevailing within the International and the Soviet Party. Consequently, the ideas of the Trotskyist opposition in the USSR and particularly the magnificent, though fruitless, campaign which Trotsky waged in exile for a united front against Hitler, had a powerful and decisive impact on our group. At the beginning, the opposition exercised a fairly large influence. In Warsaw, where the Party counted at that time, it seems, hardly more than a thousand members, the opposition had about three hundred members (most of whom had played an important role in the movement), not counting a large circle of sympathizers in the Party organizations. Unfortunately, the deplorable condition in which the Party found itself affected the opposition too. The Party was cut off from the workers in large industry and was relegated to a petty-bourgeois fringe, and this weakness was reflected in the opposition. Although we had attracted many militants in the capital, our influence was much weaker in the provinces, where the pulse of Party life in general had been rather feeble. The bulk of the militants viewed the opposition with much sympathy so long as they did not realize that not only adherence but even mere contact with the opposition would be punished by expulsion from the Party. The new grouping, which did not simply continue the old and sterile quarrel between minority and majority but posed the problem of Party policy on a new plane, was at first greeted with relief. The Party leaders retorted by expelling and slandering us in the best Stalinist style. The same leaders who, a few years hence, were to be liquidated as police agents now branded the opposition as the 'agency' of 'social-fascism', then simply of fascism, and as a gang of 'enemies of the USSR'.

By the use of such methods, the leadership succeeded in stifling all discussion and terrorizing Party members to such an extent that they began to shun us with the superstitious fear with which faithful members of the Church used to shun excommunicated heretics. The opposition was hermetically isolated from the Party, and by 1936 had almost no contact with it. Thus the charge that the Polish CP had become a Trotskyist 'agency' was sheer invention. But nevertheless, the doubts and ideas that the opposition had sown in the Party continued to germinate. Even while Party members remained conformist, many of them never ceased to listen to the voice of the opposition, and they were influenced by it to a greater or lesser degree — at any rate sufficiently to be sceptical about the holy writ of Stalinism. And since nothing in nature is ever lost completely, the Luxemburgist tradition had not vanished completely either, in spite of the years which had been spent on uprooting it. The opposition's influence and the effect of that tradition was such that even after years of 'Bolshevization', the psychological profile of even the most orthodox Polish Communist left much to be desired from the Stalinist point of view. Thus it was in the 1930s; fortunately it was like this also after the Second World War: during this whole period a certain law of continuity had never ceased to operate.

Nevertheless, a question must be posed. We know that Pilsudski had his agents in all the left-wing parties. Surely he must have tried to introduce them into the CP as well?

The theory of these networks of agents which Pilsudski supposedly had created in various left-wing parties is again a crude simplification. No network of secret agents could have enabled Pilsudski to exercise on the Socialists and on a part of the peasant movement the influence he did exercise as a result of his long and above-board connections with these parties. He was one of the founding fathers of the Polish Socialist Party and was for many years its chief leader and inspirer. He had been the Commander of the Legion, to which men of the patriotic left had rallied. Even after he had left the Socialist Party, he continued to represent something that belonged to its essence: social-patriotism pushed to the extreme. It was that which formed the basis of Pilsudski's 'magical' influence. The worship of Polish 'statehood', the dreams of the 'One and Sovereign' Poland, old loyalties, friendships, and ties of sentiment — these gave birth to those Pilsudskist 'networks' in parties of the moderate and patriotic left, which at times of conflict he attempted to destroy from within. There was not, and there could not have been, any similar basis for a Pilsudskist network in the Polish CP. The left-wing socialists who, after 1918, found themselves in the ranks and in the leadership of the Communist Party, had to their credit more than ten years of bitter struggle against Pilsudski. As for the old Luxemburgists, it is hardly necessary to dwell on their attitude towards him. However, even in the moderate, patriotic, left parties (PPS or *Wyzwolenie*) Pilsudski's 'agents' achieved very little. Very quickly these parties overcame the confusion and splits provoked by the 'networks'. Only the Polish CP, if we are to believe Stalin, was *completely* in the hands of Pilsudski's 'agents'. In 1938, when this accusation was made and one wanted to refute it, one felt overwhelmed by the sheer nonsense of it all. It is true that during the 1930s the Polish Party had suffered particularly from police provocations. The fall in the ideological level of most of the militants, the bitterness of the factional struggles, the ultra-revolutionary policy of the years 1929–35 — all this had facilitated to a certain extent the penetration of police agents into the Party. It would in any case have been surprising if the police had had no agents whatsoever in the Polish CP in the same way in which the Tsarist Okhrana had had its Azefs and its Malinowskis in nearly all the illegal Russian organizations. However, no one would have had the idea of dissolving the Bolshevik Party or the Socialist Revolutionary Party for that reason. The Stalinist provocation was a much more serious danger for the Polish CP than all the *agents provocateurs* of the Polish secret police.[16]

What, then, in your opinion were the reasons for which Stalin ordered the dissolution of the Polish Party? The view which prevails now among old Party militants is that Stalin was already preparing the ground for his 1939 agreement with Hitler and that he liquidated the Polish Party and sent its leaders to their death because he feared that they might obstruct that agreement.

This motive no doubt played a part in Stalin's decision but does not explain it fully. Warski and Kostrzewa, for years cut off from all contact with Poland (and the world), were no longer in a position to offer the slightest resistance to Stalin, even if they had wished to do so. As for Lenski and Henrykowski, I am convinced that they would have remained faithful to Stalin even in a situation as critical for Polish Communism as that of August and September 1939, in the same way as were the leaders of the French Party, not to mention the Germans and others. But here we are dealing with hypotheses. It seems to me that no single motive or sober calculation can explain Stalin's behaviour in this matter. His irrational impulses were quite as important as his 'rational' calculations; and he was impelled to act as he did by old grudges and ancient phobias, all intensified to the

---

[16]Azef was a well-known *agent provocateur* who led the terrorist organization of the Russian Social-Revolutionary Party. Malinowski, who was Lenin's friend, a deputy to the Duma, and an influential member of the Bolshevik Central Committee, was finally also exposed as an *agent provocateur*.

utmost by the persecution mania which gripped him at the time of the great Moscow trials, when he was settling his final accounts with the Leninist old guard. In this frame of mind, Stalin saw the Polish CP as the stronghold of hated Luxemburgism — the Polish 'variety of Trotskyism' — which had defied him as long ago as 1923; the Party in which some leaders were close to Bukharin and others to Zinoviev; the Party of incurable heresies, proud of its traditions and of its heroism; the Party, finally, which might well in certain international situations become an obstacle on his road . . . And so he decided to remove that obstacle by the blade of the same guillotine which, working furiously, was already destroying a whole generation of Bolsheviks.

The historian will not end his account of the fortunes of the Polish CP on the act of its annihilation. The epilogue of the story is, in a sense, its most important chapter. The 'posthumous' fate of the Polish CP will remain the most striking testimony of its greatness. Crushed, decimated, confounded and outraged, the Party's old cadre was still the spearhead of all of Poland's revolutionary forces. It was that remnant of the old Party which at the end of the Second World War, in the peculiar international situation which favoured social revolution, carried this revolution through. The survivors of the Polish CP came forward as the executors of their Party's will, although they had to do so in conditions and by methods that no philosophers dreamed of. And nearly twenty years after the massacre of the Polish CP, its spirit and, if you like, something of its old Luxemburgist tradition, showed themselves in October 1956.

Not only the historian, but also every militant Marxist, must draw certain conclusions from the tragic history of the Polish CP. Here, I must of necessity confine myself to one rather general idea: if the history of the Polish CP and of Poland at large proves anything at all, *it proves how indestructible is the link between the Polish and the Russian revolutions*. This has been proved both negatively and positively. For her attempt to place herself athwart the international revolution which had begun in Russia — the attempt made in 1918–20 — Poland had to pay with twenty years of stagnation and backwardness, of provincially narrow and anachronistic social life, and, finally, with the catastrophe of 1939. On the other hand, the revolution, isolated in old and backward Russia, isolated by the world's anti-communist forces (with Poland's eager help), underwent a distortion which not only affected tragically the peoples of the USSR but revenged itself on Poland as well. Already in 1920 Poland had felt something of that revenge. Subsequently, it led to the deformation of the working-class movement in Poland, condemning it to sterility and impotence. Then there came 1939. After the Second World War, the Russian Revolution, in spite of all its distortions, still showed itself to be sufficiently alive and dynamic to stimulate new revolutionary processes in Europe and Asia. Poland once again absorbed from the Russian Revolution its shadows as well as its lights and took over from it, together with the blessings of a progressive upheaval in social relationships, the curse of bureaucratic terror and the Stalin cult. Poland had to pay a heavy penalty for the 'miracle on the Vistula' of 1920,[17] in which she had gloried for twenty years. Having spurned the Russian Revolution in its heroic stage, she had to humble herself before this same revolution after it had degenerated. Having scorned Lenin and Leninist internationalism, Poland had to prostrate herself before Stalin and Great Russian chauvinism. Only as the Soviet Union was beginning to awaken from the nightmare of Stalinism could Poland free herself from it, and by that very act stimulate processes of recovery in other socialist countries. But only as the Russian Revolution emerges from the sidetracks onto which history drove it and at last enters the highway of socialist democracy, will the perspectives before People's Poland clear up definitely. At every step history demonstrates *ad oculos* how indissoluble are the bonds between the Polish and the Russian revolutions. But whereas hitherto history has again and again demonstrated the indissoluble nature of this bond in a negative manner — by inflicting the most cruel lessons on Poland — in October 1956 it has begun perhaps to demonstrate it in the positive, that is, in the only effective manner. History so far has not always been a good and sensible teacher. The lessons in internationalism which it attempted to teach the Polish masses were singularly involved, badly thought out, and ineffective. During almost every one of these 'lessons', history mocked and insulted Poland's national dignity and, in the first place, the dignity and independence of the Polish revolutionary movement. Is it surprising then, that the 'pupil' has not been very receptive, and, trying to escape the peculiar 'teacher', has sought refuge in the jungle of our nationalist legends? The Polish masses will understand that the bonds which unite their destiny with that of the Russian and other revolutions are indissoluble, but only after they have recovered from the blows and shocks inflicted on them in the past, and when they feel

[17]The 'miracle on the Vistula' was the name given to the battle of Warsaw, in which Pilsudski's armies inflicted defeat on the Soviet army. At the time of this battle, General Weygand was Pilsudski's adviser.

that nothing can ever again threaten their independence and national dignity. Marxists, however, must rise above the shocks and the traumas from which the masses suffer; and they must even now be deeply and thoroughly aware of the common destiny of Poland and other nations advancing towards socialism. Marxists have no right to nourish themselves, nor to feed others, on the spiritual diet of stale and warmed-up myths and legends. Socialism does not aim at the perpetuation of the national state; its aim is international society. It is based not on national self-centredness and self-sufficiency, but on international division of labour and on cooperation. This almost forgotten truth is the very ABC of Marxism.

You may say that what I am proposing is a new edition of Luxemburgism, slightly amended and adapted to the needs of 1957. Perhaps. You may tell me that this is merely a new version of the theory of 'organic incorporation'.[18] Perhaps. But what is at stake this time is the 'organic integration' of Poland into international socialism, not her incorporation into a Russian empire.

This interview was originally published in French in *Les Temps Modernes*, March 1958. The interviewer was K.S. Karol.

[18]In her theory of 'organic incorporation', which she formulated in her doctoral thesis, Rosa Luxemburg stated that the struggle for Poland's independence was hopeless and in essence even reactionary because of the 'organic' economic ties that linked Poland and Russia; neither the Polish bourgeoisie nor the Polish proletariat was interested in the restoration of a sovereign Poland: the bourgeoisie because Russian markets were more profitable to it, and the proletariat because it strove for international socialism. This conception formed the theoretical basis of Luxemburgist politics.

2

An Open Letter to Wladyslaw Gomulka

and the Central Committee
of the PolishWorkers Party*

I am addressing this letter to you in order to protest against the recent
secret trials and conviction of Ludwik Hass, Karol Modzelewski,
Kazimierz Badowski, Romuald Smiech, Jacek Kuron, and other
members of your Party.According to all available reports, these men
have been deprived of liberty solely because they have voiced views
critical of your policy or certain aspects of it, and because they have
expressed disappointment with the bureaucratic arbitrariness and
corruption which they see rampant in their country. The charge
against them is that they have circulated leaflets and a pamphlet
containing 'false information detrimental to the State and its supreme
authorities' — the public prosecutor, it seems, did not accuse them
of any crime or offence graver than that.

If this is the accusation, then the persecution of these men is
disgraceful and scandalous. Several questions must be asked: Why, in
the first instance, have the courts held their hearings *in camera*?
Surely, no matter of State security was or could have been involved.
All the defendants have been academic teachers and students, and
what they have tried to do was to communicate their views to fellow
students. Why have they not been given a fair and open trial? Why
have your own newspapers not even summarized the indictments
and the pleas of the defence? Is it because the proceedings have been
so absurd and shameful that you yourselves feel that you cannot
justify or excuse them; and so you prefer to cover them with silence
and oblivion? As far as I know, prosecutor and judges have not
impugned the defendants' motives or cast any serious doubt on their
integrity. The accused men have proclaimed themselves to be, and
have behaved like, devoted non-conformist Communists, profoundly convinced of the truth and validity of revolutionary
Marxism.

I know that one of them, Ludwik Hass, was, even before the

Second World War, a member of the Communist, so-called Trotskyist, organization of which I was one of the founders and mouthpiece. He then spent seventeen years in Stalin's prisons, concentration camps, and places of deportation. Released in 1957, he returned to Poland so free from all bitterness and so strongly animated by his faith in a better socialist future that he at once decided to join your Party; and he was accepted as a member. No one asked him to renounce his past, and he did not deny his old 'Trotskyist' views even for a moment —on the contrary, he upheld them frankly and untiringly. This circumstance alone testifies to his courage and integrity. Do you, Wladyslaw Gomulka, really believe that you have, in your 'apparatus' and administration, many people of comparable disinterestedness and idealism? Look around you, look at the crowds of time-servers that surround you, at all those opportunists without principle and honour who fawn on you as they fawned on Bierut, and as some of them fawned even on Rydz-Smigly and Pilsudski. On how many of these bureaucrats can your government, and can socialism, count in an hour of danger, as it can count on the people you have put in prison?

Recently your government claimed with a certain pride that there have been no political prisoners in Poland since 1956. This claim, if true, was indeed something to be proud of in a country the jails of which had always, under all regimes, been full of political prisoners, especially of communist prisoners. You have not, as far as I know, jailed and put in chains any of your all too numerous and virulent anti-communist opponents; and you deserve credit for the moderation with which you treat them. But why do you deny such treatment to your critics on the left? Hass, Modzelewski and their friends have been brought to the courtrooms handcuffed and under heavy guard. Eyewitness accounts say that they raised their chained fists in the old Communist salute and sang the *Internationale*. This detail speaks eloquently about their political characters and loyalties. How many of your dignitaries, Wladyslaw Gomulka, would nowadays intone the *Internationale* of their own free will and accord?

I have been informed that before the trial, during the interrogation, the official who conducted it alleged that Hass and other defendants had worked in contact with me. I do not know whether the prosecutor took up this charge in the courtroom. In any case, the allegation is a complete falsehood. Let me say that if the defendants had tried to get in touch with me, I would have readily responded. But the fact is that I have had no contact whatsoever with any of them. I have not even seen a single one of their leaflets or pamphlets. I judge their behaviour solely from reports reaching me by word of mouth or through Western European newspapers.

I ought perhaps to explain that since the Second World War I have not participated in Polish political life in any way, and that, not being a member of any political organization, Trotskyist or otherwise, I am speaking only for myself. I should add, however, that on a few very rare occasions I have broken my self-imposed political abstinence. I protested when you, Wladyslaw Gomulka, were imprisoned and slandered in the last years of the Stalin era. Knowing full well that I could not share all your views, I expressed solidarity with you. Similarly, I do not know whether I can fully approve the views and behaviour of Hass, Modzelewski and their comrades. But in their case, as in yours, I think I can recognize reactionary police terror for what it is and tell slander from truth.

Another occasion on which I allowed myself to have a say on Polish political matters was in 1957, when I explained in a special essay 'The Tragedy of Polish Communism between the World Wars'. You may remember that your censors, Stalinists of the so-called Natolin group, confiscated the essay when *Polityka* tried to publish it, and that then you, Wladyslaw Gomulka, ordered the essay to be widely distributed among Party members. In those far-off days, just after the 'Polish spring in October', you held that Polish Communists ought to know my account of the havoc that Stalin made of their Party, delivering nearly all its leaders to the firing squad. You knew that I had been one of those very few communists who, in 1938, protested against that crime and against the disbandment and denigration of what had once been our common Party. Moscow 'rehabilitated' the Polish Party and its leaders only after seventeen or eighteen years; and then you, Wladyslaw Gomulka, apologized for having kept silent in 1938, although you had not believed the Stalinist slanders. I do not believe that you are right now in persecuting and imprisoning members of your own Party and your critics on the left; and I cannot keep silent.

May I remind you of your own words spoken at the famous Eighth Session of the Central Committee in October 1956? 'The cult of the personality was not a matter just of Stalin's person,' you stated then. 'This was a system which had been transplanted from the USSR to nearly all Communist Parties . . . *We have finished, or rather we are finishing, with that system once and for all.*' (Your italics.)

But are you not to some extent re-establishing that system? Do you wish these trials to mark the tenth anniversary of your own rehabilitation and of that 'spring in October', during which you raised so many hopes for the future?

In the name of those hopes and in the name of your own record, the record of a fighter and of a political prisoner under Pilsudski and Stalin, I appeal to you and to your colleagues of the Central Committee: Do not allow this miscarriage of justice to last! Dispel the secrecy that surrounds the cases of Hass, Modzelewski and their comrades. If you think that they are guilty of grave offences, then publish the full report of the court proceedings and let it speak for itself. In any case, I appeal to you to order an immediate and public revision of the trial. If you refuse these demands, you will stand condemned as epigones of Stalinism, guilty of stifling your own Party and compromising the future of socialism.

London, 24 April 1966

Isaac Deutscher

3

Dialogue with Heinrich Brandler

15 February 1948

Brandler has· returned from Cuba and has a temporary United Kingdom visa. He is working on his memoirs. 'The more I think about my reminiscences,' he says, the more difficult it is for me to find a satisfying way of writing them. I feel that the language — *my* language — can no longer be comprehended by my reader, by the German worker of today. My friends are pressing me to write because I can do nothing sensible and worthwhile in practical politics now. And this is true. I would like to get into contact with a living and lively German worker. Even for my memoirs, such a contact is very much needed.' Brandler goes back in his story to the 1890s, to the Congresses of [German] Social Democracy. 'Only now do I realize how tremendous was the treasure of ideas which the German workers' movement acquired by its own exertions and quite independently. We were so impressed by the achievements of the Bolsheviks that we forgot our own. Take Lenin's *Imperialism,* which is quite correctly regarded as a standard work. Already at the 1907 International Congress in Stuttgart, and at other conferences at the end of the previous century, most of the ideas which Lenin developed in his *Imperialism* were already being debated, mainly by Kautsky.'

Before the First World War, Brandler belonged to the radical wing of German Social Democracy. Leader of the Chemnitz branch of the building workers' union, he was close to Rosa Luxemburg and Karl Liebknecht. About Rosa he speaks with emotion, but not uncritically. He says that the tragedy of the revolution in Germany consisted in the fact that none of the leaders had any concrete programme, or any concrete idea how to proceed, not even Rosa. Rosa was easily carried away by the mood around her; she created enthusiasm among the masses, then was carried away by that enthusiasm and overrated its power. For example, she would come to Chemnitz, inflame thousands of her listeners and then say to

Brandler: 'Well, now you will be able to move forward in your organizational work.' 'I used to answer,' continued Brandler, 'that we should be very glad to retain just a tiny part of that fever and transform it into a more permanent, more durable and more constant effort; Rosa used to reply with a wave of her hand, and turn away from me, saying: "There is no use talking to you." ' Brandler relates this in a simple and honest manner, without putting himself forward as a teacher's favourite, though he does say: 'I was the kind of cheeky good disciple who could afford to do things others could not. I used to answer her back much more sharply than others.' Brandler makes the impression on me of a mixed product of two schools: that of Bebel and that of Rosa.

I asked Brandler whether he knew about Rosa's work on the history of Poland. He had asked her about this in 1911 or 1912. She said that she had already done quite a lot of preparatory work, but that she would probably never have time to write a connected history of Poland. Brandler does not think there are any of Rosa's manuscripts still unpublished: Frölich had published nearly all of them. But there are some unpublished letters. There is, for example, one still in Brandler's possession, in which Rosa speaks lightly about her letters from prison to Liebknecht's wife: 'I do not have to tell you — these are more or less Rosa's words — that I wrote to Karl's wife to keep up her morale; but for the movement and for Marxists there is nothing in these letters.' She was definitely against the idea of publishing them and gave the impression she was embarrassed by them.

Early German Communism

On Spartacus, Brandler says that there were 3,000 members at most by the end of the war. 'And a good half of them were moral pacifists not Marxists.' Brandler was not present at the founding Congress of the KPD in December, but says the Congress was possessed by an ultra-leftist mania which Rosa Luxemburg and Jogiches tried in vain to counteract. 'Our tragedy was that we were unable to restrain the elemental forces of the revolution till the time when action was possible, unlike the Bolsheviks during the July Days. That's the source of the January tragedy.[1] When I talked with Rosa right after the Congress, she was more depressed than ever. She felt that the

---

[1] The Spartacist uprising of January 1919 and the subsequent murder of Luxemburg and Liebknecht.

current was carrying her to catastrophe and she did not even try to divert it.'

How did Rosa view the project of setting up the Third International? Brandler says it was precisely Rosa who turned the whole Central Committee against the Comintern and that he, Brandler, was the only one to vote for joining it. 'Rosa said: It will be a Russian *Krämerei* [shop] with which we shall be unable to cope. We shall perish with it.' He says he was too naïve to understand Rosa's fears. He did not fully realize the psychological and cultural differences. He knew Lenin and other Russian leaders from before the war, and from Zimmerwald and Kienthal; but he could not then understand the nature of the Russian quarrels. He was struck by one characteristic of the Russian emigration: by the fanatical hatred of Mensheviks and Liquidators towards Lenin, and by the equally fanatical admiration of Lenin among the Bolsheviks. 'For us this hatred and this adoration, this tremendous importance of a single individual, was quite incomprehensible. I understood this many many years later, too late in fact.' Was it true that Rosa retracted the criticisms of the Russian revolution contained in her pamphlet? Brandler says he could not answer that question. He had had no opportunity to discuss this with Rosa, and there were all sorts of contradictory rumours.

About Liebknecht, Brandler talks with pious sentiment but without respect. He maintains that as a personality, as an orator and agitator, Zinoviev was incomparably greater. This seems strange to me, because Brandler detested Zinoviev as he detested few people in his life. Liebknecht — says Brandler — had not a shred of demagogy in him, and without some demagogy one cannot really be a great agitator. Yes, he could arouse his audience, but he did not possess Zinoviev's power of fascination. In political questions he was erratic, indecisive and lacking in experience. As he was aware of this, he was quite satisfied with playing second fiddle. In the central organs of the party he occupied a secondary place, though he was extremely popular and liked by the masses.

Brandler speaks differently about Jogiches. Even now, thirty years after Jogiches's death, one feels from Brandler's words that Jogiches was in fact the leader of the whole group. Brandler maintains that Jogiches's death was in fact a suicide. This was not an assassination — says Brandler — this was a suicide. He spoke with Jogiches at a Berlin railway station just one hour before the latter's death. 'It was only afterwards that I understood that what Jogiches was telling me was in fact his political testament. He insisted that I should move from Chemnitz to Berlin, while I maintained that I must not abandon the Chemnitz organization. Jogiches also gave a brief characterization of all the members of the Central Committee, stressing their weaknesses and faults and the fact that they were not up to their tasks. "But you are also a member of the CC", I said. To this he answered: "Yes, but I can do nothing. I belong to a different generation." (He was then fifty years old.) "My time is over. Now you, men of the younger generation, must take over the leadership of the party." Usually Jogiches spoke little, so this conversation was all the more surprising. He was terribly depressed. Rosa's death was the ultimate blow for him, though even before that both he and Rosa were painfully aware that we were all carried by a current over which we had no control. After this talk with me he — the master of conspiratorial work — went to a place where he must have known that danger awaited him: he went to visit Mathilde, Rosa's secretary. Counter-revolutionary squads were all around and many people in the house were arrested. He stood at an open window shouting at the top of his voice all manner of insults addressed to the counter-revolutionary squads. They shot him straight away. It was obvious that he was seeking death.'

We talked then about the Halle Congress, the March events and the expulsion of Paul Levi. Brandler describes the split among the Independents in Halle as '*Das Theater*'.[2] He was against the split. His view was that the Communist Party, after the split with the KAPD,[3] should be given time to get stronger and, *gradually*, to attract militants from among the Independents and the Social Democrats. Because of the Halle split, the party became suddenly inflated. It expanded so rapidly that the leadership was unable to control the huge influx of members. However, Zinoviev's great speech in Halle impressed Brandler very much. 'Against all my fears, which later proved well founded, Zinoviev converted me to his view. And yet in Halle I really came to hate Zinoviev, his way of speaking and behaving, and all his detestable demagogy. I then thought: This man will prove disastrous for our movement.'

Brandler sees a direct link between the Halle split and the March insurrection. 'The party had grown so big that many members

[2]The split in the USPD (Independent Social Democratic Party of Germany) at its Halle Congress of October 1920, after which a majority of the Independents entered the KPD.

[3]To be precise, the expulsion of the ultra-left opposition from the party at the Heidelberg Congress of October 1919, which was followed six months later by the formation of the KAPD (Communist Workers' Party of Germany) from their ranks.

believed that the hour of revolution had struck. People were so impressed by the sheer number of party members that they refused to consider the overwhelming strength of the enemy. If we had been spared Zinoviev's *coup de théâtre*, we would have expanded more slowly and yet we should have reached our goal more certainly.

How much truth was there in Trotsky's view, expressed somewhere, that already in the Lenin period, around 1920, Zinoviev introduced the corruption of leaders of foreign parties as a matter of course? At first Brandler confirms this without reservation, and mentions the names of corrupt leaders of the Independents, among them the name of Koenen.[4] But then he corrects himself and says that the corrupt practices were not always direct and not always personal. He quotes old Adler, who used to say that he was never surprised when a party was searching for money, but was always surprised when money was searching for a party. 'Without the financial help of the Comintern — says Brandler — we would have been developing in a much healthier manner. Before, we were publishing a few newspapers with pennies contributed by workers. We were dependent on workers, we had to be in constant touch with them, and we would not have embarked on enterprises which were above our real political strength. All this changed from the moment when we received money from the Comintern. Suddenly we owned twenty newspapers; we had not enough editors — we had either workers who could not write, or "drop-out" students who could write but had very little in common with the workers' movement. Thalheimer employed them in *Die Rote Fahne* and dismissed them after two months at the latest. Our financial means were all the time greater than our political possibilities, and we began to judge our strength and importance according to the length of our purse and not according to the support of the workers. This was bound to lead to disaster.'

Although Brandler was in '90 per cent agreement' with Paul Levi's criticism of the March Action, he himself spoke for Levi's expulsion because he considered that in the circumstances Levi should have presented his arguments in a different manner. After March, Brandler fled to Moscow. There he spent several evenings with Lenin, who questioned him closely: 'He questioned me as only Lenin used to do. He did not discuss big problems, but asked about

---

[4] No doubt this is Wilhelm Koenen (1886–1963), on the executive of the USPD in 1920, and immediately elected to the *Zentrale* of the KPD after the Unification Congress of December 1920. He retained this position until 1924, when the left faction removed him as a Centrist.

all sorts of small details through which he arrived by himself at great general conclusions.'

The Events of 1923

When asked about Stalin's letter (of August 1923 to Bukharin and Zinoviev) on the need for purely defensive tactics in Germany, Brandler confirms that the letter was authentic and that the version of the letter which Trotsky published was indeed correct. Brandler was the first to translate this letter from Russian into German, in Moscow; but he did this only a year after the letter had been written. He says further that he 'had no idea of the quarrels within the Politbureau about the policy for Germany'. Brandler was at that time vice-chairman of the Comintern — Zinoviev's Deputy. The Executive of the Comintern was then only a modest office. Lenin was present at its meetings only two or three times; he simply had no time to come more often. After the March events, however, he became alarmed and returned to Comintern work, but only for a short spell — preparing for the Third Congress. The Soviet delegation to the Comintern presented, outwardly, a united front, so that other members knew little or nothing about the disagreements among the Russians. At that time, there were no private or confidential talks with them. This is how Brandler explains the differences between his version of the 1923 events and Trotsky's. 'It is quite possible that at Politbureau meetings Trotsky's position was indeed as he described it later. But in the Executive of the Comintern, these differences between him and the rest of the Soviet delegation were concealed.'

Brandler further maintains, firstly, that the whole Soviet delegation considered the situation in Germany as a revolutionary one and, in spite of his — Brandler's — protests, was determined to set a date for the revolution; and secondly, that the whole delegation insisted that he and the others should join the Saxon Social-Democratic government in order to arm the workers. 'I kept on explaining to them that the Saxon government was in no position to arm the workers, because since the Kapp Putsch all weapons had been taken away from Saxony and neighbouring provinces, so much so that even the police were not armed. When the police needed arms, very small quantities of weapons were brought from Berlin. In answer to that Zinoviev thundered, banged his fist on the table and so on. We were instructed to move the headquarters of the Party from Berlin to Saxony, because the revolution was allegedly to begin in Saxony. When I tried to persuade them that this would mean a complete destruction of the Party apparatus, the same scenes were repeated; Zinoviev thundered and banged his fist on the table. In the end, a ridiculous compromise was reached. Part of the Central Committee was to be left in Berlin and part moved to Chemnitz. I spent the whole evening with Trotsky, who tried to persuade me that I should submit to the decisions of the Comintern.'

Brandler does not answer clearly on whether Trotsky was in fact personally convinced that the revolutionary situation in Germany was ripe, or that Brandler should enter the Social-Democratic Government in Saxony. With Stalin, Brandler did not talk about this; and anyhow, he says, nobody on the Executive at the time paid any attention to Stalin. The latter was, however, present at the last meeting, shook Brandler's hand and together with others toasted 'the future victorious leader of the German revolution'. 'Only Radek,' says Brandler, 'was convinced of the unreality of all these decisions.' Outvoted, Brandler declared that he would submit to the decisions of the Comintern. This is how he explains his motives: 'I told myself that these people had made three revolutions. To me their decisions seemed nonsensical. However, not I but they were considered seasoned revolutionaries who had achieved victory. They had made three revolutions and I was just about to try to make one. Well, I had to follow their instructions. During my return journey from Moscow to Berlin I bought a newspaper at the railway station in Warsaw. From this newspaper I learned that I had become a Minister in the Saxon government. What a situation! Things were being done behind my back and I knew nothing. All this was meant to put me before a *fait accompli.*'

Asked whether today he would consider the 1923 situation as revolutionary, Brandler does not give a clear answer. From the way in which he describes events, one has the impression that his answers would, on the whole, be affirmative. But he does not draw any final conclusion. He maintains that the Social-Democratic government of Saxony was completely helpless in the face of the communists, and that even the Central government was at their mercy. He recalls that after his return to Germany, the Labour Minister of the Central government sought to meet him. When they did meet, he told Brandler: 'Listen, we are accepting all your conditions without any reservations, but you should not keep your revolver at our heads; tell the workers to return to work.' All this seems to point to a revolutionary situation, but Brandler mentions another circumstance. All strikes were economic, connected with inflation. All rises in wages were wiped out within a week by rises in prices. The problem was how to pass from economic struggle to a struggle for power: 'We did not know how to do this, and we were unable to find out. Then came stabilization.' (Brandler all the time seems to identify the financial crisis of 1923 with the crisis of the regime, and the stabilization of the currency with the stabilization of the social order.)

'The fundamental problem of our movement was the gulf between ourselves and the older class-conscious part of the proletariat, which had gone through the Bebel school and was in the ranks of the Scheidemannists.[5] We had in our ranks the proletarian element who had become politically active under the influence of the War — full of revolutionary fervour, but politically absolutely raw. Such had been the position ever since 1918. Our task was to unite these two elements.[6] When in December 1918 the founding Congress of the party passed ultra-left resolutions, Rosa was so depressed that she wondered whether she should "continue to participate at all". She even thought for a moment of leaving the KPD and returning to the Independents. I tried to dissuade her — this was one of the last talks I had with her. I told her that we would achieve more with the raw workers full of revolutionary zeal than with trained cadres of a conservative frame of mind. Yet this discord, this divorce, ought to have been overcome. But the stabilization of 1924 made it even deeper.'

Moscow in the Twenties

After the *Krach* in Germany,[7] Brandler went back to Russia, where he remained from 1924 until 1928 as an 'honorary prisoner'. Immediately after his arrival in Moscow, at the beginning of January 1924, he met Krupskaya, who told him of Lenin's serious condition: he had already lost the power of speech, did not take part in any political work, but very much wanted Brandler to come and tell him all about the situation in Germany. This was only two to three weeks

---

[5]Supporters of Philipp Scheidemann, i.e. the right wing of the SPD.

[6]In this rather opaque passage, Brandler puts forward the idea that the German working-class movement became divided into two sections, partly through the events of the war and partly through the foundation of the KPD, and that the task of the KPD was to re-unite the movement. This re-unification could not take place on an ultra-left basis, hence the reference to the resolutions passed at the founding Congress; nor could it take place if external pressures did not force the older, conservative workers to the left, out of the SPD. This is why he refers to the 'stabilization of 1924' as a factor deepening the gulf between SPD and KPD.

[7]The October 1923 defeat of the KPD.

before Lenin's death, but according to Brandler Krupskaya maintained that although he was completely paralysed, his mind was quite clear and active. (Why then after his last attack in 1923 did Lenin demand to see neither Stalin nor Trotsky, though the struggle between the two had already become public knowledge?) 'The date for my visit to Lenin — Brandler goes on — kept on being postponed. There were rumours that this was "Koba's[8] doing" — he definitely did not want me to contact Lenin. I reported these rumours frankly to Krupskaya, who denied them, but she was so embarrassed and so confused that this only seemed to confirm the rumours. A few days later Lenin died.' Here Brandler recalls a telephone conversation he had with Lenin in 1921. There were crackling noises on the line all the time, and Lenin said: 'Again some idiot is trying to listen in.' Brandler adds that everybody was eavesdropping on everybody — even Dzerzhinsky's phone was tapped.

Brandler now relates his life as an 'honorary prisoner' in the Hote Lux. He also relates an episode of 1921 which throws light on the Comintern atmosphere at that early stage. One day he saw by chance on Zinoviev's desk a pile of correspondence from Germany. These were letters not from official organs of the Party, but from Zinoviev's private informants. 'I was very indignant that Zinoviev should correspond behind my back and in secret with his own informants in Germany. I raised this question at the session of the Executive in Lenin's presence. Lenin agreed with me and insisted that such behaviour should cease. However, I am convinced that when he talked alone with Zinoviev, he reproached him only for being careless with his letters, for keeping them so accessible that I had a chance to see them. But I do not think that he criticized him for conducting his private correspondence and his private detective work. This was the Russian method, to which they all got accustomed in the course of their factional struggles. To us, Western communists, such a method was then completely unacceptable. Today I have learned that I was too naive, that this was the correct method; and I only regret that I did not apply it myself — I would then have known what was going on in the organization behind my back.'

Dismissed from the post of vice-president of the IKKI, Brandler was in 1927 appointed to the vice-presidency of the Peasant International (*Krestintern*). He was also made Dzerzhinsky's assistant in the Supreme Council of the Economy (*Vesenkha*), where he co-operated closely with Pyatakov and took part in preparing the first Five-Year

---

[8]Stalin's party pseudonym in the underground before the revolution.

Plan. Brandler says that during the factional struggle, all factions sought his support, as well as the support of other foreign leaders. In that period he had long talks with Trotsky and met Radek, Pyatakov and others even more frequently. Trotsky apparently said that the Opposition would prefer to co-operate with him, rather than with Ruth Fischer, but that for the time being nothing could be done about this. (Brandler speaks with great contempt about Ruth Fischer, especially about her latest phase, just before 1948, attacking her for her 'anti-Bolshevik atrocity propaganda'.)

Asked whether Dzerzhinsky was at all qualified to be the head of the Economic Council, Brandler bursts out laughing. It becomes obvious from what he says that Dzerzhinsky's role was purely that of police surveillance. He met the latter quite often before he became his assistant; but after this appointment he saw him only once, and that during a holiday in Kislovodsk. Brandler worked with Pyatakov, who was nominally Dzerzhinsky's deputy but in fact the real director. Brandler relates how incredible the economic chaos and disorder was in the Soviet Union. The accusations of economic sabotage, so common in that period, were the result in the first instance of a complete lack of experience or any technological tradition. On theoretical questions, the experts of the Economic Council were the equals of the best European experts; but in practical questions they were completely inept. 'Every morning I looked out of my window to make sure that the Soviet Union had not yet crumbled.' Workers recruited from among the peasants broke tools and machinery. 'One day Pyatakov asked me to join him in inspecting a coal mine where there was trouble. In the train we looked through the appropriate documents. The seams were 600 metres under the ground. The "miners" to work them were recruited from among the peasants, although the director of the mine was against this and in an article in the local paper had explained that British coalmining experience had already proved that one could not send peasants so deep down under the ground, because they were unable to get acclimatized and therefore unable to work properly. The local GPU arrested the director, accusing him of counter-revolutionary activity and sabotage because he dared to compare the building of socialism with early capitalism in Britain. In the meantime, the new "miners" had indeed damaged and destroyed the ultra-modern machinery with which the mine was equipped. Pyatakov was furious: "Idiots! Barbarians! Illiterates! Even we did not know what a savage nation we had made the revolution with." When we came to the mine, we immediately freed the director, of course. But Pyatakov addressed him more or less like this: "You were right, but now we give you six months to bring order into the mine. If you cannot manage this within six months, you'll go back to prison." ' Brandler justifies Pyatakov's methods by saying that one could not deal with Russians in any other manner.

Brandler maintains that during that period he did not engage in any factional struggle in Germany. He tried to talk with German communists who were visiting Moscow, but this was not easy because foreign comrades would get into trouble if they were seen with Brandler even in the street. The situation was indeed grotesque, because at the same time all possible honours were showered upon him, and he even had the ear of the GPU. It was only while he was inspecting factories that he realized that people were terribly frightened of him, for they looked upon him as Dzerzhinsky's associate. 'Heads of department or important economic leaders thought I would revenge myself for my political demotion by harassing them and denouncing them to the GPU for some misdeed, even if they had not committed any. I gave up all these inspections, when I realized the atmosphere around me.'

'Then came the crisis of 1928, when the Comintern started to adopt the line about social-fascism, united front only from below, etc. I demanded that my personal documents be given back to me, and my return to Germany facilitated. I told Bukharin: "For four years I have submitted to your decisions, though I disagreed with them. Now this is finished. I do not intend to follow your policy any longer. Now I see it as my duty to begin a struggle against you inside the German Party." They proposed various posts abroad to me, on condition that I did not return to Germany. I was even told that "the leadership of the German party consists of such asses that we cannot allow you to return." Bukharin, seeing my stubbornness — now that he is no longer alive I can say this — suggested that I adopt a two-faced attitude (*dvurushnichestvo*). "Why get into a fight?" he was saying. "Why enter into a struggle? As a vice-president of the Peasant International you can travel around the world as much as you like; and while agreeing formally with everything, you can do what you really think is best." I told Bukharin: "I am not a born diplomat and I shall never become one." I had a farewell meeting with Stalin. It was my shortest meeting with him and in a sense the most pleasant. He said "You must be off your head! We can live in peace but you do not want it. You have persuaded yourself that your duty is to fight against us. Please yourself, go away and fight. But you know that we can also fight you, and we know how to whip and flog our opponents. We shall give you a good and proper hiding." '

Correspondence 1953–59*

From Deutscher to Brandler

16 February 1953

Lieber Genosse Brandler,

This time I am rather late in answering, and I apologize for this. I have spent the last few weeks in the British Museum, and, when after a day's work and journeyings I return home, I find little time for my correspondence. As I read various things in the Museum, I come occasionally across your name. Recently, for instance, I have re-read the Protocols of the Third CI Congress, where you are often quoted and where I found that you were elected Honorary President of the Congress.

I agree with you that my first guesses about the Prague trial need to be corrected or rather abandoned in the light of later developments. ⁹ Unfortunately, I cannot say that I have arrived at any satisfactory view or hypotheses about the latest developments in the SU. Like yourself, I have refused, for the time being, to write on these developments, because it is no use to speculate or to give vent to moral indignation before one has thoroughly understood what is going on. I have read and re-read your article in nr.2 of *Arbeiterpolitik*. While I agree with the general trend of your argument, some of your formulae still seem to me somewhat doubtful. Since you have asked for my comment, I shall say frankly that sometimes you seem

---

*The following letters are a selection from the full correspondence, published as *Unabhängige Kommunisten*, ed. Herman Weber, Colloquium Verlag, Berlin 1981. The text printed here has been marginally shortened, to eliminate purely ephemeral matter. The translation of Brandler's letters is by Ben Fowkes.

⁹The reference is to the show trial of Slansky, Clementis and other Czechoslovak CP leaders in Prague in November 1952.

to make too strong a *peregib*[10] towards Stalin. When you say that the construction of socialism demands other people than those that have grown up under capitalism and that the development of socialism is accompanied by accentuated class struggle to the end, this may be true as a general historical proposition. But it is difficult to agree that the need for the new socialist man implies the necessity of the purge trials à la Stalin-Yagoda-Yezhov. Surely you do not want to suggest that it was necessary for Stalin to destroy the old Bolsheviks as part of his struggle for the new socialist man, however necessary that may have been for him from a much narrower and less sublime viewpoint. Nor do I think that Stalinism has been educating the new socialist man. The only credit which one must and ought to give Stalinism is that it has been creating in Russia and in the countries of the Soviet orbit the *material and organizational preconditions* of socialism. In *social psychology* and *culture* it has fostered, on the contrary, bureaucratic rigidity and stupidity on the one hand and an almost zoological individualism on the other. I wish you made this distinction more clearly. It is no use quoting Marx about the weak classes and races that must inevitably perish under the pressure of economic necessity. Marx wrote this about the victims of early capitalist development and competition to which the political destruction of whole generations of Communist revolutionaries by the Stalinist terror cannot be compared. I think that I guess your motives behind these *peregiby* — your reluctance to *appear* to say the same things which are shouted now from every anti-Soviet housetop; and with this motive I am in wholehearted sympathy. But while I would be very careful about expressing moral indignation over Stalin's deeds, I would be at least as much careful not to express anything that could be taken as moral approval. You yourself take the same line when you say that under Russian conditions there developed the Stalinist *Bürokratismus*, the renunciation of Communist principles in domestic and foreign policies. Surely the renunciation of Communist principles cannot go hand in hand with the education of the socialist man, which, you suggest elsewhere, is the function of Stalinism. It is not that I object to your basic argument. My criticism applies rather to the emphasis you give to various parts of the argument.

And here are a few other, minor points: You say that the splitting up of the large estates was not in the interest of the proletariat only in the East German zone. I remember that when I was in Germany I

[10]*peregib* is a Russian expression meaning to overdo, to overemphasize, to exaggerate.

was often told that the agricultural workers were not at all satisfied with the share out. They often suggested *Genossenschaften*, but this was then very categorically discouraged by the Soviet military administration. Something similar happened in some parts of Poland. It is not correct to say that there were no broad democratic workers' organizations in pre-war Poland. The reformist parties existed legally and were mass organizations in the fullest sense of the word. So were the trade unions. The Communist party had its ups and downs. Its influence dwindled to a minimum under the unfortunate 'Third Period'-line. But previously there were times when it not only was a mass organization but when it did in fact lead a majority of the Polish working class — and this under the Warski-Kostrzewa leadership! Nor is it correct to say that the post-war Polish CP consisted only of emotional pro-Soviet enthusiasts and job-seekers. There was no lack of these elements to be sure; but there were still thousands of people who had gone through the old underground party, suffered for it in prisons, etc. Even the tradition of Rosa Luxemburg has never been altogether dead in the Polish party. Nor is it quite dead even now!

I have the impression that you may underrate the potential effectiveness of American policy. When you say that the Soviet Union achieves in the main its purposes, in contrast to the imperialists who do so to a much smaller extent, I wonder whether you make due allowance for the probability that American policy will grow more effective as the American rearmament drive begins to yield its results. The crises in which American diplomacy has found itself several times in the last two years or so have in part been due to the circumstance that the USA has not had enough military equipment both for itself and its allies. This will change in the near future, when the American war industries get into their full swing, and the impact of the change may make itself strongly felt in international affairs. You are, of course, right in underlining the advantages which planned economy gives to the Soviet Union. This letter has grown a bit too long and I must finish. I am sending you a copy of the *Documentary History of Chinese Communism*.[11] This is a most interesting volume.

Tamara joins me in sending you our best wishes

Yours Isaac Deutscher

---

[11] *Documentary History of Chinese Communism*, Conrad Brandt, Benjamin Schwartz and John Fairbank.

Dear Genosse Brandler,
I must first ask your forgiveness for my indecently long silence.
Apart from all sorts of other trouble, I have had to prepare two books
for the printers in recent months. Two — because in addition to the
book on Trotsky, I have written a book on *Russia After Stalin*, which
appeared in the United States last month and is to be published in this
country the day after tomorrow. In connection with this, we have
now delayed the publication of the book on Trotsky for a few
months, although it is already printed. Thus both Tamara and myself
were so fully occupied these last few months that we had to delay our
correspondence; and even now we are still in the maelstrom. How I
wish I could visit you in Germany and have a long and exhaustive
discussion on current affairs! So much is happening and there are so
very few people with whom one can have a fruitful exchange of
views. Apart from this I really long to see you.

In the first instance, I was more than a little taken aback by the
attitude *Arpo*[12] adopted towards the events of June 16–17. I am afraid
I cannot share your feelings over those events. It seems to me
peculiarly tragic that Germany can never find in herself enough
revolutionary energy on the right occasions and at the proper time
and somehow does find it in herself on the wrong occasions and at the
wrong time. It goes without saying that the workers of Berlin had
their very good grievances and that the Russians and their marion-
ettes have done everything to provoke the storm. Nevertheless, it
seems to me that the effect of the Berlin revolt has been objectively
counter-revolutionary and not revolutionary. In a similar way the
German bourgeoisie and the German peasants once rose in revolt
against Napoleon, who freed in some measure the bourgeoisie and
the peasants from their servitude. Napoleon offended the national
dignity of Germany and his armies plundered the peasants just as
much as the Russians have done in our days. To this extent their
revolt against Napoleon was humanly understandable and inevitable.
But in the last instance the German bourgeoisie and peasants did
yeoman service to the Holy Alliance. One cannot humanly condemn
the workers in East Germany for what they have done; and yet the
effect of their action is equally deplorable. In Napoleon's time at least
your Steins and Gneisenaus beat Napoleon with his own stick and

[12]*Arbeiterpolitik*, the organ of the *Gruppe Arbeiterpolitik*, published in Stuttgart
between 1948 and 1959.

themselves introduced bourgeois reforms. In our day nobody even tries in Germany to beat the Russians with their own stick, that is, with socialization and planned economy.

To this extent, the June days were far below the level of anything that happened in the revolts of various German classes against Napoleon. I think *Arpo* was definitely mistaken in hailing these events as the revolutionary awakening of the German proletariat. I understand the psychological motives behind this mistake. I understand how extremely difficult if not impossible it was for you not to share in the enthusiasm which the news from Berlin must have evoked in the German working class in Western Germany. And yet I would have expected you and your friends to rise above your local German viewpoint, because you are surely aware that German developments have lost their independent significance and have become part of the world-wide conflict. It is sad to say, but Eastern Germany is now in some respects in the position in which Serbia was in 1914. You remember how many times the leading Marxists of that era pointed out that Serbia's cause, if taken in isolation, was a just one. But that it was nevertheless wrong to 'side with Serbia' in the First World War. It seems similarly wrong to 'side with Berlin' now. In both cases, the local issue was merged with a much wider conflict and a local just cause was exploited for purposes which had nothing in common with it. I have sometimes been in a position where I had to write to you that I thought you went a little too far in justifying Stalin's policies. This time I am afraid that you went too far in quite the opposite direction, in associating yourself with the anti-Russian movement.

It is obvious that the events in Berlin have already had a very negative effect on the developments in Moscow. The whole trend of events in Russia from Stalin's death until the East German earthquake went consistently in the direction of a socialist democratization of the regime. This trend has suffered a very severe setback because of Berlin. There has been very clear beneath the surface of Soviet politics an intense struggle between the diehards of Stalinism and the adherents of gradual socialist democratization, with the military Bonapartist elements watching the struggle in the background and waiting for their opportunity. The Berlin revolt has compromised the idea of a gradual relaxation of the Stalinist regime. Beria's downfall is closely connected with this. Beria was one of those who stood for democratic reform, and the reformists, seeing themselves weakened and threatened, offered Beria as a scapegoat because in his position as Chief of the Police he was morally vulnerable and therefore cast for the role of a scapegoat. I have dealt with this matter at considerable length in my new book, and I am sending you out two copies, one for you, and one for your friend who was so good to get for me Thalheimer's writings of fascism. I shall await your comments with great interest.[13]

Perhaps I shall have an opportunity to come over to Germany, but for the moment I do not see how I can do it. Tamara joins me in sending you our very best regards.

Isaac Deutscher

From Brandler to Deutscher

1 August 1953

I was indeed concerned about your silence. Your 'After Stalin' is rich recompense. If you were able to come for a few days to Germany, that would be magnificent. I too have no one with whom I can have a thorough discussion. My most long-lasting impressions of London are the evenings spent in your kitchen with yourself and Tamara. Can you organize it so that your book is issued soon in German? For us it is now a matter of urgency to provide for the German workers a clear and well-informed account of developments in the Soviet Union. I am convinced that your book will have a lasting effect on all those people who are trying to understand what is happening there. For this reason I immediately mentioned it in No. 15 of *Arbeiterpolitik*, so that at least those who knew English could profit by the book. If a German translation does not come out soon, we shall print a part of it in each forthcoming number of the journal. I hope you are in agreement with this.

And now I come to your objections to our position on the events in the Eastern Zone. You write: 'it seems to me that the effect of the Berlin revolt has been objectively counter-revolutionary.' I think this is completely wrong. Not only is your analogy with the revolt of the peasants against Napoleon in 1813 rather lame, like most analogies; it is also inapplicable in every respect to the rising of the decisive strata of the working class of the Eastern Zone. These

[13]Isaac Deutscher here refers to his postcript to the second edition of *Russia After Stalin*, published also in the collection of essays *Heretics and Renegades*, London 1955, pp. 173–90, under the title 'The Beria Affair'. See too his two essays on the same question in *Russia, China and the West*, London 1969.

decisive working-class strata would not dream of reversing the genuinely progressive achievements, such as the removal of power from the bourgeoisie, the nationalization of the most important means of production, and the planned economy. Not even the Social Democrats dare propose this openly. The workers rose against the mismanagement of the SED bureaucrats, the transfer of Russian methods to Germany, and the spoliation of the country through reparations. All these things formed an obstacle to the preservation of the measures taken in the direction of the development of socialism. How can one draw a parallel between these workers and the peasants of 1813 east of the Elbe, who petitioned for the maintenance of serfdom, and did service in the militia in order to drive out Napoleon, the executor of the French Revolution, who brought serfdom to an end. Comrade Deutscher, that is not admissible. The occupation policies of the Soviet Union have driven millions into the camp of United States and German imperialism. In East and West Germany there are millions of workers who say today: if what is happening in the Eastern Zone and in the Soviet Union is socialism, then let us rather have American capitalism. But the greater part, even of those who indignantly pose this alternative, are to be won for socialist measures provided they correspond to the possibilities in Germany.

The decisive forces, who will have the leadership in every movement once it has progressed from the stage of spontaneous revolt to the organized struggle, will be first the class-conscious nucleus from the old generation, who have fought for Soviet power since 1918, who have not let themselves be corrupted either by Fascism or by the SED bureaucracy; and secondly those people between twenty and fifty years old, who are well aware that the cause of their misery is not socialist measures but bureaucratic mismanagement, Russian methods, and spoliation through reparations at the expense of current production.

You can only compare the movement in the Eastern Zone with 1813, you can only view it as tragically inappropriate to the epoch, if you overlook all these considerations. Those who have risen against the occupation policies of the Soviet Union *are* the present-day Steins and Gneisenaus — tens of thousands of them rather than two — and they want to make the Soviet Zone an ally of the Soviet Union instead of an object of barter with the USA. Their struggle takes precisely the same direction as that of the reformers in the Soviet Union who want to liquidate Stalinism. If Beria is supposed to have been liquidated because he was blamed as a reformer for the rising in East Germany, then this is a pretext which borders on the ridiculous, for it would hit all the reformers, of whom he was hardly the most important.

The spontaneous and unorganized rising of 1953 was not a consequence of the reform plans but of the terroristic repression of the experienced workers. Its objective was to carry through the plans for the economic and political construction of the Soviet Zone in a manner consonant with the interests of the workers. The rioters were the camp-followers rather than the initiators of the movement. It may be that the confusion in the SED apparatus may have stimulated the eruption of the masses. But this confusion was a result of the orders of the Kremlin, which has still not grasped that even the corrupt instruments of its policies remain Western Europeans, who cannot implement an about turn from one day to the next just because it has been ordered from above.

Like everyone else (including even the network of spies and agents paid by the Western Powers and the Adenauer government), we were surprised by the *occasion* and the *strength* of the spontaneous rising of 16 and 17 June 1953. But we had already reckoned with spontaneous uprisings in the theses adopted at our national conference in 1951. From 1946 onwards we tried to organize resistance in individual factories and localities through active intervention from below and demands for improvements in conditions. This failed owing to police and SED terror, and our comrades paid dearly for it.[14] We were unable to bring this to the notice of the public because it was beyond our strength to mobilize the masses for resistance and for the liberation of those who had been condemned, without endangering the remaining links between our comrades. According to the recent theses issued by the CC of the SED, 'Brandlerite and Trotskyist agents had the leadership in many places'. Although we still have no reliable reports of our own, I can assure you that our comrades did not encourage any counter-revolutionary activities; on the contrary, they will quite certainly have put a stop to excesses by the mob or provocations by agents. Good comrades of ours will certainly have been among the victims now delivered over to Ulbricht's campaign of vengeance. Zaisser was dismissed because he instructed the police not

---

[14] Alfred Schmidt, leader of a group in Erfurt, was condemned in 1948 to twenty-five years in a labour camp. This marked the end of a period of relative toleration in East Germany for the ex-members of the KPO, which had lasted from 1945 to 1947. The post-war agitation of the *Gruppe Arbeiterpolitik* is dealt with in the final chapter of K.H. Tjaden, *Struktur und Funktion der KPD-Opposition* [KPO], Meisenheim-am-Glan 1964.

to intervene unnecessarily.[15] This is what Ulbricht and his kind call a capitulation. Herrnstadt, chief editor of *Neues Deutschland*, has also been sacked for capitulation, because he published reports in which the critical mood of our SED members and proletarians was reflected, very faintly.[16] However, I am convinced that this victory of the Stalinist government in the Eastern Zone will be still more short-lived than the one you prophesy for the Soviet Union, if indeed that actually takes place.

I and my comrades by no means view the events in East Germany from a narrow German standpoint. I am aware that Germany stands in the centre of the Soviet-American conflict in Europe. I am also aware that it is not the pivot of the world situation. But the rising in East Germany is a gain, an accretion of strength for the socialist camp, and not an event like the Serbs' defence of their country in 1914, which could only be justified in isolation. In the conflict between rival cliques in Moscow, the rising in the Soviet Zone can, and will perhaps, be exploited against the representatives of the New Course. The decision will be reached on 5 August as to whether the Stalinists in Russia defeat Malenkov or not.[17] In this context, there are more important matters than the setback the reformers have allegedly met with in the Soviet Zone. The commercial treaties concluded by the Soviet Union on the basis of the New Course, the armistice in Korea, the clever moves undertaken in Austria and Yugoslavia, etc., have already made it possible to break through the American front in ways which are ten times as significant as the disturbance in the Soviet Zone. If the New Course prevails in the Soviet Union, the rising of the East German workers will be on the positive side of the balance, not the negative side.

From the point of view of world politics, the meaning of the New Course is that the Soviet Union is orientating itself towards the working class on an international scale. If that happens in the Soviet Zone of Germany as well, the rebels of June will be the best allies. It is impossible to exaggerate the impact such a policy would automatically have on the working class of West Germany. The USA is not yet ready to accept the pre-conditions for a simultaneous evacuation of Germany by all the occupying Powers. The time still available is

[15]Wilhelm Zaisser, Minister of State Security, February 1950 to July 1953. Expelled from the SED in 1954.
[16]Rudolf Herrnstadt, Chief Editor of *Neues Deutschland*, the central organ of the SED, from 1949 to 1953. Expelled from the SED in 1954.
[17]The Supreme Soviet of the USSR was due to meet on 5 August.

entirely sufficient, under the New Course, if it is carried through in the Soviet Zone, and with the assistance of the decisive strata of the working class who rose in revolt in June, to convert East Germany from the nightmare it is at present into a magnet for West Germany, which will change the mood there into its opposite.

For Germany itself, the rising means that the workers have demonstrated for the first time since 1945 that they can be the decisive force if they fight. Since 1945 the German workers, like the German philistines, have viewed political events in the same way as the weather, i.e. 'we can't do anything about it'. In England you will not be able to sense the new spirit. A worker, who does not belong to our group, wrote to me that he is once again proud to be part of the German proletariat. I am too.

Has Professor Carr's third volume not appeared yet? We impatiently await your *Trotsky*. If only you could visit us, even for a short time! Best regards to yourself, Tamara, and your son.

Heinrich Brandler

From Brandler to Deutscher

25 August 1953

Dear Comrade Deutscher,
The results of the negotiations in Moscow with the East German representatives have demonstrated that your fear that 16 and 17 June might harm the 'New Course' has not been confirmed.[18] On the contrary, the return of the factories removed to the Soviet Union, the abandonment of further reparations, and the limitations of the costs of the occupation would scarcely have been conceded so quickly if the workers had not entered into action. Since the USA is not at present ready to evacuate Germany, and the Soviet Union will not give up the Eastern Zone without the evacuation of the whole of Germany, there is time for the improvements in the East to work themselves out. If the workers in the Eastern Zone can attain a standard of living similar to that in the West, all that is necessary then is for the hated Ulbricht regime to be removed, and then the way will be clear for the workers of East and West not only to defend the nationalization of the means of production and the planned economy

[18]Between 20 and 22 August 1953, negotiations took place in Moscow between delegations of the GDR government and the Soviet government.

against the cupidity of German and American capitalists, but also to fulfil the tasks of the plan more effectively than they would do under the whip of the foolish bureaucracy.

I fear the French workers may be defeated if the struggle cannot be heightened so as to go beyond the framework of a trade-union fight over wages. Auriol is reacting like the Italian government did against the factory occupations of 1920. Many thanks for the Carr. I have sent you the first volume of the *Marx-Engels Werke,* which has just appeared.

Best regards,
H. Brandler

From Deutscher to Brandler

16 September 1953

Sehr Lieber und Geehrter Genosse Brandler,
Many, many thanks for the very interesting volume *Zur Deutschen Geschichte.* It is a very useful book to have and a most pleasant gift. I should have thanked you earlier, but I suffered from some ill health recently and was compelled to take a complete rest. The doctor diagnosed a 'false angina pectoris', but as it is only false I do not worry about it and I hope that I am now well on the way to recovery. I am about to undertake a long journey — to Palestine. Together with my family, I shall be embarking on a small boat at Marseilles on 3 October; we shall stay in Palestine for about five weeks and return to England late in November. I have been invited to Palestine by my Hebrew publishers (Am Oved, the publishing house of the Israeli Trade Unions); and I have in Palestine a sister, the only surviving member of my family, whom I have not seen for thirty years. All my books have been published in Hebrew, and the *Trotsky* is to appear in Hebrew simultaneously with the English edition. My writings, I am told, exercise a fairly strong influence there on the mind of the young generation. This is a somewhat paradoxical development, for, as you may imagine, I have all my adult life been a strong opponent of Zionism. It is impossible to be an opponent of Zionism now; the millions of murdered Jews have given the State of Israel a tragic if only negative justification. However, I cannot be a Zionist either, even now.

I would like to return to our argument about the meaning of the June events in Eastern Germany and their effect on Soviet policy. I am afraid your reasoning has not convinced me so far. When I denied the June demonstrations any revolutionary significance, I did not doubt for a moment that the workers in the Eastern Zone did not come out to demonstrate in favour of a capitalist restoration. They merely acted under the impulse of their immediate grievances. But beginning on a strictly economic basis, the demonstrations soon acquired the character of a political revolt against the Pieck–Ulbricht government. Because of this they inevitably strengthened the position of the Adenauer government and of its American protectors. You see in the June events the beginning of an awakening of the German proletariat as an independent force acting in its own class interests. I would like to believe that this is so, but the absolute passivity of the working class in Western Germany contradicts your assumption. If the German workers had acted with equal vigour and determination against both Ulbricht and Adenauer, your view might have been justified. But are you not struck by the strange contrast between the behaviour of the workers in the East and in the West? It is because of this contrast that one is entitled to speak about the counter-revolutionary consequences of the June events. Of course, the propagandists of the SED are simply stupid when they describe the June events as the result of machinations of Nazis and imperialist agents, although there is no doubt that the latter did what they could to fish in troubled waters. But even if they had not done so, even if no lumpenproletarian elements had joined in the demonstrations, even if the whole revolt had remained within the limits of a dignified proletarian action, its objective consequences would have still remained far from revolutionary or progressive, precisely because of the wider political context.

Curiously enough, even the most reactionary elements in the West have understood this. Far from being frightened by the 'revolutionary' élan of the East German workers, they welcomed enthusiastically the events of June. Eisenhower, Dulles, even McCarthy greeted the Berlin demonstrators as their allies in the struggle for 'freedom'. What a paradox. Or is it a paradox? Maybe I do not feel, as you say, the new wind blowing in Germany, although I doubt whether you yourself could feel much of that new wind in the recent election in West Germany. But I certainly do feel the wind blowing in America and England. Here there has been not the slightest doubt in any political grouping of any significance that the demonstrations of June were a signal victory for the West in the cold war, and not an independent revolutionary act of the German proletariat. In so far as there have been any misgivings in the West, they have troubled those elements — for instance in the British ruling circles — which are inclined to seek some conciliation with Russia, and which were afraid that the Berlin revolts would make the Americans so insolent as to rule out any chance of a conciliatory policy in the near future. One may risk the statement that 'enthusiasm' for the Berlin workers was strongest among the most extreme counter-revolutionary elements in the West. Again, all this might not have mattered much if the picture of the class relationships in Western Germany had been different from what it is.

You may not approve of my comparison with 1813 and say that it is impermissible to compare the workers of Berlin with the peasants who petitioned for the preservation of serfdom. But you yourself go on to say that both in East and West Germany there are millions of workers who say today that they prefer American capitalism to conditions in the Eastern Zone. Does not this prove the correctness of the comparison? We shall not differ about the extent to which Soviet policy must bear the blame for this. But once we have apportioned the blame, we still have to face the facts as they are. And it is unfortunately a fact that for the foreseeable future the practical alternative before Germany is between the capitalist regime of Adenauer and the bureaucratic quasi- (or if you like pseudo-) socialism of Pieck and Ulbricht. It may be that the Russians will abandon Pieck and Ulbricht; but then they will do so in favour of politicians standing for capitalism, in favour of Christian Democrats or at best of Social Democrats. And when *Arpo* now clamours for the dismissal of the hated government of Pieck and Ulbricht (and hated they indeed are), it clamours for nothing else, regardless of its excellent intentions, but the substitution of a bourgeois government for that of Ulbricht and Pieck. It may be that a bourgeois government would in a sense be a lesser evil, because it would open the prospect of a more normal class struggle in Germany, although this is highly debatable. But I have the strong impression that this is not what *Arpo* wants to say. You speak as if you imagined that it was possible in Germany today for some revolutionary socialist government to spring into the place now occupied by Pieck and Ulbricht. You speak in other words as if there existed a real revolutionary party in Germany. In your letter you even write that 'the decisive forces, who will have the leadership in every movement once it has progressed from the stage of spontaneous revolt to that of organized struggle, will be the class-conscious nucleus from the old generation, who have fought for Soviet power since 1918.'

This seems to me, frankly, a strange illusion. You know that I have the greatest respect and admiration for the revolutionary Marxist tradition in the German labour movement, and for those men of the old generation who, despite so many cruel disappointments, try to hand down that tradition to the young. But I cannot for a moment imagine that the 'class-conscious nucleus from the old generation', small and decimated as it is, can assume the effective leadership of a German revolutionary movement. Apart from individuals, exceptional individuals like yourself, who may preserve freshness of mind and strength of character when they are over seventy, the leading nucleus in any revolutionary movement must be much younger. The tragedy of the German movement, and not only of the German, consists, so it seems to me, in the gap, the vast gap, between the old nucleus — or rather its survivors — and the present young generation. You yourself have so often written about the absence of any revolutionary party in Germany that I do not see how you can forget your own words. It is this absence of a revolutionary party that has allowed the long-bankrupt Social Democracy to come back and to play its present role in West Germany, and a party of puppets to perform a quasi-revolutionary role in Eastern Germany. And as long as this is so, the German working class is paralysed as an independent revolutionary factor. And what the events of June revealed once again is that paralysis, not the beginning of any awakening. Because of this, an action which had all the outward appearances of a revolutionary deed went to strengthen the hands of counter-revolution.

You disagree with my view that the June events weakened the party of reform in Moscow. You point to the latest economic concessions Moscow made through Pieck and Ulbricht to disprove my contention. In fact, the Russian policy towards Eastern Germany initiated after June consists in the substitution of economic concessions for political reforms. The same trend can be observed since July also in domestic Soviet affairs. This new phase of policy reflects in my view the dialectical contradictions of the present situation. On the one hand, the need for reform is overwhelming both inside Russia and in Eastern Europe, including Eastern Germany. On the other, the Soviet ruling group has caught fright, the reformist elements in it have been weakened, and it seeks a way out by trying to satisfy the need for reform on the economic but not on the political ground. It goes without saying that economic concessions resulting in a higher standard of living will eventually pave the way for political reform. But the operative word here is 'eventually'. In the meantime, economic concession serves to put off political reform. It may well be that from a general point of view this is the sounder and the safer course to take for the Soviet ruling group. We are not in a position to judge this, and only the future can show.

This argument has grown far longer than I wanted it to be, and I must finish now. When are you returning to Hamburg? We still hope to pay you a visit in the autumn, after our return from Israel. Tamara joins me in sending you our warmest wishes.

Yours, Isaac Deutscher

From Brandler to Deutscher

12 January 1959

Dear Comrade Deutscher,

Thank you very much for sending me the first 170 pages of your manuscript of *The Prophet Unarmed*. Communists who read this second volume will find your work something to wonder at, for it gives an account of the struggles over the succession of Lenin on which no one will ever be able to improve. It will still remain important when this period has been presented in full, with all its dialectical contradictions, and when the role of the masses has been treated on the basis of their economic and social situation. Given the biographical form of your work, this could not be done there. Every biography which is not written by an absolute opponent of the hero becomes a justification, even when as in your biography it makes critical points about some of the hero's main weaknesses. I believe I can say this without being presumptuous.

I was in the Soviet Union from the end of October 1921 until July 1922, and then again from the beginning of May 1924 until the end of October 1928. In between, I was also present from the middle of April until the middle of May 1923, at the session of the IKKI at which we were compelled to include Thälmann and Ruth Fischer in the *Zentrale*. It was at this meeting that Trotsky discovered in the shape of Thälmann the 'proletarian gold' that was needed to provide a counterweight in the *Zentrale* to my 'Social-Democratic tendencies'. That provided extra support for Zinoviev's faction in the KDP. Stalin intervened too, winning to his side Maslow, who had been retained in Moscow at Lenin's suggestion. I was against this method, but I went along with it, just as I submitted to discipline in the session from the middle of August to the end of September. This second session was the one in which the plan of action for the revolution was decided. The pre-history of October I have just mentioned is not

without importance. For your depiction of the unarmed prophet,
1923 is only an episode, which it was in the life of Trotsky as well.
But for the KPD, this episode is the beginning of the period which led
to its collapse.

Radek introduced the April meeting, and Trotsky introduced the
one in September. Radek was too familiar with the conditions in
Germany to have demanded the entry of the Zinoviev-faction into
the *Zentrale*. Nevertheless, he organized this, on instructions from
Moscow, and not because he saw it as an appropriate way of bringing
the KPD to a state of readiness. It was not the first time Radek had
come to Berlin with commissions from Zinoviev to which we objected. In most cases, I succeeded in convincing him overnight of the
impracticability of Zinoviev's proposals. He then received a scolding
from the latter, but took this on his own account. What I did not
know in April 1923 was that a factional struggle was proceeding in
the CPSU. I knew neither of its existence nor of the issues involved.
The Maslow–Ruth Fischer faction was informed about this, if not by
Zinoviev himself, then through their connection with Shlyapnikov,
of the Workers' Opposition.

For Radek, the situation was tragi-comic: in Moscow he was
thought of as a German; for us he was a Russian. He received blows
from both sides. I often used to tell him that we found it difficult to
swallow that he negotiated as a representative of the Soviet government with Seeckt and German ministers, and at the same time as
Comintern representative with us. Objections like this made him
very angry. In Moscow, he defended our policy as far as possible.
Since I was only allowed very rarely to mention the disagreements
with Radek in the *Zentrale,* I was denounced by the Maslow–Ruth
Fischer faction as a tool of Radek's faction. It was not possible to
ignore his Schlageter speech at the Fourth Congress;[19] but the
Zentrale did not adopt his line, it was rather the Ruth Fischer faction
and the conciliator Paul Frölich who advocated it.[20] Radek was

[19]This speech, made by Radek to the Third Plenum of the Enlarged EKKI in Moscow
on 20 June 1923 (and *not* to the Fourth Congress), extolled the German nationalist
fanatic Leo Schlageter, who had just been shot by a French firing squad in the Ruhr,
and inaugurated the 'National Bolshevik' period of summer 1923 during which the
KPD tried to outbid the German Nationalists in the fight against the Versailles Treaty.

[20]Paul Frölich had been a member of the *Zentrale* since 1919, with one interval;
throughout 1923 he was an adherent of Brandler. But in January 1924, in common
with several other members of the Brandlerite majority, such as Ernst Meyer, he went
over to an intermediate position between Right and Left. For some years afterwards,
the 'conciliators' Frölich and Meyer tried to provide a bridge between Right and Left
in the KPD.

accused by Moscow of being the author of my definition of the five forms of the workers' government.[21] In reality, he tried to prevent this definition from being adopted; not because he thought it incorrect but, as I learned years later, because it irritated Zinoviev, and Radek found this inconvenient for his factional struggle in Moscow.

Neither in Moscow, nor during Radek's and Pyatakov's stay in Germany, did we learn anything of the Russian factional struggles. That is hard to believe, but it is a fact. Only in December 1923 did we learn of these conflicts, after Zinoviev's letter accusing me of treachery to the revolution — which was a complete volte-face on his part from his initial attitude. We — that is, Thalheimer and myself — replied that we would take up a position on the factional struggles when we had familiarized ourselves with the material. That was in January 1924. Not because I wanted to save my position, as you write on page 145. It is not true that I or Thalheimer (whose position on the question of October 1923 was the same as mine) gave our support to the Triumvirate. Nor did the *Zentrale* issue any such declaration. When I travelled to Prague in the middle of December, from where I was supposed to proceed to Moscow, Ulbricht assured me that he would be careful to prevent any stupidities, and said I should remain firm and that the majority of the Party stood firmly behind me.[22] Only after a week of waiting did I get a false passport for my journey to Moscow, and I arrived when the negotiations had already come to an end. All that was required of me was my assent, i.e. my signature. *I refused it.*

Walcher and Pieck tried to convince me by saying that if I refused I should not get into the new *Zentrale*. That the KPD delegation had given its support to the troika during my absence is possible, even likely, but I knew nothing of this myself. After all, the resolution, which received the assent of Klara Zetkin too, corresponded to the troika's view of the situation.[23] But neither Thalheimer nor myself accepted it. As late as the Fifth Congress [of the Comintern], I opposed the resolution as incorrect — see the official minutes —and declared that although I would submit to party discipline, I would

[21] This definition put forward by Brandler at the Eighth Party Congress in January 1923, was part of an attempt to lay down the conditions under which the KPD might enter a possible workers' government in Saxony. It was strongly opposed by the Left.

[22] Walter Ulbricht was at this time a member of the Brandlerite majority leadership on the *Zentrale*. He dissociated himself from the Right in 1924, but was unable to secure re-election until 1927.

[23] The resolution of 21 January 1924 on the 'Lessons of the German Events', adopted by the Presidium of the EKKI, detailing the 'mistakes' of the KPD in the course of 1923.

still strive for a revision of it.[24] This revision could not take place, because the question of the German October was entangled with the factional struggle in the Soviet Union. And that is how the KPD was ruined.

I do not understand the basis for your assertion that Radek and Pyatakov advised me to call off the uprising. When this decision was made, at the time of the Chemnitz Conference, neither Radek nor Pyatakov was in Germany. They could not give any advice at all, for they were both *en route*. It would be correct to say, instead, that Radek and Pyatakov told me afterwards that I had done the right thing — Zinoviev too said the same at the beginning. Responsibility for the 'cancellation' falls on me alone. I communicated this proposal to all the members of the *Zentrale* who were present in Chemnitz, and they all accepted it. Graupe, the minister, informed us that the interventionist troops were on the march, and that they had been sent for protection against an invasion from Bavaria.[25] He would have to leave the Conference, he said, if a general strike were decided on and proclaimed, because that would constitute the signal for an uprising. In the plenary meeting I immediately came out sharply against this mystification, and declared that we should not allow ourselves to be held back from doing anything by this exercise in camouflage.

After discussions with the other members of the *Zentrale*, I advised against the proclamation of a general strike, and in this course I received the assent of all the *Zentrale* members present, including Ruth Fischer. My decision was based on the following reflections: in spite of all our own information services, we had only the announcement by Graupe, and confirmation from the Dresden police after I had asked them by telephone. If the information was correct, this would mean that we had been taken by surprise by the enemy in the strategically important region of Saxony-Thuringia, and would have to fight on the defensive. I was of the opinion, and I still am today, that a defensive uprising is condemned to defeat, and should only be risked if there is no other possible way out.

The united front policy, with which we had conquered the leadership of all those fighting against the miseries caused by the galloping inflation, was bound to collapse the moment the government was able to procure the means of subsistance and could not only promise but also issue money which retained its value. The so-called Cuno

[24]The text of Brandler's speech in his defence is in *Protokoll. Fünfter Kongress der Kommunistischen Internationale*, vol. 1, Hamburg 1925, pp. 218–36.

[25]George Graupe, SPD Minister of Labour in Saxony, April to October 1923.

Dialogue with Heinrich Brandler 161

strike in Berlin was an especially prominent example of this tendency — whereas you use it to illustrate your adoption of the common assertion that the Berlin workers were burning with revolutionary fighting spirit.[26] We had this experience with all the strikes, demonstrations and attempts to control food and market prices in 1923. It is one thing to make radical speeches, of the kind tossed around by Ruth Fischer, and not only by her, in 1923; but it is quite another thing to make the transition from the fight against everyday shortages to the revolutionary, life-and-death struggle for power. This was not a piece of knowledge first obtained by me in 1923; all the struggles since 1918, the Kapp Putsch and so on, had taught me this.

When Lenin asked me in November 1921 why, despite my opposition to the armed resistance mounted against the Severing–Hörsing disarmament action in Central Germany,[27] I had accepted and published Béla Kun's appeal — 'Communists, do not let yourselves be disarmed, take weapons where you can find them' — I replied that I not only considered this to be the correct line in general, but even more so in this case; for there were tendencies present in the German working class, and in the KPD as well, which admittedly did not openly reject armed struggle, but which looked upon it with indifference, after the defeats of the period 1918 to 1920. I was opposed to armed resistance against the action of Hörsing, which itself had the objective of provoking an armed struggle, because we could bring this proclamation to nothing more effectively if we did not allow ourselves to be provoked. The weapons the Central German workers had hidden after the Kapp putsch in the copper mines near Leuna, and in other good hiding-places in the Thüringer Wald and the Erzgebirge, could never have been fetched in time. We should have had to march out empty-handed, under the scornful laughter of the other workers. In this context, I informed Lenin of my anxieties, and requested him to send us a dozen experienced civil war experts, with whom I hoped to change the situation in the party. Lenin agreed, and at the end of 1922, after my return to Germany thanks to the Rathenau amnesty, we were sent some.[28] Only after the

[26]The general strike in Berlin and elsewhere began on 9 August. It brought down Cuno on the 11th, and continued until the 15th.

[27]This is a reference to the March Action of 1921, which took the form of resistance to the occupation of the mining district around Halle by the police, who had been sent in by the SPD head of the local administration, Otto Hörsing, and the Prussian Minister of the Interior, the leading SPD politician Carl Severing.

[28]After the assassination of Walter Rathenau, and in connection with the campaign for the defence of the republic which followed, some of the participants in the March

162

Anti-Fascist Day, for which I issued a proclamation, was there any
readiness demonstrated in the party for this task. Trotsky described
my proclamation as a sign of the revolutionary situation. 'If Brandler
is writing proclamations like this . . . then we are almost there.' That
is what he said to Walcher, when the latter visited him in the
Caucasus.

Thus I did not oppose the preparations for the uprising of 1923. I
simply did not view the situation as acutely revolutionary yet,
reckoning rather with a further sharpening. But in this affair, I
considered Trotsky, Zinoviev and other Russians to be more competent — mistakenly. I strongly objected to the attempt to hasten
the revolutionary crisis by including communists in the Saxon and
Thuringian governments — allegedly in order to procure weapons. I
knew, and I said so in Moscow, that the police in Saxony and
Thuringia did not have any stores of weapons. Even single sub-
machine guns had to be ordered from the *Reichswehr*'s arsenal near
Berlin. The workers had already seized the local arsenals twice, once
during the Kapp putsch, and again in part in 1921. I declared further
that the entry of the communists into the government would not
breathe new life into the mass actions, but rather weaken them; for
now the masses would expect the government to do what they could
only do themselves.

I did not understand why a fixed date was to be set for the
revolution, and said that for this purpose they would have to send us
someone with expert knowledge. I was given the choice between
Zinoviev and Trotsky, and I chose Trotsky, the organizer of the Red
Army, as against Zinoviev, the agitator. This had nothing to do with
taking up a position towards the factional struggle in Russia, because
I simply knew nothing of it. Nor was there any personal sympathy or
antipathy involved. In secret discussions I was offered not only
deliveries of weapons, but also eventual military assistance in East
Prussia. Now, plenty of money was given out for the purchase of
weapons, but weapons were not acquired — only in some places
comrades were corrupted, e.g. in Hamburg. I was given assurances
about weapons which were already available, but these never corresponded to the truth. Not even in the case of the Hamburg rising
were there any weapons; this is why it started with the plundering of
a few police stations.

Action were amnestied, including Brandler (August 1922). He was working with the
Czech communists in Prague at the time, and made his way back to Germany in
September.

The minutes of the KPD Congress of 1924 prove that Thalheimer and myself did not offer to make our submission to the troika. Things were quite different from this. Our friends demanded that we should refuse to submit to the order exiling us to Moscow and take up the fight at home, and be prepared even to split the party. I rejected this idea for the following reasons: 1. This would not further the continuance of the party's active united front policy, with the objective of liquidating the SPD by winning over their most active working-class members to communism. Moscow would fight us with the cynical accusation 'They capitulated to Ebert and Seeckt; they fight against the Comintern and the Soviet Union.' 2. The KPD was financed by the Comintern, which enabled it to issue twenty-seven newspapers and pay 200 functionaries. Even if, as our supporters claimed, we were to win over half the membership, we would not be able to publish even as many as four newspapers or pay a dozen functionaries from our own resources. I saw no other possibility, I said, than to take up an attitude of critical expectation that the new *Zentrale* would make a mess of things, and to make sure that the nucleus of lesser functionaries remained active. This nucleus would rapidly come into concrete conflict with the factory and trade-union line adopted by Ruth Fischer and Maslow. This development alone could provide a fresh and firm basis for the party to recover from its sickness. And so we travelled to Moscow, into exile.

Best regards to yourself and Tamara,
from Heinrich Brandler

From Deutscher to Brandler

4 February 1959

Sehr Lieber and Geehrter Genosse Brandler,
Both Tamara and I were very sad to hear that you were ill and had to go to hospital. We do hope that the treatment will improve your health and we send you our best wishes and warmest regards. Your general comment on the first two chapters of *The Prophet Unarmed* gave me much satisfaction. I could let you have the rest of the volume in page proofs, but I hesitate to inflict this on you in your present position, unless you definitely want to read it.

Let me once again explain, in general terms, the attitude from which as a historian I have viewed the 1923 controversy over Germany. I have done my best to approach it objectively and to weigh carefully the conflicting evidence, without taking sides. This approach, of course, has nothing to do with any liberal objectivism. Wherever I deal with the conflicts between revolution and counter-revolution or communism and anti-communism and reformism, I stand as a historian on the side of those who fight for the revolution, without ceasing to present the counter-revolution objectively. But when it comes to the internal factional struggles in the communist camp, I feel that as a historian I must be above them and not commit myself to any apologetics for one faction or another, even where my sympathies either went or still go one way or the other. I think that in 1923 both Trotsky and yourself were in an impasse, and that consequently both you and Trotsky were right and wrong at the same time. I think that Trotsky underrated, as Marx and Lenin did so often, the objective factors which worked towards a temporary stabilization of capitalism — temporary yet very long-lasting indeed. I am coming back to this problem in the third volume, where I am putting together all the crises of the inter-war years: 1919, 1921, 1923, 1929–33, 1936–38, and showing how in all these crises Trotsky committed the same mistake. Yet, this was a mistake which as a revolutionary he was as if compelled to make — mistakes which underlay his tragedy and do not detract from his greatness.

You, on the other hand, saw in 1923 more clearly the objective difficulties in the way of a revolutionary party. (This comes out in, among other things, your speech at the Congress of the Polish Communist Party in September 1923, which the Polish *Histpart* has now published in *Z Pola Walki*.[45]) Yet at the same time you were under pressure not only from IKKI but also from your own position as a leader of a revolutionary party, to commit yourself to a revolutionary course of action. You were, therefore, torn between your sense that objectively the situation was not revolutionary and your acceptance of a revolutionary line of action. This conflict in yourself again reflects itself very strikingly in your speech at the Polish Congress. If you had followed your own sense of the objective difficulties only, you would have refused to act on Zinoviev's and Trotsky's advice. You would have said: 'Comrades, I consider your policy to be wrong, I cannot carry it out, I wish to bear no responsibility for it, and I stand aside.' You would then have spared yourself all the subsequent criticisms which were so often unjust, but were

[29] *Z Pola Walki*, I, 4, Warsaw 1958, pp. 134–40.

also inevitable, because in the eyes of so many communists you were associated with a policy of defeat. But you could not stand aside. You committed yourself to prepare the German October. Yet, having done so, you did not really act on your commitment. You hesitated, you were torn by contradictions in your attitude. I do not think that the historian can blame you for this, much though contemporaries did blame you. Your predicament reflected the tragedy of the German and international communist movement at that time. I think that this view is implied in the first two chapters of *The Prophet Unarmed,* and will be absolutely clear to the reader who will have read vol. III.

However, I cannot blame Trotsky for the things for which you are still blaming him — they have to be seen in a historical perspective and not merely in the context of an inter-factional struggle. I do not think that Trotsky was wrong when he favoured in April 1923 the introduction of Thälmann into the German leadership. Thälmann did represent an important current in the German Party, and it was only right that that current should be represented at the top. Trotsky acted, of course, on the assumption that the German party would be directed in the spirit of democratic centralism, on the basis of a collective leadership, where no communist current would be excluded and no group or clique would have a monopoly on the leadership. That Thälmann subsequently acquired that monopoly does not make Trotsky's action in 1923 wrong. In politics as in law we should beware of retroactive condemnation. In April 1923 Trotsky could surely not foresee what a fatal role Thälmann would play one day. Nor do I think that it is right to speak of Thälmann as belonging to the Zinoviev faction in *April* 1923.

As you say, the German events of 1923 are in Trotsky's biography an episode, and this compels me to treat it much more summarily than I would have liked to do, and to condense the narrative to the utmost. This results in some unavoidable imprecision. Thus, at one point I write: 'And so when the moment of rising arrived, Brandler, supported by Radek and Pyatakov, cancelled the battle orders.' This sentence implies clearly enough that you cancelled the orders on your initiative, and that Radek and Pyatakov only supported you. On the same page I say that they 'advised you' to cancel the orders. Now, the English 'advised' is not quite as specific as the German *'Rat geben'* — it is more vague. However, it would have been better if I had said that they 'backed Brandler when he cancelled the orders for insurrection'. Unfortunately, the page proofs have gone back to the printer, and I doubt whether I shall still have an opportunity to correct this. I shall certainly do so in any subsequent edition. Politically, however, in the context of my narrative, this slight imprecision is not important at all: what I have argued in this context is that the two Trotskyists, Radek and Pyatakov, took up the same position as you did, and that the triumvirs therefore blamed Trotsky and Trotskyism for the German defeat. This was so, regardless of whether Radek and Pyatakov 'advised' you to act as you did, or whether they merely approved your decision *post factum*.

In explaining your behaviour, I say that you were 'anxious to disentangle the German question from the Russian issues'. This I give as your main motive. You do not object to this, but you deny that you 'declared your support for the official Russian leadership, that is the triumvirs'. You say that you arrived in the January session of IKKI after everything had been settled, and that you had no idea of the conflict betewen the triumvirs and Trotsky. Here as a historian I have to take into account the evidence of other witnesses, your friends as well as your opponents, and to make allowance for a possible slip of your memory. You spoke in the session of IKKI on 11 January 1924. Five days later, on the 16th, there assembled the 13th conference of the Russian party, which was occupied mainly with the excommuni-cation of Trotsky. It is impossible that you should not have known this, and that the main theme of the Russian conference should not have been the subject of some talk at IKKI, at least behind the scenes. Thalheimer in *Eine Verpasste Revolution* makes no bones about the fact that your group turned against Trotsky as early as it could. The record of the session of IKKI shows that Warski and the other Poles were defending Trotsky against the attacks from the triumvirs, and that they were doing this at this same January session of IKKI. They were for this reason attacked by Zinoviev and his people during the session. You were there and you kept silent. Your silence spoke for itself, and the historian cannot but deduce from it that you decided not to defend Trotsky, who defended you through Radek. When one has in mind your subsequent and long-lasting antagonism to Trotsky, one is entitled, I think, to interpret your silence of January 1924 as an act of support for the triumvirs. I am saying this without any polemical intention and without any desire to blame you, but merely in order to explain why I brought in the consideration of your 'support for the official leadership, that is the triumvirs' among the many factors of the situation.

I have not taken over the 'assertion that the Berlin workers were burning with revolutionary fighting spirit'. What I say is that in Berlin the *party organization* was in a militant mood, and this I state

as a fact without going into its evaluation. Surely, this was so —
otherwise the opposition of the Berliners to you and their support of
Maslow and Fischer would have been inexplicable. That I have not a
shade of sympathy for the 'militancy' of Fischer and Maslow I have
given several very clear hints in various places, hints which I am sure
you have not missed.

All these are small details, however. I am very grateful to you for
your comments and for your very exhaustive and informative letter. I
am sure that I shall have an opportunity to write at greater length
about the events of 1923, and then I shall, with your permission, use
your explanations. Once I have finished with the third volume of the
Trotsky, I am going to write an analysis of the development of
socialism in this century, beginning with the origin of German
revisionism and ending with the present situation. In this context
1923 will, of course, be of great importance.

Once again, we are sending you our heartfelt wishes.
Isaac Deutscher

Heinrich Brandler to Tamara Deutscher

Hamburg, 20 August 1967

Dear Comrade,
The first news of today was the report in the midnight radio bulletin
that Isaac Deutscher had died of a heart attack in Rome. And I, who
cannot move, cannot work any longer, I am still here. The last of my
friends in Leipzig died. Death is not so bad for those it strikes, but for
their nearest, their friends. We were already so much looking
forward to Isaac Deutscher's dispute with Leonhard in Cologne.
That's not to be. The large circle of Isaac Deutscher's friends will not
find a substitute for him; nor will all those who valued his activity,
though they may not have agreed with him on everything.

Dear Comrade Tamara, please accept the expression of my deepest
sympathy at the loss of Deutscher; and convey it also to your son. If I
can at all be of help to you, please do let me know.

With heartfelt greetings,
Heinrich Brandler

Tamara Deutscher to Heinrich Brandler

31 August 1967

Dear Comrade Brandler,

Thank you so much for your letter. You know what immense respect Isaac had for you, and how greatly he admired you. You were for him one of those very, very few people — perhaps the only one — with whom he could find a common language. He was rejoicing at the sight of the new generation, those youngsters 20–22 years old, who were beginning to look for a real socialist, Marxist *Weltanschauung*. Isaac used to say that only the old — like you — or those very, very young understand him: the generations in-between were ground to dust between the heavy millstones either of Stalinism or McCarthyism.

I need not tell you with what sentiment we remember our rich evenings over the poor meals in our kitchen in our London flat.

I am sending you my respect, and also my love.
Tamara Deutscher

4

Conversation with Trygve Lie

Oslo, 28–29 April 1956

Trygve Lie is now the Governor of Oslo and lives in an American-style skyscraper a few kilometres from the city. The skyscraper looks a little incongruous, all the more so because it is surrounded by shacks and inferior tenement houses. Trygve Lie's flat is on the 14th floor: it consists of enormous rooms furnished in ultra-modern style, and looks like a luxurious gigantic first-class waiting room at a railway station. From the window there is an extensive view over fjords, forests and hills, and with a little imagination one might think one was looking at Manhattan and the Hudson River. As he led me into the room, I said:

'You seem to have brought a bit of New York here.'

My host was visibly flattered and started telling me in detail how, when he was still at his United Nations headquarters and learned about the building of this skyscraper in Oslo, he had arranged to have this flat reserved for him. At the door his first question was whether the taxi driver knew his address.

'Did you tell him: take me to Trygve Lie's home?'

'Yes, he knew,' I said though I was not sure whether it was not the hotel porter who had actually directed him. Again, I could not miss the satisfaction on Trygve Lie's face.

He sat opposite me. He looked exactly as in the newspaper pictures, but even more expressionless: very large, with elephantine — as if swollen — head and fishy eyes.

I spent several hours with him. He talked volubly, though with a very restricted English vocabulary and in rather primitive and crudely constructed sentences — which was surprising if one considers that he had spent so many years in England and the United States, and held so high an office. Much of the time he spoke to me as if I were his, not Trotsky's, biographer. He was still proud of the reprisals he took against Trotsky, boasted of them, had no idea that he was giving himself away until the moment when I made him feel a little of what I thought of all this. Then he got nervous and raised his voice, shouting at me repeatedly:

'Beware what you write, Mr Deutscher. Beware what you write!'

There was a hint of a threat in the intonation, though not so much in the words. For a moment I felt in this essentially parochial Scandinavian a streak of the New York gangster who suspects someone of the intention to expose some of his dirty doings and is on the point of blackmailing the suspected denunciator. I did my best to calm him in order to get the information I was seeking. As he talked about himself and Trotsky, he dwelt on his role as the man who saved the Norwegian Labour Party from communism — and that not only in connection with Trotsky — as if he were trying to ingratiate himself with a conservative, right-wing bourgeois public. At other moments he was boasting of what he did, as if he were talking to a good Stalinist. He was not quite sure where I stood and how he should treat me. And so imperceptibly, even to himself, he was switching from one viewpoint to the other, until late in the conversation he began to guess something and said:

'Ah, I see you are an admirer of Trotsky!' And again: 'Beware what you write, Mr Deutscher. Beware what you write!' Altogether a flea boasting that it once buzzed in the nostril of a lion, and even stung the lion.

'Did you ever meet Trotsky personally? Did you know him before he came to Norway? How did it happen that you gave him the right of asylum in 1935?'

'I first met Trotsky in 1921, when a delegation of the Norwegian Labour Party went to Moscow to negotiate with the Communist International and to clear the conflict we had as member party with the Executive of the International. We were received by the Executive, by Lenin, Trotsky and Zinoviev. Trotsky said nothing. He spent with us only an hour and then left excusing himself — he was busy elsewhere. I did not see Trotsky again until 1935. In March of that year the Labour Party took over the government in our country. I was then, in 1935, as a young Minister of Justice, approached by Olaf Schöffle and asked to give Trotsky a visa. Olaf Schöffle was one of the great leaders of our party in its Comintern period and headed the left wing of the party till the end of his life. He was not a Trotskyist but was always a great admirer and respecter of Trotsky and was, of course, closer to him than anyone of us, including Tranmael who was also Trotsky's great wellwisher.

'As to the asylum, I tell you most emphatically that we never gave

Trotsky the right of asylum. But I must also say that as a young and inexperienced minister I committed in this matter two mistakes. Mistake number one was that I let Trotsky in. Yes, my mistake was not that I expelled him but that I let him in. Listen to the story how it really was. My civil servants were strongly against admitting him, but Schöffle and the other party leaders all wanted him to come. There was a vote in the government and against two votes it was decided to let him in. But we did not give him asylum. I instructed our consul in Paris that he should give him an entry visa on two conditions: 1. that he should first obtain a French return visa; 2. that during his stay in Norway he should not interfere either in Norwegian or in any international politics. But Trotsky was smart and he never signed any such commitment. And the consul never communicated these conditions to Trotsky.'

At this point I interrupted, asking rather gently whether, if the consul had never communicated these terms to Trotsky, Trotsky's behaviour could in this matter be really described as 'smart'.

'Oh, yes, Mr Deutscher, oh, yes. He was a smart man, you do not know how smart he was. And I was a young and inexperienced minister. He outmanoeuvred me at every step, at every step. It is difficult to describe this. For he was an incredibly smart man.'

This was one of the refrains of the conversation: 'He was a smart man, he outmanoeuvred me all the time.'

'True, the consul told him nothing about these conditions, so he came to us without a French return visa. What could I do? I let him in. And the party was for letting him in. But then Schöffle told Trotsky that he must not interfere in Norwegian or international politics. But Trotsky was a smart man and he never signed anything. Only Schöffle told me that Trotsky accepted the conditions. And here my mistake number two: the party leaders, Tranmael and Schöffle, told me that I should go with them and pay a formal visit to Trotsky in Knudsen's home. I should not have gone. But I was young and inexperienced, and so I went. When we came to him, Tranmael said we must interview him for the *Arbeiderbladet*. Trotsky was a great man, a great historic figure, and they were all very proud to have him here and they wanted to have him interviewed for the party paper. Trotsky refused. He was a smart man. He said: Well, you made it a condition that I must not interfere in politics, so I don't. He talked to us about the weather all the time, and did not want to answer any political questions. So I as Minister of Justice said that for this occasion I waive the restriction. In the end we persuaded him to give us the interview. But I said I waive the restriction for this occasion only. I checked the interview. I had no objection to anything he said about world affairs, and I authorized publication. This was my mistake number two.'

'Mr Lie, tell me as a socialist and as a lawyer, did you think that you were entitled to demand from Trotsky that he should refrain from any political activity concerning international, not Norwegian affairs? Would you say that this was the traditional liberal conception of the right of asylum? Do you imagine how, for instance, Marx who lived and worked most of his life in London, would have reacted if the English governments a hundred years ago, had interpreted political asylum in this way?'

'What you are saying, Mr Deutscher, is exactly what the liberal party in our parliament was saying when they attacked me. Also some comrades in my own party. However, no political refugee has the right of asylum; it is not a right but a government's prerogative to grant asylum. We did not give Trotsky any asylum. We only thought that his life was in danger and we let him come here to save his life, nothing else. I must say that for a long time Trotsky adhered to the conditions we set. He was beleaguered by journalists who wanted interviews, but he refused. He did not — or so it seemed to me, a young and inexperienced minister — interfere in any politics. I knew this very well because I had some police control over what he was doing. It was not an efficient control; there was no censorship of his mail. But I knew that he kept strictly to the terms of his entry permit and refused to give any interviews.'

'When then did relations begin to deteriorate?'

'We began to get some alarming information about Trotsky's activities in connection with the Fourth International. We had at the time a special contact with the international police through which various governments exchanged information of mutual interest. We had from the Belgian police some alarming reports which were also confirmed by the French police. There was still not enough in those reports to justify reprisals against Trotsky or even any ground to warn him. But we were suspicious of his secretaries who went to Paris and back, and so we withdrew entry permits of some of these secretaries. Among them was Wolf, who was later killed in Spain. Then, on 5 August there came the Nazi attack on Knudsen's and Trotsky's home. They got hold of some documents, but they were of no importance. I assure you, Mr Deutscher, that the action I later took against Trotsky had nothing to do with these documents which were of no importance. But this was also the time of the election campaign in our country. The conservatives and the Nazis made of

Trotsky's stay here the most important electoral issue. I talked to Koht [at the time Foreign Minister] and to other members of the government, and we all saw that the election will be decided on the Trotsky question. We were afraid we were to lose the election. Trotsky appeared in court twice as witness in the case of the Nazis who attacked his home. And so I said to myself: It was time I did something about this. First I had Trotsky brought to my office at the Ministry of Justice. He was brought under police escort, but this was still before I ordered his internment. The talk we had was not very friendly. We spoke in German. I reminded Trotsky that he was not to interfere in any politics — Norwegian or international. Trotsky argued that he was granted asylum, that he never did and never would interfere in Norwegian affairs, but would not take any obligation as far as international affairs were concerned. I told him: You must sign such an obligation now.

'You should have seen the look he gave me when I told him this. I cannot describe to you that look. He was a proud man, you know. He stood up and said: Do you think, I, Leon Trotsky, with my past, with my record, that I am going to sign such a document? He spoke so about himself: "I, Leon Trotsky". You do not know what a proud and egocentric man he was. Then I told him: Leon Trotsky (I did not call him Mister and I did not call him Comrade, but just Leon Trotsky), Leon Trotsky, I said, and what about the Norwegian Labour Party and the election? That made Trotsky laugh. He was a great man. What did he worry about Norway and its Labour Party? He said: What do I care about your elections? You are a rotten gang and you have no idea about international affairs.

'And you know what? He came to my office, and though he had never been there before, he knew where every minister had his office, and he pointed through the window at the office of the Prime Minister and said to me: You and your *Pantoffel* Prime Minister who sits over there, you will all be refugees driven out of your country in two years from now. Well, we were refugees, and when we were driven from Norway, we remembered his words, but this was after four not after two years.

'Well, this was my first talk with Trotsky in my office. It must have been in August, soon after the attack. Then the electoral campaign got into full swing and the business of Trotsky was becoming more and more a central issue. Then I ordered him to be interned and had him again brought to the Ministry of Justice. I told him that I have taken the necessary steps to prevent him from participating in politics. You should have seen that proud man. "I, Leon

Trotsky" — he spoke of himself. Yes, he was a great man. I have met five great men in my life. You know who they were: Lenin, Stalin, Trotsky, Churchill and Roosevelt. Trotsky was perhaps the greatest of them, except for Roosevelt and perhaps Lenin. Oh, he was a great man. And he was so well educated, he knew everything. And his logic was sharp like a knife. And he was humane, very humane. Quite a different man from Stalin. When I sat with Stalin, I felt something was freezing in my back. I just felt I was afraid to death of that man. With Trotsky it was different. He was very humane. But I was frightened all the same, frightened of his sharp logic, of his shrewdness, of his smartness. He could outmanoeuvre me, and all of us and you too, Mr Deutscher. At every step he outmanoeuvred us all.

'It was enough to meet these two men — Stalin and Trotsky — to know that Trotsky was by far the more intelligent and able. He was a genius. You felt it when you talked to him. And so I thought he was the more dangerous of the two. You see, he was the only man who could bring communism to complete success. So I hated him. Do not forget that in our party there was a considerable communist or near-communist element. And I was opposed to it. I am proud of this that I played a role, quite an important role, in defeating the pro-communist element in our party. No, I could not have been Trotsky's friend. He was a great danger to us all. And I hate dictators. I fought Trotsky in 1936 and I fought Hitler in 1940. I could only intern him by a royal decree, and so I got the royal decree which enabled me to intern him, otherwise our Constitution gave no power to do this. But I hate dictators.'

'Excuse me, Mr Lie, but in 1936 it was not Trotsky who was a dictator but you. It was you who ruled by decree then, wasn't it?'

'Yes, I did it by decree all right. But are you, Mr Deutscher, Trotsky's admirer? I see you are his admirer. You think I acted wrongly, do you? Now, tell me frankly what do you think of my behaviour? You do not approve of it?'

'Well, Mr Lie, if you ask my frank opinion I will tell you. If one day somebody writes your biography, someone who admires you, he will perhaps not be very proud of this particular chapter in your career.'

'Oh, I see, you are Trotsky's admirer, you are. Beware what you write, Mr Deutscher, beware what you write. I have documents, documents, and documents to show that I was right. I told Trotsky: You broke the conditions and I am going to intern you and allow you no contact whatsoever with the outside world. And I established a censorship over all his mail. I hired a villa at Hurum and I put him and his wife there, and I placed twenty policemen to guard him. And you know who was in charge of the police guard: Jonas Lie. Later Jonas Lie was one of the wartime traitors, one of the leaders of Quisling's party. He was in charge of the place and he was sending me reports every day about what Trotsky did and how he behaved in the course of the day. So I thought I knew very well what Trotsky was doing. But you know what a smart man he was? He outmanoeuvred me again, me, a young and naive minister. His friends sent him a cake into his internment place. And, you know, in the cake they smuggled in some documents to him. Then he said he had to visit a dentist in town. I allowed him to go. He left the policeman outside the dentist's door to stand guard. But in the waiting room there was already a comrade of his waiting for him and getting some documents from him. We learned all this later. At first we had no idea. But Trotsky knew how to do clandestine work, he knew it. He was a genius at this, too.'

'Mr Lie, you interned him at the time of the first of the great purge trials, the Zinoviev and Kamenev trial in Moscow. And he, Trotsky, was the chief defendant in these trials. You cut him off from all contact with the world. As a lawyer, do you think that you were right in refusing him every opportunity to answer the accusations? Perhaps he smuggled his answer to Vyshinsky? Indeed, I am sure that this was what he smuggled out. Now, tell me, if someone accused Trotsky in Norway of a burglary, would you as a lawyer refuse him the right to defend himself? And here was Trotsky, accused of poisoning thousands of Soviet workers, plotting to assassinate Stalin and other Soviet leaders, presented as Hitler's agent and spy and you, Mr Lie, refused him any possibility of defending himself. You think you were right in doing that?'

'But why did he not apply to me and said that he wanted to answer Vyshinsky? I might have permitted him. Yes, I cut him off from all contact with the world, that is true. And he had the right to defend himself, that's also true. But we did not give him asylum. And why should our little country have to be dragged into his struggle with Stalin? We could not take the risk. We were a small country, with Hitler on one side and Stalin on the other, and we could not afford embroiling ourselves. There were bigger countries, bigger democratic countries than we, and none wanted to give him asylum. Why should we have risked our existence? He was a great man, but too great for our little Norway, too great for us. And he was in the wrong because he did not observe the conditions of his residence permit.'

'But are you not, Mr Lie, putting forward two different and even conflicting arguments which cancel each other? First you say that as a small country exposed to pressure from two great powers you could not risk giving Trotsky asylum and all the rights that that implied. One can understand this viewpoint — there is truth in it. What this amounts to is that you were perhaps morally in the wrong, but that you could not afford to be morally in the right. And then you go on to say that it was Trotsky who was morally in the wrong. Surely, you cannot have it both ways? But let me ask you another question which is of the greatest importance in this story. Did the Soviet Ambassador ever ask for Trotsky's expulsion or internment or extradition? Did the Soviet government, as some believe, ever threaten you with stopping their imports from Norway or with a financial boycott?'

'No, never. They never asked for Trotsky's expulsion. They never threatened us with any economic reprisals. We acted of our own accord, for our own motives because of the domestic situation, because of the elections, and because of Trotsky's behaviour. Only once Yakubovich, the Soviet Ambassador here, came to see me at the Ministry of Justice, but this was already after I had interned Trotsky. He came to me, but I did not even let him talk, and before he said anything I smiled and told him: "We have taken care of the Trotsky case. I have ordered Trotsky to be interned." Yakubovich smiled and left without saying a word. That was all.'

'Could you tell me how and why you decided to expel him from Norway? And how did it happen that he went to Mexico?'

'We could not afford to keep him interned here. It involved us in too large expenses. I had to hire a villa; I had to keep twenty policemen on the spot. So when I had him in my office for the second time I told him this. You should have seen him! You should have seen how he reacted. A year before, he was an ordinary modest refugee. Now he was a cock again and a proud man. He had been impolite to the guards, he cheated their vigilance, and so on. Then I asked him who might possibly give him a visa. He had mentioned Diego Rivera several times as his friend and suggested that Mexico may be a possible refuge. But he said he would not go there unless he were invited: and unless he were given safe transport. I sent a man to the Mexican envoy in Stockholm, and they at once agreed to give him asylum. I was a little uneasy, because I expected them to ask us whether he would get a Norwegian return visa. You can imagine how happy I was when they did not ask for that. I then informed Trotsky about the arrangements for the journey. I had hired a tanker *Ruth*. Then I gave Trotsky a passport and asked him to sign some sort of a document. He refused to sign and said he would not go on that tanker. I was telling him that this was a very good solid vessel, with very comfortable accommodation and excellent food. But he was not interested. He said "Stalin knows all about your *Ruth*. The tanker would be torpedoed, it will never reach the British Channel. What kind of defences has that ship?" — he asked. I guaranteed him that we would maintain absolute secrecy. I told him that nobody knew about all this except me, him, and the owner of the ship. But he still refused to go on the *Ruth*. Then I told him that I shall order the police to take him aboard the tanker. And he had to yield. But he still refused to sign the document, and he signed it only when he stood on Mexican soil. The ship was not allowed to use her radio or to give any signals, and only when she was in mid-Atlantic did the news leak out.'

On this the interview was practically concluded. There came still a few 'Beware, Mr Deutscher, beware' and Lie was obviously alarmed at what I might write about him. When we got out of the lift and he politely arranged to get a taxi for me, he still said: 'So you think that a biographer will blame me for all this, and that's what you are going to do?' To this I answered:

'I said, Mr Lie, that your biographer may blame you. But surely, you realize that I am Trotsky's biographer not yours. And it is not my job to judge your behaviour in my book.'

This put his mind at rest. He once again inquired, as he had done at the beginning of the conversation, about the American sales of my books and was evidently impressed when I told him that they were selling very well; his autobiography was apparently not a success. We parted in a friendly way, he assuring me once again of his admiration for my *Stalin* which he said he consulted regularly — the volume was indeed on his desk and had many marks in the margin.

Coulsdon, Surrey.
4 May 1956

Part Four
China

1
Maoism — its Origins and Outlook

I

What does Maoism stand for? What does it represent as a political idea and as a current in contemporary communism? The need to clarify these questions has become all the more urgent because Maoism is now openly competing with other communist schools of thought for international recognition. Yet before entering this competition Maoism had existed as a current, and then as the dominant trend of Chinese communism for thirty to thirty-five years. It is under its banner that the main forces of the Chinese revolution waged the most protracted civil war in modern history, and won their victory in 1949, making the greatest single breach in world capitalism since the October Revolution, and freeing the Soviet Union from isolation. It is hardly surprising that Maoism should at last advance politically beyond its national boundaries and claim world-wide attention to its ideas. What is surprising is that it has not done so earlier and that it has for so long remained closed within the confines of its national experience.

Maoism presents in this respect a striking contrast with Leninism. The latter also existed at first as a purely Russian school of thought; but not for long. In 1915, after the collapse of the Second International, Lenin was already the central figure in the movement for the Third International, its initiator and inspirer — Bolshevism, as a faction in the Russian Social Democratic Party, was not much older then than a decade. Before that the Bolsheviks, like other Russian socialists, had lived intensely with all the problems of international Marxism, absorbed all its experience, participated in all its controversies, and felt bound to it with unbreakable ties of intellectual, moral and political solidarity. Maoism was from the outset Bolshevism's equal in revolutionary vitality and dynamism, but differed from it in a relative narrowness of horizon and a lack of any direct contact with critical developments in contemporary Marxism.

One hesitates to say it, yet it is true that the Chinese revolution, which in its scope is the greatest of all revolutions in history, was led by the most provincial-minded and 'insular' of revolutionary parties. This paradox throws into all the sharper relief the inherent power of the revolution itself.

What accounts for the paradox? A historian notes first of all the total absence of any Socialist-Marxist influence in China prior to 1917.[1] Ever since the middle of the nineteenth century, from the Opium Wars and the Taiping Rebellion, through the Boxer Rising and till the overthrow of the Manchu dynasty in 1911, China had been seething with anti-imperialism and agrarian revolt; but the movements and secret societies involved in the risings and revolts were all traditional in character and based on ancient religious cults. Even bourgeois liberalism and radicalism had not penetrated beyond the Great Wall till the beginning of this century: Sun Yat-sen formulated his republican programme only in 1905. By that time the Japanese labour movement, of which Sen Katayama was the famous spokesman in the Socialist International, had officially embraced Marxism. In Russia the invasion of Western socialist ideas had begun by the middle of the nineteenth century; and ever since Marxism had gripped the minds of all revolutionaries, Populists and Social Democrats. As Lenin put it, Bolshevism stood on the shoulders of many generations of Russian revolutionaries who had breathed the air of European philosophy and socialism. Chinese communism has had no such ancestry. The archaic structure of Chinese society and the deeply ingrained self-sufficiency of its cultural tradition were impermeable to European ideological ferments. Western imperialism managed to sap that structure and tradition, but was unable to fructify the mind of China with any vital liberating idea. Only the revolutionary explosion in neighbouring, yet remote, Russia shook the immense nation from its inertia. Marxism found a way to China via Russia. The lightning speed with which it did so after 1917, and the firmness with which it then struck roots in China's soil, are the most stupendous illustration of the 'law of combined development': here we see the most archaic of nations avidly absorbing the most modern of revolutionary doctrines, the last word in revolution, and translating it into action. Lacking any native Marxist ancestry, Chinese communism descends straight from Bolshevism. Mao

[1]The first Chinese translation of the *Communist Manifesto* appeared only in 1920; it was then that Mao, at the age of twenty-seven, read the *Manifesto* for the first time. The year before he still went on a pilgrimage to the grave of Confucius, although he was not a believer.

stands on Lenin's shoulders.[2]

That Marxism should have reached China so late and in the form of Bolshevism was the result of two factors: the First World War, exposing and aggravating to the utmost the inner contradictions of Western imperialism, discredited it in the eyes of the East, intensified socio-political ferments in China, made China 'mature' for revolution and extraordinarily receptive to revolutionary ideas; while Leninism, with its original, vigorous emphasis on anti-imperialism and the agrarian problem, rendered Marxism, for the first time in history, directly and urgently relevant to the needs and strivings of the colonial and semi-colonial peoples. In a sense, China had to 'jump over' the pre-Bolshevik phase of Marxism in order to be able to respond to Marxism at all.

Yet the impact of undiluted Leninism on China was very brief. It lasted only through the early 1920s till the opening of the 'national' revolution in 1925. Only a very small *élite* of the radical intelligentsia acquainted itself with the programme of Leninism and adopted it. At the foundation Congress of the Chinese Communist Party in 1921 only twelve delegates were present — Mao Tse-tung was one of them — representing a total membership of fifty-seven! At the second Congress, in the following year, the same apostolic number of delegates spoke for a membership of 123. There were still no more than nine hundred party members in the whole of China at the beginning of 1925, shortly before the communists were to find themselves at the head of insurgent millions.[3] On these first communist propaganda circles the basic ideas of Leninism left a deep impression. No matter how much the Stalinized Comintern did later to confound the mind of Chinese communism, the germ of Leninism survived, grew, and became transformed into Maoism.

Leninism offered its Chinese adepts a few great and simple truths rather than any clear-cut strategy or precise tactical prescriptions. It taught them that China could achieve emancipation only through revolution from below, for which they must work as tirelessly, indomitably and hopefully as the Bolsheviks had worked for their

---

[2] A parallel may be drawn here between the fortunes of Marxism and revolution in Europe and Asia. Just as in Europe Marxism first exercised a wide influence in industrial Germany, so in Asia it found its first important following in industrial Japan, the 'Prussia of the Far East'. But in neither of these two 'advanced' countries did Marxism go beyond propaganda and agitation. On both continents it fell to the great 'backward' nations to accomplish the revolution.

[3] Ho Kan-chih, *A History of the Modern Chinese Revolution*, Peking 1959, pp. 40, 45, 63, 84.

revolution; that they ought to distrust any bourgeois reformism and hope for no accommodation with any of the Powers that held China in subjection; that against those Powers they ought to join hands with patriotic elements of the Chinese bourgeoisie, but that they must distrust any temporary bourgeois allies and be ever ready for their treachery; that Chinese communism must look for support to the destitute masses of the peasantry and unfailingly be on their side in their struggles against war-lords, landlords and money lenders; that China's small urban working class was the sole consistently revolutionary and potentially the most dynamic force in society, the only force capable of exercising leadership ('hegemony') in the nation's struggle for emancipation; that China's 'bourgeois-democratic' revolution was part of an 'uninterrupted', or 'permanent', revolution, part of a global upheaval in which socialism was bound to overcome imperialism, capitalism, feudalism and every form of archaic Asian society; that the oppressed peoples of the East should rely on the solidarity with them of the Soviet Union and the Western working classes; that the Communist Party, acting as the vanguard of the movement, must never lose touch with the mass of workers and peasants, but should always be ahead of them; and, finally, that they must guard jealously the party's total independence in policy and organization *vis-à-vis* all other parties.[4] This was the quintessence of Leninism which the few pioneers of Chinese communism had absorbed before the revolution of 1925–27.

As far as Maoism is concerned, these were still the years of its 'pre-history'. It was only during the revolution that Maoism began to announce itself; and only in consequence of the revolution's defeat did it form a special trend in communism. The 'pre-historical' period is nevertheless of obvious importance, because some of the lessons Maoism had learned in the school of Leninism, although they were to be overlaid by other ideological elements, entered firmly into its political make-up.

II

The next formative influences were the revolution itself and the traumatic shock of its defeat. The years of 1925–27 brought to

[4] The Second Congress of the Communist International occupied itself, in 1920, especially with the problems of the colonial and semi-colonial countries; and Lenin was the primie mover of the theses and resolutions on this subject. See Lenin, *Sochineniya*, Moscow 1963, vol. 41.

eruption all the national and international contradictions by which China had been torn; and the eruption was astounding in suddenness, scale and force. All social classes — and all the Powers involved —behaved as Leninism had predicted they would. But the most outstanding feature of the events — a feature that was not to be found in the next Chinese revolution and is therefore easily forgotten or ignored — was the revelation of the extraordinary political dynamism of China's small working class.[5] The main centres of the revolution were in the industrial and commercial cities of coastal China, especially Canton and Shanghai. The most active organizations were the trade unions (which had almost overnight become a great mass movement). General strikes, huge street demonstrations and workers' insurrections were the main events and turning points of the revolution, as long as the revolution was on the ascendant. The agrarian upheaval in the background, widespread and deep, was far slower in the take-off, scattered over immense areas, and uneven in tempo and intensity. It gave a nation-wide resonance to the action of the urban proletariat but could not affect the events as directly and dramatically as that action did. It cannot be emphasized too strongly that in 1925–27 China's working class displayed quite the same energy, political initiative and capacity for leadership that Russia's workers had shown in the revolution of 1905. For China these years were what the years 1905–06 had been for Russia — a general rehearsal for revolution, with this difference, however, that in China the party of the revolution drew from the rehearsal conclusions very different from those that had been drawn in Russia. This fact, in combination with other, objective factors, discussed later, was to be reflected in the differences between the socio-political alignments in the China of 1949 and the Russia of 1917.

At the time of the Chinese 'rehearsal', official Moscow was already reacting against its own high hopes and international-revolutionary aspirations of the Lenin era — it had just proclaimed Socialism in One Country as its doctrine. The Stalinist and Bukharinist factions, which still jointly exercised power, were sceptical of the chances of

---

[5]Mao gives the number of Chinese industrial workers employed in large-scale enterprises as two million. There were about ten million coolies, rikshas, etc. (Mao Tse-tung, *Izbrannye proizvedeniya*, Moscow 1952, vol. I, pp. 24–5.) Mao explains the decisive role of the workers in the revolution by the high degree of their concentration in big factories, their extraordinarily oppressive conditions, and exceptional militancy. Russia had no more than three million workers employed in modern industry about the time of the revolution; and Trotsky explains their decisive role in much the same way.

186

Chinese communism, afraid of international 'complications', and resolved to play for safety. To avoid challenging the Western Powers and antagonizing the Chinese bourgeoisie, Stalin and Bukharin acknowledged the Kuomintang as the legitimate leader of the revolution, cultivated 'friendship' with Chiang Kai-shek, proclaimed the necessity of a 'bloc of four classes' in China, and instructed the Communist Party to enter the Kuomintang and submit to its guidance and discipline. Ideologically, this policy was being justified on the ground that the Chinese revolution was bourgeois in character, and must be kept within the limits of a bourgeois revolution. No proletarian dictatorship was therefore on the order of the day — only 'a democratic dictatorship of the workers and peasants', a vague and self-contradictory slogan which Lenin had advanced in 1905, when he still held that the Russian revolution would be only 'bourgeois democratic'.

To follow this course, the Chinese communists had to give up almost every principle Moscow had inculcated in them quite recently. They had, as a party, to resign their independence and freedom of movement. They had to give up, in deeds if not words, the aspiration of proletarian leadership and accept bourgeois leadership instead. They had to trust their bourgeois allies. In order to bring about and keep in being the 'bloc of four classes', they had to curb the militancy of the urban workers and the rebelliousness of the peasantry, which constantly threatened to explode that bloc. They had to abandon the idea of continuous (or permanent) revolution, for they had to 'interrupt' the revolution whenever it tended to overlap the safety margins of a bourgeois order, which it constantly tended to do. They had to break the proletarian-socialist momentum of the movement — or else Moscow would denounce them as adherents of Trotskyism. Socialism in One Country, in the USSR, meant no socialism in China.[6]

At this point Chinese communism fell a prey to its own weaknesses as well as Moscow's opportunism and national egoism. Having no Marxist tradition of their own to fall back upon, being dependent on Moscow for inspiration, ideas and the sinews of their activity, finding themselves raised by events of dizzy suddenness from the obscurity of a tiny propaganda circle to the leadership of millions in revolt, lacking political experience and self-confidence, bombarded by an endless stream of categorical orders, instructions and remonstrances from Moscow, subjected to persuasion, threats

[6]See my account of these events in *The Prophet Unarmed*, pp. 316–38.

and political blackmail by Stalin's and the Comintern's envoys on the spot, bewildered and confounded, the pioneers of Chinese communism gave in. Having learned all their Leninism from Moscow, they could not bring themselves to say, or even think, that Moscow was wrong in urging them to unlearn it. In the best circumstances they would have found it very hard to rise to their task and would have needed firm, clear, absolutely unequivocal advice. The advice they got from Moscow was unequivocal only in prompting them to equivocate, to shirk their responsibilites, and to abdicate. They did not know that the Trotskyist Opposition was defying Stalin's and Bukharin's 'General Line'; and that Trotsky himself opposed the idea that the Chinese party must enter the Kuomintang and accept its dictates. (They had no contact with the Opposition and Trotsky was criticizing Stalin's and Bukharin's 'friendship' with Chiang Kai-shek in the privacy of the Politburo.) To the Chinese therefore Stalin and Bukharin spoke with the voice of Bolshevism at large.

It was at that moment, the moment of the surrender to the Kuomintang, that Mao first registered his dissent. His expression of dissent was only oblique; but within its terms it was firm and categorical. In the second half of 1925 and at the beginning of 1926 Mao spent much time in his native province of Hunan, organizing peasant revolts, and participated in communist activity in Canton and Shanghai, representing the party within some of the leading bodies of the Kuomintang. His experience led him to assess the social alignments, especially the class struggle in the countryside, in two essays (*The Classes of Chinese Society*, written in March 1926, and *A Study of the Peasant Movement in Hunan Province*, March 1927). He did not attempt to analyse China's social structure in depth or to criticize the party line in general; but he made his assessment in terms that conflicted implicitly and irreconcilably with every premiss of the party's and the Comintern's policy.

'. . . There has not been a single revolution in history,' he wrote in March 1926, 'that has not suffered defeat when its party guided it along the wrong road. To gain confidence that we shall not lead the revolution along the wrong road . . . we must take care to rally our genuine friends and strike at our genuine enemies . . . [we must be able] to tell our genuine friends from our genuine enemies . . .' The 'genuine friends' of the revolutionary proletariat were the poor peasants and the semi-proletarian elements in the villages; the 'genuine enemies' — the landlords, the wealthy peasants, the bourgeoisie, the Right wing of the Kuomintang. He characterized the behaviour of all these classes and groups with such total lack of illusion and such clarity and determination that, in the light of what he said, the 'bloc of four classes', the party's submission to the Kuomintang, and the idea of a containment of the revolution within bourgeois limits appeared as so many absurdities, suicidal for the party and the revolution. He was not yet turning his eyes from the town to the country, as he was to do presently, although he already responded far more sensitively and fully to what the peasants were feeling and doing than to the workers' movement. But he still insisted, in good Leninist style, on the workers' primacy in the revolution; and his emphasis on this reflected the actual relationship of workers and peasants in the events of that period.

By this time in the Soviet Union only the Trotskyists and Zinovievists still spoke such language;[7] Mao was something of a 'Trotskyist' Jourdain unaware of what kind of prose he was using. His role in the party was not prominent enough for the Comintern to notice his heresy; but already in 1926 he was at loggerheads with the Chinese Central Committee and Chen Tu-hsiu, the party's undisputed leader and his own erstwhile intellectual and political guide. In the *Study of the Hunan Peasant Movement*, written shortly before Chiang Kai-shek's *coup d'état*, Mao vented his indignation at those Kuomintang leaders and those 'comrades within the Communist Party' who sought to tame the peasantry and halt the agrarian revolution. 'Quite obviously,' he castigated them, 'this is a reasoning worthy of the landlord class . . . a counter-revolutionary reasoning. Not a single comrade should repeat this nonsense. If you are holding definite revolutionary views and happen to be in the country even for a while, you can only rejoice at seeing how the many millions of enslaved peasants are settling accounts with their worst enemies . . . All comrades should understand that our national revolution

[7]A comparison of the documents contained in Trotsky's *Problems of the Chinese Revolution* with Mao's writings of 1926–27 shows the complete identity of their views on these points. Ho Kan-chih in op. cit (which is the official Maoist account of the Chinese revolution) unwittingly gives many other illustrations of that identity. Thus, he relates that early in 1926 Mao protested against the Chinese party's decision to vote for the election of Chiang Kai-shek to the Executive Committee of the . . . Kuomintang and to back his candidature to the post of Commander-in-Chief of the Armed Forces. About the same time Trotsky protested in Moscow against Chiang's election as an Honorary Member of the Executive of the Comintern. The Maoist historian blames only Chen Tu-hsiu for the 'opportunist' policy, pretending not to know that Chen behaved as he did on Moscow's orders and that Chiang was Stalin's candidate to the post of the Commander-in-Chief. The fact that Chiang was Honorary Member of the Comintern's Executive is not even mentioned in the Maoist *History*.

requires a great upheaval in the country . . . and all should support that upheaval — otherwise they will find themselves in the camp of counter-revolution.'

This attitude cost Mao his seat on the Central Committee. He was to regain it a year later; but the streak of radicalism or of 'pristine Leninism' was to survive in him, even underneath many later accretions, and was to bring upon him the charge of Trotskyism . . . thirty-six years later.

III

It was, however, from the defeat of the revolution that Maoism took its proper origin, and that it acquired those features that distinguished it from all other currents in communism and from — Leninism.

The defeat caused much heart-searching among the Chinese communists, especially after they had learned the truth about the struggle over China that had gone on in the Russian Politburo. There were several conflicting reactions to what had happened. Chen Tu-hsiu ruefully acknowledged that he had misguided his party but pleaded that he himself (and the Central Committee) had been misguided by Moscow. Exposing dramatically the inner story of the revolution, relating the many acts of pressure and blackmail to which Moscow had subjected him, he acknowledged that Trotsky had all along been right over China. He was for this expelled from the party, slandered and persecuted by both the Kuomintang and the Comintern.[8] Chen Tu-hsiu and his few friends, arguing from an analogy with the Russian revolution (and accepting Trotsky's guidance), saw ahead of them a period of political stagnation, an interval between two revolutions; and they proposed to act as the Bolsheviks had acted during the interval between 1907 and 1917: retreat, dig in, and hold out

---

[8]Chen Tu-hsiu's fate — denounced as 'traitor' by the Comintern, he was imprisoned and tortured by the Kuomintang police — was a terrible warning to Mao who henceforth avoided any *open* breach with Stalinist orthodoxy, even while he was at loggerheads with its successive Chinese guardians. Mao was never to risk a conflict with both Stalin and Chiang Kai-shek. His cautious, ambiguous attitude towards Stalinism reflected something of the sense of weakness and ultimate dependence on Soviet backing which had caused Chen Tu-hsiu to accept Stalin's and Bukharin's dictates in 1925–27. But unlike Chen, Mao, for all his outward deference to Stalin, was never to give up his own judgement on Chinese affairs and swerve from his own course of action.

primarily among the industrial workers; regain and build up strong-holds in the cities which would be the main centres of the next revolution; combine clandestine work with open propaganda and agitation; struggle for 'partial demands', wage claims and democratic freedoms; press for the unification of China and call for a National Constituent Assembly; support the peasantry's struggles; use all discontents against Chiang Kai-shek's dictatorship and so gather strength for the next revolution, which would at last be the unin-terrupted revolution Lenin and Trotsky had preached.

This was, theoretically at least, a comprehensive prospect and a coherent programme of action. What the Comintern, through its nominees, Li Li-san and Wang Ming, offered was an utterly inco-herent combination of basic opportunism and ultra-left tactics, designed to justify the policy of 1925–27 and to save Stalin's face. The canon was upheld that the next revolution would also be only 'bourgeois democratic' — the canon could be used in future to justify a renewal of a pro-Kuomintang policy and a new 'bloc of four classes'. (Stalin always held that policy in reserve, even during his wildest ultra-left zigzags.) Meanwhile the Comintern, denying that the Chinese revolution had suffered any defeat, encouraged the Chinese party to stage hopeless coups and armed risings. These tactics, initiated with the armed Canton insurrection in December 1927, fitted in well with the Comintern's new 'General Line', which consisted in a forecast of imminent revolution in East and West alike, a call for 'direct struggle for power', rejection of any socialist-communist united front in Europe, refusal to defend democratic freedoms, slogans about social-fascism, etc. In Germany this policy led to the disaster of 1933. In China the hopeless risings, coups and other mad adventures demoralized and disorganized what had been left of the Chinese labour movement after the 1927 defeat.

It was against this background that Maoism made its entry. Although its official historians (and Mao himself) never admit it, Mao shared Chen Tu-hsiu's view that the revolution was in decline and that a political lull was ahead. He rejected the Comintern's ultra-left tactics, beginning with the Canton rising and ending with the various versions of 'Li-Li-sanism'. He held, however, that com-munism would for a long time to come have no chance at all of re-entrenching itself in the cities and regaining footholds in the working class — so deep, as he saw it, was the moral debacle that followed the surrenders of 1925–27. He did not as yet give up the hope that eventually the urban proletariat would rise again; but he turned his eyes wholly to the peasantry, which had not ceased to struggle and rise up in revolts. What was supposed to be merely the agrarian 'accompaniment' of the revolution in the cities could still be heard, loud and stormy, after the cities had been reduced to silence. Was it possible, Mao wondered, that this was no mere 'accompaniment'? Were perhaps the revolts of the peasants not just the backwash of a receding wave of revolution, but the beginning of another revolution of which rural China would be the main theatre?

A historian of Maoism may follow the subtle gradations by which Mao arrived at the affirmative answer to this question. Here it will be enough to recall that late in 1927, after his quarrel with the Central Committee, he retired to his native Hunan; then, after the defeat of the Autumn Harvest Rising, he withdrew at the head of small armed bands into the mountains on the Hunan–Kiangsi border; and from there he urged the Central Committee to 'remove the party as a whole', its headquarters and cadres, 'from the cities to the countryside'. Official Chinese textbooks now credit Mao with having conceived already then, in 1927–28, the far-sighted strategy that was to bring victory twenty years later. Mao's contemporary writings suggest that at first he thought of the 'withdrawal into the countryside' as a temporary expedient and possibly a gamble, but not as desperate a gamble as were the party's attempts to stir the urban workers back into insurrectionist action. Again and again he argued that the 'Red Base' he and Chu Teh had formed in the Hunan–Kiangsi mountains was only a 'temporary refuge' for the forces of the revolution.[9] Yet this temporary and provisional expedient did already point to the later Maoist strategy. The party leaders, 'opportunists' and 'ultra-radicals' alike, rejected Mao's advice, holding that it amounted to a break with Leninism. And, indeed, who could imagine Lenin, after the 1905 defeat, 'withdrawing the party' from Petersburg and Moscow and going at the head of small armed bands into the wilderness of the Caucasus, the Urals, or Siberia? The Marxist tradition, in which the idea of the supremacy of the town in modern revolution held a central place, was too deeply ingrained in Russian socialism for any Russian socialist group to embark upon such a venture. Nothing like it occurred even to the Social Revolutionaries, the descendants of the Narodniks, Populists and agrarian socialists.

[9]Mao, *op. cit.* vol. I, pp. 99–110 and 117ff. and *passim.*

IV

Mao gradually became aware of the implications of his move and in justifying the 'withdrawal from the cities', he recognized more and more explicty the peasantry as the sole *active* force of the revolution, until, to all intents and purposes, he turned his back upon the urban working class. He treated his new 'road to socialism' as a 'uniquely Chinese phenomenon', possible only in a country which was neither independent nor ruled by a single imperialist Power, which was the object of an intense rivalry between several Powers, each with its own zone of influence, and its own war-lords, *compradores* and puppets. That rivalry, he argued, made it impossible for China to achieve national integration; the Kuomintang would no more be able to achieve it, and to set up a cohesive national administration, than previous governments had been. Chiang Kai-shek could smash with a few military blows the concentrated strength of the urban workers, but would not be able to deal likewise with the peasantry, which, being dispersed, was less vulnerable to the white terror and could fight on for many years. There should therefore always exist 'pockets' in rural China where forces of the revolution could survive, grow and gather strength. Renouncing the prospects of a revolutionary revival in the towns, Maoism banked on the permanence of the agrarian revolution.

Mao assumed in effect a prolonged stalemate between the defeated urban revolution and a paralytic counter-revolution, a prolonged and unstable equilibrium between the divided imperialisms, the impotent Kuomintang bourgeoisie, and the apathetic working class. The stalemate would allow the peasantry to display its revolutionary energies, and to support the communists and their Red Bases as scattered islands of a new regime. From this assumption he drew (in 1930) this broad generalization about the international prospects of communism:

> If . . . the subjective forces of the Chinese revolution are weak at present, so are also the reactionary ruling classes and their organiza- tion . . . based on a backward and unstable socio-economic system . . . In Western Europe . . . the subjective forces of the revolution may at present be stronger than they are in China; but the revolution cannot immediately assert itself there, because in Europe the forces of the re- actionary ruling classes are many times stronger than they are in China. . . *The revolution will undoubtedly rise in China earlier than in Western Europe.*[10]

[10]Mao, *ibid*, p. 196. My italics.

This assumption, so characteristic of Maoism, was not altogether original — it had appeared fleetingly in some of Lenin's, Trotsky's, Zinoviev's and Stalin's reasonings a decade earlier.[11] But Mao made of it the cornerstone of his strategy, at a time when no other communist school of thought was prepared to do so. In retrospect, the events have amply justified him. Yet if the Maoist orientation and action are judged not retrospectively, but against the background of the late 1920s, and early 1930s, they may not appear as faultless as they seem now. It may be argued that the superiority of the 'reactionary ruling classes' in Western Europe would not have been so overwhelming, and that it might even have crumbled, if the Stalinist and Social-Democratic self-defeating policies (passivity *vis-à-vis* rising Nazism, and the shams of the Popular Fronts) had not worked to preserve and enhance it. One may further argue that the Maoist road of the Chinese revolution was not necessarily predetermined by the objective alignment of social forces, that the Chinese working class might have reasserted itself politically, if the Comintern had not recklessly wasted its strength and if the Chinese party had not 'withdrawn from the cities', and so deserted the workers, at a time when they needed its guidance more than ever. As so often in history so here, the objective and subjective factors are so enmeshed and intertwined after the events that it is impossible to disentangle them and determine their relative importance.

It should further be noted that the period of the middle 1930s was extremely critical for Maoism; its major premises were brought under question and nearly refuted by the events. In the south of China, the area to which Mao's action had been confined till 1935, the peasantry was utterly exhausted by its many revolts and was crushed by Chiang Kai-shek's punitive expeditions. The Red Bases of Hunan and Kiangsi, having held out against Chiang's 'extermination drives' for seven years, were succumbing to blockade and attrition. Mao and Chu Teh just managed to lead the Partisans out of the trap and start on the Long March. They thereby acknowledged their defeat in that part of China which had been the main theatre of their operations. It looked as if the counter-revolution, far from being impotent in the countryside, had demonstrated its superior strength there and gained a decisive advantage. In the meantime, the workers of Shanghai and other coastal cities had shown a new defiance and staged turbulent strikes and demonstrations. But, lacking competent leadership and organization, they were defeated

[11]See *The Prophet Armed*, pp. 456–7 and *The Prophet Outcast*, p. 61.

again and again. Maoist historians cast a veil of obscurity over this chapter of the movement in the cities, precisely because it raises the question whether under effective guidance those struggles of the urban workers might not have opened up a new revolutionary situation much earlier than it could be opened up from the country. Was it inevitable that the interval between the two revolutions should last not ten years, as it lasted in Russia, but more than twice as long? Or had the Maoist withdrawal from the cities something to do with it? Whatever the truth of the matter — the historian can pose the question but not answer it — around 1935 the Maoist strategy was on the point of collapse and nearly bankrupt. These facts are recalled here not for any polemical purpose, but because they lead to a conclusion of some topical relevance, namely, that Maoism as a strategy of revolution owes its ultimate vindication to an extraordinarily complex and largely unpredictable set of circumstances.

In 1935 Mao fought his way out of the impasse by means of the Long March, which has since become the heroic legend of Chinese communism. Yet at the end of the Long March Mao had under his orders only one-tenth of the force he had before the March — 30,000 out of 300,000 Partisans.[12] What saved Maoism and decisively contributed to its further evolution were, apart from its own heroic determination to survive, two major events or series of events: the Japanese invasion, and the deliberate de-industrialization of coastal China by the invader. The Japanese conquest deepened the contradictions between the imperialist Powers and interrupted the unification of China under the Kuomintang. It thus reproduced that impotence of the reactionary ruling class on which Mao had based his calculations. Northern China was in turmoil; the Kuomintang was unable to assert its military control there and to prevent the emergence and consolidation of the Northern 'Soviets'. Maoism derived fresh strength from the Kuomintang's inability to secure the nation's independence and form its own revolutionary-patriotic, 'Jacobin', stand against Japan. On the other hand, with the systematic de-industrialization of coastal China, the small working class was removed from the scene. As the Japanese dismantled industrial plant in Shanghai and other cities, the workers dispersed, became déclassés, or vanished in the country.[13] From this fact Maoism obtains a kind of

[12]Ho Kan-chih, *op. cit.* p. 270. The author blames the recklessness of the 'ultra-lefts' in the party and army for these disastrous losses.

[13]A most instructive description of this process and of its political effects is to be found in Chen Tu-hsiu's correspondence with Trotsky (The Trotsky Archives), quoted in *The Prophet Outcast*, pp. 423–4.

retroactive vindication. Henceforth no one could hope for the rise of a new 'proletarian wave' in the cities. The class alignments of 1925–27 could not be expected to reappear in the next revolution. The Marxist–Leninist scheme of class struggle became inapplicable to China. The peasants were the sole force struggling to subvert the old order; and Mao's party focused and armed all their rebellious energies. It was now, in the late 1930s, that Mao finally formulated the main and most original principle of his strategy: The Chinese revolution, unlike other revolutions, will have to be carried from country to town.[14]

V

The relationship between Maoism and Stalinism was ambiguous from the beginning. The motives which had led Maoism to take on the protective colour of Stalinist orthodoxy are obvious enough. In the late 1930s, Mao and his colleagues were aware of the weight of the influence on Chinese affairs that Stalin's government would exercise in consequence of the Second World War; and they feared that it might exercise it in a narrowly self-interested manner, and as opportunistically as in 1925–27. They knew their dependence on Moscow's

---

[14]From what has been said it is clear that the validity of the Maoist method of revolution is of necessity limited. Mao himself, in the early days of Partisan warfare, used to underline this — he spoke of the 'unique Chinese character' of the conditions in which his method could be applied. Only in primitive countries, where the body politic has not achieved national integration (or where it has disintegrated) and where there does not exist any bourgeoisie capable of exercising national leadership, can Partisans enjoying the peasantry's support carry revolution from the country to the towns; and then it depends on the revolutionaries' 'ideology' and international connections whether they can impart a socialist impulse to their revoltuion. An analysis of the social alignments in the Cuban and Algerian revolutions, and in other Afro-Asian upheavals, may show to what extent, and with what variations, the 'Chinese' conditions have or have not been reproduced in those countries. Victorious leaders of a Partisan movement are, of course, inclined to claim for their experience wider validity than it inherently possesses. Thus Che Guevara, in his essay on guerrilla warfare, recommends the Castroist strategy to revolutionaries all over Latin America. In those Latin American countries, however, where the bourgeois regime is more broadly based, integrated, and centralized than it was in Cuba under Batista, Che Guevara's recommendation, if acted upon, may lead to abortive coups.

We may mention here as a grotesque curiosity that the leaders of the French counter-revoltuion in Algeria, the OAS colonels, also tried to 'apply some lessons of Maoism'. Mao is undoubtedly a great authority on the military aspects of Partisan warfare. But the main secret of the success of his strategy lies in its close combination with agrarian revolution. It is impossible to apply his military prescriptions without his social strategy, as the leaders of the OAS have learned to their detriment.

goodwill; but they were determined *not* to allow Moscow to use them as it had used Chen Tu-hsiu, Li Li-san and Wang Ming. They were determined to prevent another abortion of the Chinese revolution. They played, therefore, a most intricate game, pursuing their independent strategy without arousing Stalin's suspicion and wrath. Stalin could not have been quite unaware of this. Yet the Comintern neither sanctioned nor condemned Mao's 'un-Marxist' and 'un-Leninist' strategy. Stalin would not have tolerated anything like the Maoist heresy in any Communist Party situated in a sphere of world politics which he considered more vital to his interests. But Maoism had started upon its career on what looked to Stalin like a remote periphery; and Mao behaved as some heretics had once behaved in the Catholic Church who, defying their local bishop or cardinal, strenuously avoided any collision with the Pope himself. Later, when Maoism moved closer to the centre of Chinese politics, it was already too strongly entrenched — yet was outwardly still sub-missive enough — for Stalin to conclude that to excommunicate Mao was both risky and unnecessary. He did not himself believe, not even as late as 1948, that Mao's Partisans would ever be able to conquer the whole of China and carry out a revolution; he was willing to use them as bargaining counter or instruments of pressure on Chiang Kai-shek, whom he again considered his chief ally in Asia.

In the Comintern the years after 1935 were again a period of 'moderation', the period of Popular Fronts. Translated into Chinese terms, the policy of the Popular Fronts meant the re-establishment of the 'bloc of four classes' and of the 'friendship' between the Kuomintang and the communists, this time in a united front against the Japanese invader. The old, never abandoned and now emphati-cally reasserted canon about the exclusively bourgeois-democratic character of the Chinese revolution served as the 'ideological' justifi-cation of this turn of policy. For Maoism, engaged as it was in civil war against the Kuomintang, the Comintern's new demands were a severe trial. Only the show of an unreserved acceptance of the Comintern's line could prove that Mao and his comrades remained loyal to Stalinism. And so Mao 'moderated' his Yenan regime and his propaganda and agitation; he appealed to the Kuomintang for patriotic solidarity and joint action against Japan; and he even used his influence to save Chiang Kai-shek's position and probably even his life during the Sian incident. Yet the Partisans never yielded to the Kuomintang even as much as an inch of their territory and power.

Mao's Stalinism was in some respects, however, more than sheer mimicry. The persistence with which Mao asserted and reasserted the

purely bourgeois character of the Chinese revolution accorded well
with the complete identification of his Partisans with the peasantry.
To the great mass of the peasantry the perspective of an 'uninterrupted revolution', that is of a revolution solving the land problem,
unifying China and also *opening up a socialist upheaval*, was either
meaningless or unacceptable. In the primitive pre-industrial society
of Shensi and Ninghsia — where Mao's writ ran during the Yenan
period — there was no room for the application of any measures of
socialism. It was only after its conquest of the cities in 1949 that
Maoism was to run up against the inevitability of the uninterrupted
(permanent) revolution and obey its dictates.

VI

From the theoretical, Marxist viewpoint the central question posed
by all these events is how a party, which had for so long based itself
only on the peasantry and acted without any industrial working class
behind it, was after all able to go beyond the 'bourgeois' agrarian
upheaval and initiate the socialist phase of the revolution.
Communist writers have so far avoided discussing this embarrassing
question frankly and have allowed anti-communist 'Marxologists' to
monopolize it. Has not the course of events in China, the latter
argue, refuted once and for all the Marxist and the Leninist con-
ceptions of revolution and socialism? Surely, the idea of proletarian
revolution in China belongs to the sphere of mythology — and,
surely, the Chinese experience shows up the Russian revolution too
to have been the work of a ('power-hungry', 'totalitarian') intelligentsia which used the workers and their allegedly socialist aspirations only as the ideological cover for its own ambitions. All that
both these revolutions have achieved, M. Raymond Aron, for
instance, is quick to point out, is merely to change the ruling elites,
which is nothing surprising to anyone who has learned his lessons
from Pareto and Max Weber. (Even a writer like the late C. Wright
Mills, convinced of the relevance of Marxism to the problems of our
age, concluded that not the working class but the revolutionary
intelligentsia is the real historic 'agency' of socialism.) Ex-Marxists,
who have found out that socialism has been 'the illusion of our age',
and that the reality behind it is state capitalism or bureaucratic
collectivism, invoke the old Marxist dictum that 'socialism will be the
work of the workers or it will not be at all'. How then, they ask, is it

possible to speak of a revolution in which the workers have played no part as being socialist in any degree whatsoever. In a different context and on a different level of argument, the question arises whether the famous Russian controversy between Narodniks and Marxists over the relative roles of workers and peasants in modern revolution has in fact been as irrevocably resolved as it seemed to have been until recently. Even if the Marxists were right in Russia, are the Narodniks not vindicated in China? Has not the peasantry there turned out to be the sole revolutionary class, the decisive agent of socialism?

There is no question that the record of Maoism compels a critical review of some habitual Marxist assumptions and reasonings. How this is necessary is illustrated *inter alia* by the assessment of Maoism which Trotsky gave in the 1930s. Grasping all the intensity of the agrarian upheaval in China, but apprehensive about the Maoist withdrawal from the cities, Trotsky bluntly ruled out the possibility of the consummation of the Chinese revolution without a previous revival of the revolutionary movement among the urban workers. He feared that Maoism, despite its communist origin, *might* become so completely assimilated with the peasantry as to become nothing but its mouthpiece — that is, the champion of the small rural proprietors. If this were to happen, Trotsky went on, Mao's Partisans, on entering the cities, might clash in hostility with the urban proletariat and become a factor of counter-revolution, especially at that critical turn when the revolution would tend to pass from the bourgeois into the socialist phase. Trotsky's analysis, reverberating unmistakably with decades of the Russian Marxist–Narodnik controversy and the experience of the Russian revolution, was reduced *ad absurdum* by some of his Chinese disciples who denounced the victory of Maoism in 1949 as a 'bourgeois and Stalinist counter-revolution'.[15]

The phenomenon of a modern, socialist (or be it even 'bureaucratic collectivist') revolution of which the working class had not been the chief driving force stood indeed without precedent in history. What drove the Chinese revolution beyond the bourgeois phase? The peasantry was interested in the redistribution of land, the abolition or reduction of rents and debts, the overthrow of the power of the landlords and money-lenders, in a word in the 'bourgeois'–agrarian upheaval. It could not give the revolution a socialist impulse; and

[15]See the controversy over this among the Chinese Trotskyists, reproduced in several issues of the *International Information Bulletin* of the Socialist Workers Party (New York), for the year 1952. Trotsky's articles on the Chinese Partisans had appeared in the *Byulleten Oppozitsii*.

Maoism, as long as it operated only within the peasantry, could not have been more reticent than it was about the prospects of socialism in China. This changed with the conquest of the cities and the consolidation of Maoist control over them. Yet the cities were almost dead politically, even if a galvanized remnant of the old labour movement stirred here and there.

We are confronted here, on a gigantic scale, with the phenomenon of 'substitutism', i.e. the action of a party or a group of leaders which represents, or stands in the stead of, an absent, or inactive, social class. The problem is familiar from the history of the Russian revolution, but it presents itself there in quite a different form. In Russia the working class could not have been more conspicuous as the driving force of the revolution than it was in 1917. Yet, after the civil war, amid utter economic ruin and industrial collapse, the working class shrank, disintegrated and dispersed. The Bolshevik Party set itself up as its *locum tenens,* and as trustee and guardian of the revolution. If the Bolshevik Party assumed this role only some years *after* the revolution, Maoism assumed it long *before* the revolution and during it. (And Mao and his followers did this without any of the scruples, compunction and *crises de conscience* that had troubled Lenin's party.)

Liberal or 'radical' Paretists, who see in this yet another proof that all that revolutions achieve is a change of ruling elites, have still to explain why the Maoist elite was determined to give the revolution a socialist (or collectivist) turn, instead of keeping it within bourgeois limits. Why has the Chinese communist elite behaved so differently from the Kuomintang elite? This was not even the case of a 'young' elite replacing the old and 'exhausted' one, for the two elites were contemporaries and had entered the political stage almost simultaneously. Why then have Mao and his comrades given China a new social structure, while Chiang Kai-shek and his friends floundered hopelessly in the wreckage of the old? And what accounts for the stern puritanical morale of Maoism and for the notorious corruption of the Kuomintang? The answer surely is that Chiang Kai-shek and his men identified themselves with the classes that had been privileged under the old order, while Mao and his followers embraced the cause of those that had been oppressed under it. Behind the change of the elites there was a profound transformation in the basic social relationships of China, the decline of one social class and the rise of another. No one doubts the extent to which the peasantry backed the Partisans during the twenty-two years of their armed struggle —without that support they would not have been able to hold out, to make the Long March, to shift their bases from one end of China to the other, to keep the Kuomintang's greatly superior military strength engaged all the time, to repulse so many 'annihilation drives', etc. So strong and intimate were the ties between the Partisans and the peasantry that at one time Mao appeared to many, to friend and foe alike, as the commander of a gigantic jacquerie rather than as the leader of a Communist Party — as a kind of Chinese Pugachev.

Yet this Chinese Pugachev, or super-Pugachev, had gone through the school of Leninism; and no matter how far he deviated from it in his methods of action, some general ideas of Leninism continued to govern his thought and action. He did not abandon his commitment to socialism (or collectivism) in favour of the peasants' individualism and attachment to private property, even while he was doing his best to satisfy that individualism and unfold its bourgeois-revolutionary potentialities. Nor should it be forgotten that revolutionary agrarian movements have always produced their Utopian communists, their Münzers and Anabaptists. Of the peasants' 'two souls' — the expression is Lenin's — one is craving property, while the other dreams of equality and has visions of a rural community, the members of which own and till their land in common. It might be said that Maoism expressed both 'souls' of the peasantry, were it not for the fact that it never was just the peasantry's mouthpiece. It always looked upon itself as the legatee of the defeated revolution of 1925–27, of which the industrial workers had been the driving force. Identifying itself ideally with those workers, Maoism continued to echo their socialist aspirations. Was this arrogance or usurpation? But what else could a party, committed to the communist programme, do after the dispersal of the urban working class and the political decline of the cities?

In carrying the revolution beyond the bourgeois phase Maoism was actuated not merely by ideological commitments but also by a vital national interest. It was determined to turn China into an integrated and modern nation. All the experience of the Kuomintang was there to prove that this could not be achieved on the basis of a belated, and largely imported, capitalism, superimposed upon patriarchal landlordism. National ownership of industry, transport and banking, and a planned economy were the essential preconditions for any even half-way rational deployment of China's resources and for any social advance. To secure these pre-conditions meant to initiate a socialist revolution. Maoism did precisely that. This is not to say that it has turned China into a socialist society. But it has used every ounce of the nation's energy to set up the socio-economic framework indispensable for socialism and to bring into being, develop, and educate the working class, which alone can make of socialism a reality eventually.

International factors, in the first instance the relationship between China and the USSR, co-determined the course and outcome of the revolution. That relationship has been much wider and more positive than the ambiguous connection between Maoism and Stalinism. Whatever the mutations of the political regime of the USSR, the Chinese revolution could not — and cannot — be dissociated from the Russian. Although the Partisan armies had received little or no Soviet support and had overthrown the rule of the Kuomintang in the teeth of Stalin's obstruction, Red China, born into a world split into two power blocs, and herself confronted by American hostility and intervention, could not but align herself with the USSR. In this alignment, Maoism found another potent motive for carrying the revolution beyond the bourgeois phase. The ultimate guarantee of the solidity of that alignment lay in the collectivist structure of the Chinese economy. As I have pointed out elsewhere, 'the revolutionary hegemony of the Soviet Union achieved [despite Stalin's initial obstruction] what otherwise only Chinese workers could have achieved — it impelled the Chinese revolution into an anti-bourgeois and socialist direction. With the Chinese proletariat almost dispersed or absent from the political stage, the gravitational pull of the Soviet Union turned Mao's peasant armies into agents of collectivism.'[16]

No Marxist textbook has or could have foreseen so original a concatenation of national and international factors in a revolution: Maoism does not fit into any preconceived theoretical scheme. Does this refute the Marxist analysis of society and conception of socialism? When Marx and Engels spoke of the working class as *the* agency of socialism, they obviously presupposed the presence of that class. Their idea had no relevance to a pre-industrial society in which such a class did not exist. It should be recalled that they themselves pointed this out more than once; and that they even made allowance for the possibility of a revolution like the Chinese. They did this in the exchanges of views they had with the Russian Narodniks in the 1870s and 1880s. The Narodniks, we know, saw Russia's basic revolutionary force in the peasantry — no industrial working class existed as yet in their country. They hoped that by preserving the

[16]*The Prophet Outcast*, p. 520.

obshchina, the rural commune, the Russia of the *muzhiks* could find her own way to socialism and avoid capitalist development. Marx and Engels did not dismiss these hopes as groundless. On the contrary, in a well-known letter addressed, in 1877, to *Otechestvennye Zapiski* Marx declared that Russia had 'the finest chance [to escape capitalism] ever offered by history to any nation'; and that even as a pre-industrial agrarian society she could start moving towards socialism. For this, as he saw it, one condition was necessary: namely, that Western Europe should make its socialist revolution before Russia had succumbed to capitalism. Russia would then be carried forward by the gravitational pull of Europe's advanced, socialist economy. Marx repeated this view some years later in correspondence with Vera Zasulich, pointing out that his scheme of social development and revolution, as he had expounded it in *Das Kapital* and elsewhere, applied to Western Europe; and that Russia might well evolve in a different manner. Engels expressed himself in the same sense even after Marx's death.[17]

All this has been well known and many times discussed. What have been less clear are the implications of this argument. How did Marx view the social alignments in that hypothetical Russian revolution which he anticipated? Evidently he did not see the industrial working class as its chief driving force. The revolution could find its broad base only in the peasantry. Its leaders had to be men like the Narodniks, members of the intelligentsia, who had learned something in the Marxist school of thought, had embraced the socialist ideal, and considered themselves to be the trustees of all the oppressed classes of Russian society. The Narodniks were, of course, the classical *zamestiteli,* the arch-substitutists, who acted as the *locum tenentes* for an absent working class and a passive peasantry (the *muzhiks* did not even support them) and who championed what they considered to be the progressive interest of society at large. Yet Marx and Engels encouraged them to act as they did and trusted that their action would be fruitful for socialism, if revolution in more advanced countries transformed the whole international outlook early enough.

True, Marx's prospect failed to materialize in Russia because, as Engels pointed out much later, the Western European working classes had been 'far too slow' in making their revolution and in the

[17] *Perepiska K. Marksa i F. Engelsa s russkimi politicheskimi deyatelyami,* pp. 177–9, 241–2 and *passim.* [See Teodor Shanin, ed. *Late Marx and the Russian Road,* London 1984, ed. note.]

meantime Russia had succumbed to capitalism. But on an incomparably larger scale, and against a changed international background, that prospect has materialized in China. It should be noted that the Maoists were far more broadly based on the peasantry than the Narodniks had ever been, that their socialist consciousness was far more mature — they engaged in mass action not in individual terrorism; and that, on assuming power, they could lean on the advanced collectivist structure of the USSR, which even as an economic Power was rising to the second place in the world. In proclaiming that socialism can be the work only of the workers, Marxism did not preclude the inception of socialist revolution in backward pre-industrial nations. But even in such nations the working class remains the chief 'agency' of socialism in the sense that fully fledged socialism cannot be attained without industrialization, without the growth of the working class and its self-assertion against any post-revolutionary bureaucracy, in a word, without the real, social and political ascendancy of the 'proletariat' in post-capitalist society.

VII

The present outlook of Maoism has crystallized in the post-revolutionary period, which has now lasted nearly fifteen years. Yet the seizure of power was not for the Chinese communists the sharp and decisive turn in their fortunes it had been for the Bolsheviks: even as Partisans they had controlled considerable areas of their country; their leaders and cadres had been half-rulers and half-outlaws before they became full rulers. On gaining national victory, the party had to 'urbanize' itself and to cope with a wide range of new tasks. But it was less dependent on the old bureaucracy for the business of government than the Bolsheviks had been, and therefore probably less exposed to infiltration by socially and ideologically alien elements.

It is unfortunately impossible to be categorical or precise about these questions, because the Maoists do not provide us with enough information. Such is their secretiveness that we know incomparably less of the 'inner story' of the fifteen years of their rule than we know from official Bolshevik sources about the early periods of the Bolshevik regime. However, a comparison between Maoism and Bolshevism, viewed at approximately the same remove from the moment of the revolution, a comparison between the China of 1963–64 and the Soviet Union of the early 1930s, based only on the generally established facts, brings out certain crucial similarities, differences and contrasts which may help to illumine the picture of Maoism in the post-revolutionary era.

It is a truism that the Chinese revolution has occurred in a socio-economic environment far more backward than that in which the Russian revolution took place. China's industrial output had never been more than a fraction of the Russian, an infinitesimal fraction in relation to the needs of a far larger population. The predominance of the archaic rural structure of society was almost absolute. The Chinese peasantry was even more primitive than the Russian (although, unlike the latter, it had not been subjected to centuries of serfdom, a fact which may show to some advantage in its character — in the greater independence, sobriety and industriousness of the Chinese peasants). Age-old economic, technological and social immobility, rigid survivals of tribalism, despotic ancestral cults, immutable millenary religious practices — all these have made the task of the Chinese revolution even more difficult and have affected Maoism itself, its methods of government and ideological outlook. Bent on industrializing China, Maoism has had to initiate primitive socialist accumulation on a level far lower than that on which accumulation had proceeded in Russia. The extraordinary scarcity of all material and cultural resources has necessitated an unequal distribution of goods, the formation of privileged groups, and the rise of a new bureaucracy. National history, custom and tradition (including the deep philosophical influences of Confucianism and Taoism) have been reflected in the patriarchal character of the Maoist government, the hieratic style of its work and propaganda among the masses, and the magic aura surrounding the leader. Like Stalinism (and partly under its influence), Maoism allows no open discussion or criticism of its high priest and hierarchy. And the fact that for two decades before its rise to power the party existed as a military organization has favoured the perpetuation of unquestioning discipline and blind obedience in its ranks.

Yet encumbered as it is by the greater backwardness of its environment, the Chinese revolution has in some respects been more advanced than the Russian, if only because it has come after it. It has never experienced the fearful isolation that has cramped and crippled the mind and the character of Bolshevism. It has come into the world as a member of the 'socialist camp', with the USSR as its powerful, though difficult, ally and protector; even the exposed flanks of Red China have to some extent been protected by the high tide of anti-imperialist revolt that has swept Asia. Despite American hostility,

Mao's China did not have to beat off anything like the 'Crusade of fourteen nations' that the Russia of Lenin and Trotsky had to repulse. In embarking upon primitive socialist accumulation China was not wholly reduced to her own meagre resources: Russian assistance, limited though it was, helped her in priming the pump of industrialization. More important than the material aid was the Russian experience from which the Maoists could learn: China did not have to pay the terrible price for pioneering in socialization and economic planning Russia had had to pay. Her industrialization, despite the partial failure of the Great Leap, has proceeded more smoothly than Russia's did in the early stages. And, despite a long sequence of natural calamities and bad harvests, Red China has not known any of the terrible famines that the Soviet Union suffered in 1922 and 1930–32, when millions of people starved to death.

Altogether, the social tensions have not been even remotely as acute and dangerous in China as they were in the Soviet Union. Nor has the post-revolutionary conflict between the rulers and the ruled been as severe and tragic. Maoism in power has enjoyed the peasants' confidence to a degree which Bolshevism has never attained. The Chinese have been far less reckless and brutal in collectivizing farming; and for a long time far more successful. Even the rural communes do not seem to have antagonized the peasants as disastrously as Stalin's collectivization did.

The fact that the Chinese peasantry has not been driven into a mortal enmity towards the regime has influenced the behaviour of all other social classes, of the workers who, recruited from the peasantry, are bound to reflect its moods; and of that section of the intelligentsia which has its roots in the country. Nor has the Chinese bourgeoisie been as hostile and aggressive towards the new regime as the Russian bourgeoisie, feeling the peasantry's backing, was in its time; and Mao's government has treated the bourgeoisie more prudently than Lenin's government did; wherever possible it has preferred to buy off the entrepeneurs and merchants rather than expropriate them.

Yet another vital difference in the starting points of the two revolutions has decisively contributed to making the social climate in China milder than in the Soviet Union. In Russia the civil war was waged *after* the revolution, whereas in China it had been fought *before* the revolution. The question whether communists enter the civil war as a ruling party or as a party of opposition is of the greatest consequence for their subsequent relationship with all classes of society. If, like the Bolsheviks, they have to fight as a ruling party, they bear in the eyes of the people the odium for the devastation, suffering and misery caused by civil war — as a rule, the people's despair and fury at its conditions of existence turn against those in office. In 1921–22 the Bolsheviks had wielded power for four or five years, during which they could do nothing to improve the lot of the workers and peasants, or rather to prevent its disastrous worsening. 'Is this what we have made the revolution for? Is this how the Bolsheviks keep their promises?' — these were the angry questions the Russian workers and peasants asked. A gulf was already fixed between the rulers and the ruled, a gulf which it was impossible to bridge, a gulf to which the Bolsheviks reacted with a self-defensive, panicky distrust of society and which they perpetuated and deepened thereby until there was no escape from it; a gulf which yawns ominously through the whole record of Stalinism.

In China, by contrast, the people blamed Chiang Kai-shek's government for all the devastation and misery of the civil war. The revolution came as the conclusion, not the opening of hostilities. The communists, having seized power, could at once give their undivided attention to their economic problems and use at once all available resources constructively, so that very soon the lot of the people began to improve and went on improving steadily. And so the first years of the new regime, far from producing disillusionment, were characterized by rising popular confidence. If the Bolsheviks set out to industrialize Russia after they had nearly exhausted their political credit with the masses, the Maoists were able to draw on an immense and growing credit. They had far less need to use coercion in the realization of their ambitious programme. They did not have to resort to the inhuman labour discipline Stalin had imposed on the workers; or to send punitive expeditions to the villages in order to extract grain, to deport huge masses of peasants, etc. Lenin once said that it had been easy to make the revolution in Russia, but far more difficult to build socialism; and that in other countries it would be far more difficult to overthrow the bourgeoisie, but much easier to cope with the constructive tasks of the revolution. Lenin made this prediction with an eye to Western Europe, but to some extent it has come true even in China. Although the material resources of the Chinese revolution were so much poorer than those of the Russian, its moral resources were larger; and in revolution as in war the Napoleonic rule holds good that the moral factors are to the material ones as three to one.

Maoism has therefore been far less hag-ridden with fear than Stalinism was. As in the nation at large so within the ruling party the tensions have been less explosive and destructive. Here, paradoxically, Maoism benefits from certain advantages of backwardness, whereas Bolshevism suffered from progressiveness. The establishment of the single party system in China was not the painful and dramatic crisis it had been in Russia, for the Chinese had never had the taste of any genuine multiparty system. No Social Democratic reformism had struck roots in Chinese soil. Maoism has never had to contend with opponents as influential as those that had defied Bolshevism: there were no Chinese Mensheviks or Social Revolutionaries. And, lacking Marxist tradition, and the habits of inner party freedom, the habits of open debate and criticism, Maoism was never in the throes of a deep conflict with its own past, such as troubled the Bolshevik mind when it was being forced into the monolithic mould. Maoism had so much less to suppress both within itself and in society that it did not have to give to suppression (and self-suppression) the prodigious mental and physical energy the Soviet Communist Party had to waste on that job.

Nor has the Chinese party become the ruthless promoter of inequality and the champion of the new privileged strata that the Soviet party became. While in China too, amid all the prevailing want and poverty, the recrudescence of inequality has been inevitable, this has *not* so far been accompanied by anything like Stalin's frantic and shameless drives against egalitarianism. This circumstance throws fresh light on the problem of inequality in post-revolutionary society. Although 'general want and poverty' are, according to Marx, the objective causes for the recrudescence of inequality, the intensity of the process depends on subjective human factors such as the character of the ruling group, the degree of its identification with the new privileged strata, and the viciousness (or the lack of it) with which it is prepared to foster inequality. The fact that Mao and his colleagues have spent the best part of their lives in the midst of the poorest peasants, hiding with their Partisans in the mountains, sleeping in the caves, fighting, marching and starving together, allowing no estrangement between officers and men, and no differences in food rations and uniforms — this extraordinary experience of the Maoists, an experience of over two decades which no other ruling group has gone through, may have left its imprint on their character and in some measure shielded them from the worst corruption of power. Characteristically, the Chinese party insists that its brain workers and dignitaries should periodically descend from their high offices to the factories and farms and, for about a month every year, perform manual labour, so as not to lose touch with the workers and peasants. Such practices, sometimes bizarre in form, cannot overcome the contradictions between the rulers and the ruled and between brain workers and manual labourers; but they may help to keep these contradictions within certain limits, and they indicate that the egalitarian conscience is not dead even in the ruling group. (On the other hand, Chinese officialdom, like the Russian, refuses to disclose just how wide are the discrepancies between high and low wages and salaries, which suggests that it is afraid of disclosing the real scope of the existing inequality.)

Against these features which distinguish so favourably Maoism from Stalinism must again and again be set the marks of its backwardness, which make for its affinity with Stalinism. The Chinese party is strictly monolithic, far more so than the Soviet party is now, in the post-Stalin era. Having had no proletarian background and no Marxist, socialist-democratic traditions of its own — having formed itself at a time when the whole Communist International was already Stalinized — Maoism was born into the monolithic mould and has lived, grown and moved within it, as the snail moves within its shell. Except for one pregnant moment (when the Hundred Flowers were to blossom all over China), Maoism has taken its monolithic outlook for granted. The Leader's infallibility is at least as firmly established as it had ever been in Russia, with this difference that for about twenty-five years no one has seriously challenged it. The Chinese party has not so far been involved in any convulsions as terrible as those that once shook the Russian party. It has had its important and obscure purges, one of which resulted in the 'liquidation' of Kao Kang in 1955; but the composition of the ruling group has not significantly changed since the days of the revolution or even of the Partisan struggle. Mao has not had to contend against a Trotsky, a Bukharin, or a Zinoviev. But neither do the assemblies and conferences of the Chinese party resound with the abject recantations of defeated Opposition leaders that had poisoned Soviet political life by 1932, and were to end in the Moscow trials.

VIII

The Maoist challenge to Moscow's 'leadership' of the Communist movement is partly a result of the consolidation of the Chinese revolution — the Maoists would not have risked such a conflict with Moscow earlier; and consolidation and growth of strength and confidence are expressed in a 'shift to the left' and in the Maoist ambition to speak for all militant elements of world communism.

Here again, a comparison with the Soviet Union of the early 1930s lights up a signal contrast. The prevalent mood in the Soviet Union at that time was one of moral–political weariness and of a reaction against the high revolutionary internationalism of the Lenin era. In the name of Socialism in One Country, the ruling group had initiated ideological 'retrenchment', and was seeking to disengage the Soviet Union from its commitment to world revolution — Stalin was already then practising the revisionism of which Mao is now accusing Khrushchev. The fact that at a comparable remove from the revolution, opportunism and national egoism ruled supreme in the Soviet party, while the Chinese party proclaims its radicalism and proletarian internationalism, is of immense historic and political consequence.

We have seen how the radical Leninist streak, now submerged and now coming into the open, has run through every phase of Maoism, and in decisive moments did not allow it to yield or surrender, under Stalinist pressure, to the Kuomintang and abandon the road of revolution. It is this, the Leninist element in Maoism that is at present asserting itself more strongly than ever and that seems to be transforming the outlook of Chinese communism. If Bolshevism after some years in power was morally declining, its enthusiasm withering and its ideas shinking, Maoism is on the ascendant, discovers new horizons, and enlarges its ideas. The debacle of official Bolshevism was epitomized in its vehement and venomous repudiations of permanent (continuous) revolution, which was not merely Trotskyist doctrine but the principle Lenin's party had deeply and passionately held in the heroic years of the Russian revolution. Maoism, on the contrary, had long and stubbornly dwelt on the limited bourgeois character of the Chinese revolution; yet now it is solemnly proclaiming that permanent revolution is the principle by which it lives, the *raison d'être* of international communism. At the close of his career, Mao appears once again as the Trotskyist Jourdain he was at its beginning. Like Trotsky, though without the latter's deep roots in classical Marxism yet with all the resources of power at his command, Mao is calling communism to return to its source, to the irreconcilable class struggle Marx and Lenin had preached.[18]

[18]Mao's view of class antagonisms in post-revolutionary society is also far closer to Trotsky's than to Stalin's. Recently Maoist theorists have written about what Trotsky called the Thermidorian spirit of the Soviet bureaucracy very much along the lines of his argumentation. And several decades after Trotsky, they hint at the 'danger of capitalist restoration' in the . . . USSR.

Part of the explanation for this shift to the left lies certainly in the West's attitude towards Red China, in the continuing American blockade, in the fact that so many Western Powers have not yet recognized the Peking government and have barred it from the United Nations. It should not be forgotten that the first great wave of opportunism came over the Soviet Union in the years 1923–25, after Clemenceau's and Churchill's *cordon sanitaire* had broken down, when most Western governments established diplomatic relations with Moscow. Beneficial in so many respects, this change in the international position of the Soviet Union had its adverse side: it encouraged the ruling group to practise *Realpolitik*, to take distance from the oppressed classes and peoples of the world, and to make far-reaching concessions of principle to the 'class enemy'. China's ruling group has not so far been exposed to such temptations. On the contrary, events constantly remind it that to capitalism's unabated hostility it has one reply only — its own unflagging defiance. Moreover, the ideological retreat of the Russian party was also a reaction to the many defeats the revolution had suffered in Germany and in the rest of Europe between 1918 and 1923; whereas Maoist militancy has drawn nourishment from the upsurge of anti-imperialism in Asia, Africa and Latin America. Here too, China is benefiting from the fact that she has not been the first country to embark upon the road of socialism. It is proving much more difficult for the capitalist world to tame or intimidate the second major revolution of the century than it was to contain, if not to 'roll back', the first.

Of course, grave dangers may be lurking behind the breach between the USSR and China. How will Maoism react to isolation from the Soviet Union, if the isolation deepens and hardens? How will it be affected by a relative stabilization of the 'national bourgeois' regimes in most of the formerly colonial or semi-colonial countries? And if some Western Powers were to try to play China against the Soviet Union, instead of playing the latter against the former — might Peking not succumb to the temptation? The prospect would be clearer than it is if one could be sure that Maoist professions of revolutionary internationalism are not merely a response to Western provocation but genuinely reflect the frame of mind of the Chinese masses. But we know far too little, next to nothing, about that aspect of the problem.

The credibility and effectiveness of the Chinese call for a restoration of Leninist principles would be far greater if Maoism did not seek to rescue the myths of Stalinism from the discredit into which they have deservedly fallen. In this Maoism is acting from motives of self-defence: it has to vindicate its own record, its past commitments, and its rigidly ritualistic party canon which, like every such canon, requires that is formalistic continuity be unalterably upheld. The infallible leader could not have been in error on any of those past occasions on which he extolled the Stalinist orthodoxy. The obeisance Mao paid to the living Stalin compels him to pay obeisance to the dead as well. Maoism's affinity with Stalinism lies precisely in this need to uphold established cults and magic rituals designed to impress primitive and illiterate minds. No doubt, one day China will grow out of these crude forms of ritualistic ideology, as the USSR is growing out of them; but that day has not yet come. Meanwhile, the conservative element in Maoism, its backwardness, is at loggerheads with its dynamic element, especially with its revolutionary inter-nationalism. In a similar way, elements of backwardness and advance, differently assorted, have been in constant collision with the Soviet Party after Stalin. The prospects would be infinitely more hopeful if it were possible for the diverse progressive urges in the two great Communist parties to release themselves from the grip of retrograde factors, and to coalesce — if the Chinese fervour for Leninist internationalism went hand-in-hand with a zeal for a genuine and consistent de-Stalinization of the Communist move-ment. The impossibility of disentangling progress from back-wardness is the price that not only Russia and China but mankind as a whole is paying for the confinement of the revolution to the under-developed countries. But this is the way history has turned; and now nothing can force its pace.

Written for *Socialist Register* and *Les Temps Modernes* in 1964.

2

The Meaning of the 'Cultural Revolution'

As one reads the endless official reports on the 'cultural upsurge of the masses' in China one may be tempted to dismiss the upsurge as mere farce. The Chinese News Agency has described in detail the 'fierce offensive against all old ideas, culture, customs and habits' that the 'Red Guards have taken to the streets of Peking since 20 August'. But one looks in vain for any positive indication of what the new ideas and the new cultural customs and habits are. In the name of Marxism and Leninism the Guards have denounced Balzac and Hugo, and Shakespeare and Beethoven, as the products of a rotting bourgeois culture; they have defaced Pushkin's monument in Shanghai, and have vented their contempt for the works of Cherny-shevsky and Herzen, the progenitors of the Russian revolutionary movement of the nineteenth century. Peking's 'cultural revolution-aries' are, it seems, quite unaware of Marx's lifelong admiration for Shakespeare and Balzac, of Lenin's love for Pushkin and Beethoven, and of the decisive formative influence Chernyshevsky had on him. We have been presented with long lists of streets and boulevards, the names of which have been changed from 'Eternal Peace' to 'The East is Red', from 'Well of the Prince's Palace' to 'Prevent Revisionism', from 'Glorious Square' to 'Support Vietnam', from 'Eastern Peace Market' to 'East Wind Market', and so on. We are asked to rejoice in the fact that certain culinary establishments are no longer called 'Collection of All Virtues', but 'Peking Roast Duck Restaurants'. Hosts of hairdressers and dressmakers have pledged themselves to produce no more outlandish haircuts, such as 'ducktail' and 'spiral-ling' hairdoes, or cowboy jeans and tight-fitting shirts and blouses and various kinds of Hongkong-style skirts. 'We should not regard these matters lightly,' the Chinese Agency says gravely, 'because it is here that the gates to capitalist restoration are wide open.' And so the floodwaters of the great proletarian cultural revolution are now pounding the various positions of the bourgeoisie; and the hotbeds of capitalism are no longer safe. Poor Karl Marx — he had no inkling when, exactly a hundred years ago, he was preparing *Das Kapital* for publication, where the real 'hotbeds of capitalism' were to be found.

Undertaking the all-too-easy task of ridiculing these exploits the Soviet press has recalled Proletkult, the Russian literary and artistic movement of the early years of the revolution, which renounced bourgeois art and promised to create a proletarian culture. A writer in *Pravda* has described Trotsky as Proletkult's inspirer, which should presumably be enough to make both Proletkult and the Chinese 'cultural revolution' stink in our nostrils. The truth is that, by comparison with the Chinese riot, the Russian Proletkult, which was akin to Western European Futurism fashionable in those years, was a harmless and almost civilized affair; it was supported by Bukharin and Lunacharsky, while Trotsky, far from being its inspirer, wrote a whole book, *Literature and Revolution*, to repudiate it. *Pravda* could have found a much closer parallel to the latest events in China nearer home: in the Stalinist Russia of the late 1940s and early 1950s, when Stalin, Zhdanov and *Pravda*'s writers 'disciplined' the intelligentsia, thundered against 'kowtowing to decadent Western culture', banned the works of Einstein, Freud, Mendel and many other foreign thinkers, and indulged in a hysterical glorification of all things Russian. *Pravda* avoids drawing this parallel because even now Russia has not yet fully lived down the legacy of that period, and quite a few of the old bans are still in force. But the parallel is close enough; and it suggests that the Maoist 'cultural revolution' is a deadly serious affair. Its effect on China's spiritual and intellectual life is, in all probability, going to be just as devastating and lasting as were the consequences of the Stalinist witch-hunts. Its political meaning is also comparable. Like Russia in the last years of the Stalin era, so China has now plunged headlong into a self-centred isolationism and nationalism and has shut herself off more hermetically than ever from the outside world and from all its political and cultural influences. To achieve this Mao had to organize a pogrom of the intelligentsia, whom he suspects of being vulnerable to foreign, especially 'revisionist', influences.

This is not to say that these developments foreshadow any new aggressive phase in China's foreign policy. True, in the last few weeks Peking and Shanghai have resounded with the cry for the liberation of Taiwan, Macao and Hongkong. But nothing indicates that Marshal Lin Piao is preparing marching orders for the liberation campaigns (even though all Chinese, communists and anti-communists, Maoists and anti-Maoists alike, consider these territories as belonging to their country by right). China is even less ready than Russia was in Stalin's last years for war-like adventures or territorial expansion. Her ideological aggressiveness and her shrill contempt for Western cultural values are manifestations, no doubt morbid ones, of her intensely self-defensive mood and of her sense of complete isolation in a hostile world. Since Khrushchev withdrew, with utter ruthlessness, all economic assistance from China in 1960, that sense of isolation has grown heavy and stifling; and recent setbacks — above all, the collapse of the pro-Maoist Communist Party of Indonesia and the slaughter of hundreds of thousands of its members — have aggravated it to the utmost. Despite Peking's thunderous rhetoric about the 'rising wave of revolution in Asia', the Indonesian events mark a deep ebb of revolution and a disaster for Maoism. The defection of the Japanese and North Korean Communist Parties from the Chinese camp has been a further setback; and the ambiguous behaviour of the North Vietnamese, who are more than ever dependent on Soviet aid, is causing much discomfiture to Peking. Above all, the Chinese believe that the threat of an American attack on their country is real and imminent.

One way of getting out of the isolation would be to try a reconciliation with Khrushchev's successors in Moscow. But since Mao Tse-tung has ruled this out, he has had to contrive some extra-powerful booster to national morale. Three nuclear explosions have demonstrated China's new technological capacity to the nation and the world. But this feat is not enough to dispel the malaise; for many Chinese realize at what cost, and under what back-breaking handicaps their nation has entered, so belatedly, the nuclear arms race. Nor does Maoism offer China the pride in rapid industrialization that Stalinism once offered Russia — China's tempo of economic advance is relatively much slower. The 'cultural revolution' and an almost mystical apotheosis of Maoism are to provide a moral compensation for all these disappointments and frustrations.

It can be said in advance that the 'positive' effect of this booster on national morale will be short-lived, but that its adverse consequences will be felt for a long time. The Party, its hierarchy and cadres, will not recover quickly from the humiliation the 'Red Guards' have inflicted on them. The old intelligentsia — the scientists and the technicians, but more especially the writers and artists — who have been associated with the broad current of the Maoist revolution and have directed the educational work among the masses since 1949, are being degraded and ousted from their posts. They have not been destroyed as their counterparts were in Stalinist Russia; but they are forced to make room for a new intelligentsia, who have been brought up since the revolution and have far fewer ties either with their own native cultural tradition or with the cultural heritage of the outside world. To some extent this change of generations is inevitable in any post-revolutionary society. But when it is carried out as abruptly, brutally and demagogically as it was in Stalinist Russia and as it is now being effected in China, the change entails an irreparable loss to the nation: a gap in its cultural consciousness, a lowering of standards, and an impoverishment of spiritual life. Post-Stalinist Russia is still smarting under the loss, and so will Maoist and post-Maoist China . . .

What next? It remains to be seen whether Mao will proceed to stage purges in the Stalinist style or whether he will find a less bloody way of dealing with inner-party opposition. Beyond these immediate issues there loom the great unresolved problems of China's domestic and foreign policy. Dwelling on the dangers threatening the country from American imperialism, Mao is calling the nation to live the kind of Spartan life that the Red Partisans led during the heroic Yenan period. The newspapers have been quoting this sentence from the diary of a Maoist hero: 'I must remember Mao's teachings to set myself *high* political standards and *low* living standards'; and the mass of citizens are called upon to follow this maxim. The phrase sums up a programme. Yet it must be doubted whether the sentiment it expresses, admirable though it may be in heroic individuals, can animate an entire people and form the basis of national policy. It is an unwitting confession of how little Maoism has now to offer China. The countryside, though it no longer suffers from the mass famines so familiar under the *ancien régime,* remains backward, primitive and terribly overpopulated; and in the cities industrialization is not progressing fast enough to absorb the surplus. This year a new Five Year Plan, the first since the economic disasters of 1958–62, has been put into effect; but its industrial targets have not been announced. Is it because production statistics are considered a military secret? Or because the targets are not inspiring enough for the propagandists to make much play of them? Either explanation may be correct.

In any case, the government is now placing far less emphasis on rapid economic development than it did in the 1950s and than Soviet governments have always done. Mao has not shown anything like Stalin's ruthlessness in harnessing the nation's manpower and resources and in forcing town and country alike to make the most terrible sacrifices for the sake of industrialization. Ever since the partial failure of the Great Leap, he has kept to the view that China's industrialization and modernization is a matter of many, many decades and that it may take the lifetime of two, three or four generations to accomplish it. He does not call China 'to catch up with and to surpass the capitalist West', and he does not seek to dazzle the people with promises of quick successes. Realistic though this view may be basically, it holds out no solution to China's pressing needs, no method for dealing with her over-population, her open or latent unemployment, with the social antagonisms between town and country, and with the demands that the international situation places on China's economy.

Behind the call for 'high political standards and low living standards' is the desire and the hope of settling within the framework of what the Russians once described as 'War Communism' — on the basis, that is, of a roughly egalitarian distribution of extremely scarce economic resources. In Russia this policy led to an impasse and had to be abandoned only three years after the October Revolution. China is practising it — true, with considerable modifications — seventeen years after her revolution. But for how long can Party and government adhere to a policy which does not offer the people sufficient material incentives for development and growth? Yet, if China's rulers do not wish to embark upon forcible industrialization, they cannot initiate a more ambitious policy as long as China remains isolated and is denied foreign, especially Soviet, aid. But this only means that all issues of policy, domestic as well as foreign, lead back to the same question, namely, whether China has any possibility of emerging from isolation in the foreseeable future. Has she any chance of resuming contact with the Soviet Union and regaining massive Soviet aid? We have seen that Mao has answered these questions in the negative, and that he urges China to 'go it alone' economically, politically and militarily. This, however, implies virtual reconciliation with China's economic and social backwardness.

It is difficult to believe that political stabilization can be achieved on such a basis. Pressures for a more ambitious policy of economic progress will make themselves felt. A few years ago such pressures caused Mao and his colleagues to undertake the Great Leap. But the resulting disappointments brought about a pause in industrialization. Yet the slow tempo creates its own insurmountable difficulties and is certain to revive the demand for a more forward policy. Mao may then call for another Great Leap or else his entire approach will have to come under review. The fact is that, as a dynamic revolutionary power, China cannot 'go it alone'; and that the Maoist policy, committed as it is to isolationism, will be unable to cope with the crises to come. Whether these will develop in Mao's lifetime or later must, of course, remain an open question.

In the inner-party struggle the problem of the succession to Mao has loomed large behind the more topical issues. For the time being Lin Piao has emerged as the winner, and Liu Shao-chi looks like the loser. But it is perhaps too early to take the outcome of the struggle for granted. For one thing, in post-revolutionary regimes the heir apparent appointed in the dictator's lifetime is not necessarily the man who exercises power after the dictator's death. Stalin's heir apparent — Malenkov — did not succeed in imposing himself upon his colleagues; he had to yield his place to Khrushchev who had been well below him in the Party hierarchy. But even if Lin Piao were to be Mao's real successor, it does not follow that he will necessarily continue the policy with which he is at present associated. When the call for a revision and change of Mao's policy, the call now so furiously silenced, rises again, Lin Piao may well have to yield to it. Mao's departure, even though he may still be able to swim the Yangtse, is not likely to be far off; and with it some reaction against the latest version of Maoism is all too likely to set in. The reaction need not be as severe as was the Russian revulsion against Stalinism, for Mao's place in the history of the Chinese revolution, whose presiding spirit he has been for so long, is much more solidly assured than Stalin's place was in Moscow's mausoleum. Mao has been in one person China's Lenin and Stalin. But at the end of his road he shows more and more similiarity to Stalin; and the latest orgy of his personality cult underlines the likeness. It is as if he had outlived himself and is already a relic of the past, an embodiment of China's backwardness and isolationism. When the reaction against these aspects of Maoism comes, his successor or successors, whoever they are, will have to act as its mouthpieces and agents. *A la longue* China cannot keep up her ideological aspirations and 'go it alone'.

21 September 1966

Part Five

Marxism and Our Time

The Roots of Bureaucracy

I

We are presently witnessing an obvious tendency toward the increasing bureaucratization of contemporary societies, regardless of their social and political structure. Theorists in the West assure us that the momentum of bureaucratization is such that we now live under a managerial system which has, somewhat imperceptibly, come to replace capitalism. On the other hand, we have the huge, stupendous growth of bureaucracy in the post-capitalist societies of the Soviet bloc and especially in the Soviet Union. We are justified in attempting to elaborate some theory of bureaucracy which would be more comprehensive and more satisfying than the fashionable and to a large degree meaningless cliché: 'managerial society'. It is not, however, easy to come to grips with the problem of bureaucracy; in essence it is as old as civilization, although the intensity with which it has appeared before men's eyes has varied greatly over the ages.

If I have undertaken to discuss the roots of bureaucracy, it is because I believe we have to dig down to find the deepest causes — the initial ones — of bureaucracy, in order to see how and why this evil of human civilization has grown to such terrifying proportions. In the problems of bureaucracy, to which the problem of the state is roughly parallel, is focused much of that relationship between man and society, between man and man, which it is now fashionable to describe as 'alienation'.

The term itself suggests the rule of the 'bureau', of the apparatus, of something impersonal and hostile, which has assumed life and reigns over human beings. In common parlance we also speak about the lifeless bureaucrats, about the men who form that mechanism. The human beings that administer the state look as if they were lifeless, as if they were mere cogs in the machine. In other words, we are confronted here in the most condensed, the most intensive, form with the reification of relationships between human beings, and with the appearance of life in mechanisms, in things. This, of course, immediately brings to mind the great complex of fetishism: over the whole area of our market economy man seems to be at the mercy of things, of commodities, even of currencies. Human and social relationships become objectified, whereas objects seem to assume the force and power of living elements. The parallel between man's alienation from the state and the representatives of the state — the bureaucracy — on the one hand, and between his alienation from the products of his own economy, on the other, is obviously very close, and the two kinds of alienation are similarly interrelated.

There is a great difficulty in getting beyond mere appearance to the very core of the relationship between state and society, between the apparatus that administers the life of a community and the community itself. The difficulty consists in this: the appearance is not *only* appearance, it is also part of a reality. The fetishism of the state and of the commodity is, so to say, 'built into' the very mechanism in which state and market function. Society is at one and the same time estranged from the state and inseparable from it. The state is the incubus that oppresses society; it is also society's protective angel without which it cannot live.

Here again some of the most hidden and complex aspects of the relationship between society and state are clearly and strikingly reflected in our everday language. When we say 'they', meaning the bureaucrats who rule us, 'they' who impose taxes, 'they' who wage wars, who do all sorts of things which involve the life of all of us, we express a feeling of impotence, of estrangement from the state: but we are also conscious that without the state there would be no social life, no social development, no history. The difficulty in sifting appearance from reality consists in this: the bureaucracy performs certain functions which are obviously necessary and indispensable for the life of society; yet it also performs functions which might theoretically be described as superfluous.

The contradictory aspects of bureaucracy have, of course, led to two contradictory and extremely opposed philosophical, historical and sociological views of the problem. Apart from many intermediate shadings, traditionally there have been two basic approaches to the question of bureaucracy and the state: the bureaucratic and the anarchist approach. The Webbs liked to divide people into those who evaluated political problems from the bureaucratic or from the anarchist point of view. This is, of course, a simplification, but nevertheless there is something to be said for it. The bureaucratic approach has had its great philosophers, its great prophets, and its celebrated sociologists. Probably the greatest philosophical apologist of the state was Hegel, just as the greatest sociological apologist of the state was Max Weber.

There is no doubt that old Prussia was the paradise of the bureaucracy, and it is therefore not a matter of accident that the greatest apologists for the state and for bureaucracy have come from Prussia. Hegel and Weber, each in a different way and on different levels of theoretical thinking, are in fact, the metaphysicians of the Prussian bureaucracy, who generalize from the Prussian bureaucratic experience and project that experience onto the stage of world history. It is therefore necessary to keep in mind the basic tenets of this school of thought. To Hegel, the state and bureaucracy were both the reflection and the reality of *the* moral idea, that is the reflection and the reality of supreme reason, the reality of the *Weltgeist*, the manifestation of God in history. Max Weber, who is in a way a descendant, a grandson of Hegel (perhaps a dwarf grandson), puts the same idea into his typically Prussian catalogue of the virtues of bureaucracy:

> Precision, speed, unambiguity, knowledge of the files, continuity, discretion, unity, strict subordination, reduction of friction and of material and personal costs — these are raised to the optimum point in the strictly bureaucratic administration, and especially in its monocratic form . . . bureaucracy also stands . . . under the principle of *sine ira ac studio*.[1]

Only in Prussia perhaps could these words have been written. Of course, this catalogue of virtues can very easily be invalidated by a parallel catalogue of vices. But to me it is all the more surprising and in a sense disquieting that Max Weber has·recently become the intellectual light of so much of Western sociology. (Professor Raymond Aron's gravest reproach in a polemic against myself was that I write and speak 'as if Max Weber never existed'.) I am quite prepared to admit that probably no one has studied the minutiae of bureaucracy as deeply as Max Weber; he catalogued the various peculiarities of its development, but failed to understand its full meaning. We all know the characteristic feature of that old German so-called historical school which could produce volumes and volumes on any particular industry, including the bureaucratic

---

[1] Hans H. Gerth and C. Wright Mills, eds. and trans., *From Max Weber: Essays in Sociology*, Oxford 1953, pp. 214–15.

industry, but could rarely see the mainstream of its development.

At the other extreme we have the anarchist view of bureaucracy and the state, with its most eminent representatives — Proudhon, Bakunin and Kropotkin — and with the various derivative liberal and anarcho-liberal trends. This school, when you look at it closely, represents the intellectual revolt of the old France of the bourgeoisie and of the old Russia of the *muzhiks* against their bureaucracies. This school of thought specializes, of course, in composing catalogues of bureaucratic vices. The state and the bureaucracy are seen as the permanent usurpers of history; they are seen as the very embodiment of all evil in human society, evil which cannot be eradicated other than by the abolition of the state and the destruction of all bureaucracy. When Kropotkin wanted to show the depths of the moral deterioration of the French Revolution, he described how Robespierre, Danton, the Jacobins and the Hébertists changed from revolutionaries to statesmen. In his eyes, what vitiated the revolution was bureaucracy and the state.

In fact each of these approaches contains an element of truth because in practice the state and bureaucracy have been the Jekyll and Hyde of human civilization. They have indeed represented the virtues and the vices of human society and its historical development in a manner more concentrated, more intense, than any other institution. State and bureaucracy focus in themselves this characteristic duality of our civilization: every progress achieved so far has been accompanied by retrogression; every advance that man made has been bought at the price of regress; every unfolding of human creative energy has been paid for with the crippling or stunting of some other creative energy. This duality has been, I think, very striking in the development of bureaucracy throughout all social and political regimes.

*   *   *

The roots of bureaucracy are indeed as old as our civilization, or even older, for they are buried on the border between the primitive communistic tribe and civilized society. It is there that we find the remotest and yet the very distinct ancestry of the massive, elaborate bureaucratic machines of our age. They show themselves at the moment when the primitive community divides into the leaders and the led, the organizers and the organized, into the managers and the managed. When the tribe or the clan begins to learn that division of labour increases man's power over nature and his capacity to satisfy his needs, then we see the first germs of bureaucracy which become also the very earliest signs of a class society.

The division of labour begins with the process of production, with which the first hierarchy of functions appears as well. It is here that we have the first glimpse of the gulf that was about to open in the course of civilization between mental work and manual labour. The organizer of the first primitive process in cattle breeding might have been the forebear of the mandarin, of the Egyptian priest, or the modern capitalist bureaucrat. The primary division between brain and brawn brought with it the other manifold sub-divisions, between agriculture and fishing, or trade and craft and sea-faring. The division of society into classes followed in the course of fundamental processes of historic development. In society, from the threshold of civilization to our own day, the basic division has been not so much that between the administrator and the worker as between the owner and the man without property, and this division absorbed into itself or overshadowed the former one. Administration has been, in most epochs, subordinated to the owners of property, to the possessing classes.

One could broadly categorize the various types of relationship between bureaucracy and basic social classes. The first one might call the Egyptian–Chinese type; then comes the Roman–Byzantine type with its derivative of an ecclesiastic hierarchy in the Roman Church; then we have the Western European capitalist type of bureaucracy; the fourth would be the post-capitalist type. In the first three types, and especially in the feudal and slave-owning societies, the administrator is completely subordinate to the man of property, so much so that in Athens, in Rome and in Egypt it is usually from among the slaves that the bureaucracy is recruited. In Athens the first police force was recruited from among the slaves because it was considered beneath the dignity of the free man to deprive another free man of freedom. What a sound instinct! Here you have the almost naively striking expression of the dependence of the bureaucrat on the property owner: it is the slave who is the bureaucrat because bureaucracy is the slave of the possessing class.

In the feudal order the bureaucracy is more or less eclipsed because the administrators either come directly from the feudal class or are absorbed into it. Social hierarchy is, so to say, 'built into' the feudal order, and there is no need for a special hierarchical machine to manage public affairs and to discipline the propertyless masses.

Later, much later, bureaucracy acquires a far more respectable status and its agents become 'free' wage-earners of the owners of property. Then it pretends to rise above the possessing classes, and indeed above all social classes. And in some respects and up to a point bureaucracy indeed acquires that supreme status.

The great separation between the state machine and other classes comes, of course, in capitalism, where the earlier clearly marked hierarchy and dependence of man on man, so characteristic of feudal society, no longer exists. 'All men are equal' — the bourgeois fiction of equality before the law makes it essential that there should function an apparatus of power, a state machine strictly hierarchically organized. Like the hierarchy of economic power on the market, so the bureaucracy, as a political hierarchy, should see to it that society does not take the appearance of equality at its face value. There grows a hierarchy of orders, interests, administrative levels, which perpetuates the fiction of equality and yet enforces inequality.

What characterizes the bureaucracy at this stage? The hierarchical structure in the first instance; then the seemingly self-sufficient character of the apparatus of power enclosed within itself. The tremendous scope, scale and complexity of our social life make the management of society more and more difficult, we are told; only skilled experts who possess the secrets of administration are able to perform the organizing functions. No, indeed, we have not moved a very long way from the time when the Egyptian priest guarded the secrets which gave him power and made society believe that only he, the divinely inspired, could manage human affairs. Self-important bureaucracy, with its mystifying lingo which is to a very large extent a matter of its social prestige, is, after all, not far removed from the Egyptian priesthood with its magic secrets. (Incidentally, is it not also very close to the Stalinist bureaucracy with its obsessive secrecy?)

Many decades before Max Weber, who was himself so impressed by the esoteric wisdom of bureaucracy, Engels saw things in a more realistic and objective light:

> The state is by no means a power imposed upon society from the outside . . . It is rather the product of society at a certain stage of development. It is an admission that this society has involved itself in an insoluble contradiction with itself, that it has become split in irreconcilable contradictions . . . In order that . . . classes with conflicting economic interests should not consume themselves and society in fruitless struggle, a power had become necessary which seemingly stands above society, a power that has to keep down the conflict and keep it within bounds of 'order'. That power emerging from society but rising above it and becoming more and more estranged from it is the State.

Even the welfare state, we may add, is, after all, only the power that emerges from society but rises above it and becomes more and more estranged from it. Engels goes on to say: 'In possession of public force and power and of the right to levy taxes, the officials now stand as the organs of society above society.' He describes the process of the emergence of the state from the primitive community:

> They [the officials] are not content with the free and willing respect that had been paid to the organs of a tribal community . . . Holders of a power estranged from society, they must be placed in a position of respect by means of special laws which assure them the enjoyment of a special halo and immunity.[2]

However, there is no use being angry with bureaucracy: its strength is only a reflection of society's weakness, which lies in its division between the vast majority of manual workers and a small minority which specializes in brain work. The intellectual pauperism from which no nation has yet emancipated itself lies at the roots of bureaucracy. Other fungi have grown over those roots, but the roots themselves have persisted in capitalism and welfare capitalism, and they still survive in post-capitalist society.

II

I would like to redefine my subject of discussion more rigorously. I am not interested in the general history of bureaucracy, nor do I wish to give a description of the varieties and modalities of bureaucratic rule that can be found in history. The focus of my subject is this: What are the factors that have historically been responsible for the political supremacy of bureaucracy over society? Why has no revolution so far succeeded in breaking down and destroying the might of the bureaucracy? On the morrow of every revolution, regardless of its character and the *ancien régime* which preceded it, a state machine rises like a phoenix from the ashes.

I have already pointed out — with some overemphasis — the perennial factor working in favour of bureaucracy, namely, the division of labour between intellectual work and manual labour, the gulf between the organizers and the organized. This contradistinction is in fact the prologue to class society; but in further social

---

[2] Engels, *The Origin of the Family*, London 1942, pp. 194–95.

development that prologue seems to become submerged by the more fundamental division between the slave-owner and the slave, between the serf-owner and the serf, between the man of property and the propertyless.

The real, massive ascendancy of bureaucracy as a distinct and separate social group came only with the development of capitalism, and it did so for a variety of reasons, economic and political. What favoured the spread of a modern bureaucracy was market economy, money economy and the continuous and deepening division of labour of which capitalism is itself a product. As long as the servant of the state was a tax farmer, or a feudal lord, or an auxiliary of a feudal lord, the bureaucrat was not yet a bureaucrat. The tax collector of the sixteenth, seventeenth or even eighteenth century was something of an entrepreneur; or else he was a servant of the feudal lord or part of his retinue. The formation of bureaucracy into a distinct group was made possible only by the spread and the universalization of a money economy, in which every state employee was paid his salary in money.

The growth of bureaucracy was further stimulated by the breaking down of feudal particularisms and the formation of a market on a national scale. Only on the basis of a national market could national bureaucracy make its appearance. By themselves these general economic causes of the growth of bureaucracy explain only how bureaucracy in its modern form became possible, but they do not yet explain why it is grown and why, in some definite historical circumstances, it has acquired its political importance. To these questions one should seek an answer not in economic changes but in sociopolitical structures. We have, for instance, the striking fact that England, the country of classical capitalism, was the least bureaucratic of all capitalist countries, while Germany, until the last quarter of the nineteenth century an underdeveloped capitalist country, was the most bureaucratic. France, which held a middle position, also held a middle position with regard to the strength of bureaucracy in political life.

If one were to seek certain general rules about the rise and decline of bureaucratic influence in capitalist society, one would find that the political power of bureaucracy under capitalism has always been in inverse proportion to the maturity, the vigour, the capacity for self-government of the strata constituting a given bourgeois society. On the other hand, when in highly-developed bourgeois societies class struggles have reached something like a deadlock, when contending classes have lain as if prostrate after a series of exhausting social and political struggles, then political leadership has almost automatically passed into the hands of a bureaucracy. In such situations the bureaucracy establishes itself not only as the apparatus regulating the functioning of the state, but also as the power imposing its political will on society. The real cradle of modern bureaucracy was, of course, the pre-bourgeois absolute monarchy — the Tudors in England, the Bourbons in France, or the Hohenzollerns in Prussia — the monarchy which was maintaining the uncertain equilibrium between a decaying feudalism and a rising capitalism. Feudalism was already too weak to continue its supremacy, capitalism was still too weak to establish its domination; a stasis in the class struggle, as it were, between feudalism and capitalism left room for the absolute monarchy to act as the umpire between the two opposed camps.

The stronger the opposition of feudal and bourgeois interests and the more paralysing the stalemate between them, the more scope was there for the bureaucracy of the absolutist monarchy to play the role of arbiter. Incidentally, England (and also the United States) was the least bureaucratic of all capitalist countries precisely because very early in history that feudal-capitalist antagonism was resolved through the gradual merger of the feudal and capitalist interests. The feudal-bourgeois notables, the great aristocratic English families, assumed some of the functions which on the continent were exercised by the bureaucracy. In a sense, the *embourgeoisé* feudal elements administered the state without becoming a distinct and separate social group. The United States too was in its history free from that strife between feudal and capitalist interests, the strife which acted as a stimulus for the growth of bureaucracy.

Quite a different and peculiar case was Russia, where the great power of state and bureaucracy resulted from the underdevelopment of both social strata: neither the feudal element nor the bourgeoisie was ever strong enough to manage the affairs of the state. It was the state that, like the demiurge, created social classes, now inducing their formation and expansion, now impeding and thwarting it. In this way its bureaucracy became not only an umpire but also the manipulator of all social classes.

If I were to give a sub-title to my further remarks, it would probably be a very general one: on bureaucracy and revolution. At this point I would like to clear up some confusion, and I fear that in the process I shall clash with several established historical schools. As this is unavoidable in any case, I shall pose the problem in its most provocative form: Was the English Puritan Revolution a bourgeois revolution? Was the Great French Revolution bourgeois in character? At the head of the insurgent battalions there were no bankers, merchants or shipowners. The *sans-culottes*, the plebs, the urban paupers, the lower-lower middle classes were in the forefront of the battle. What did they achieve? Under the leadership of 'gentlemen farmers' (in England) and lawyers, doctors and journalists (in France) they abolished the absolutist monarchy and its courtier bureaucracy and swept away feudal institutions which were hindering the development of bourgeois property relations. The bourgeoisie had become strong enough and sufficiently aware of its power to aspire to political self-determination. It no longer wanted to accept the tutelage and the dictates of the absolutist monarchy; it wanted to rule society by itself. In the process of the revolution the bourgeoisie was driven forward by the plebeian masses — on the morrow the bourgeoisie attempted by itself to rule society at large.

The process of the revolution with all its crises and antagonisms, with the constant shifting of power from the more conservative to the more radical and even to the utopian wings of the revolutionary camp — all these led to a new political stalemate between the classes which came freshly to the fore: the plebeian masses, the sans-culottes, the urban poor were tired and weary; but the victorious, now dominant class — the bourgeoisie — was also internally divided, fragmented, exhausted from the revolutionary struggle and incapable of governing society. Hence in the aftermath of bourgeois revolution we see the rise of a new bureaucracy somewhat different in character: we see a military dictatorship, which outwardly looks almost like the continuation of the pre-revolutionary absolutist monarchy or an even worse version of it. The pre-revolutionary regime had its centralized state machine — a national bureaucracy. The revolution's first demand was the decentralization of this machine. Yet this centralization had not been due to the evil intentions of the ruler but reflected the evolution of the economy, which required a national market, and this 'national soil', as it were, fed the bourgeois forces which in their turn produced the revolution. The aftermath of the revolution brings renewed centralization. This was so under Cromwell; this occurred under Napoleon. The process of centralization and national unification and the rise of a new bureaucracy was so striking that Tocqueville, for example, saw in it nothing more than the continuation of pre-revolutionary tradition. He argued that what the French Revolution had done was merely to carry further the work of the *ancien régime*, and had the revolution not taken place this trend would have gone on all the same.[3] This was the argument of a man who had his eyes fixed on the political aspect of the development only and completely ignored its social background and deeper social motives; he saw the shape but not the texture or the colour of society.

Political centralization after the revolution went on as before, yet the character of the bureaucracy had completely and thoroughly changed. Instead of the courtier bureaucracy of the *ancien régime*, France now had the bourgeois bureaucracy recruited from different layers of society. The bourgeois bureaucracy established under Napoleon survived the Restoration and in the end found its proper head in the Citizen King.

The next phase, in which we see another rise of bureaucracy and a further promotion of centralist tendencies of the state, occurs again at a moment of political paralysis of all social classes. In 1848 we find a situation in which different class interests are again opposed to each other; this time it is the interest of the established bourgeoisie and that of the nascent proletariat. To this day nobody has described this process of mutual exhaustion better than Karl Marx, especially in the *18th Brumaire*. He also demonstrated how the prostration of all social classes secured the triumph of the bureaucracy, or rather of its military arm, under Napoleon III. At the time this situation was characteristic not only of France but also of Germany, especially Prussia, where the deadlock was many-sided: between the feudal and semi-feudal interests of the Junkers, the bourgeoisie, and the new working class. And in Prussia it resulted in the rule and dictatorship of Bismarck's bureaucracy. (Incidentally, Marx and Engels described Bismarck's government as a 'Bonapartist' regime, although outwardly there was, of course, very little or nothing of the Bonaparte in Bismarck.)

III

I am well aware that because of the vastness of the subject I can do no more than indicate schematically the main points which need further elaboration. I am not going to deal with reformist socialism and bureaucracy. This, important though it is politically, especially in England, presents from my viewpoint very little theoretical interest.

[3] Alexis de Tocqueville, *The Old Regime and the French Revolution*, New York 1955, pp. 32–41.

To my mind it is part of 'capitalism and bureaucracy'. The bulk of the economy remains capitalist whether or not fifteen percent or twenty-five percent of industry is nationalized, and here quantity also determines quality. The whole background of social life is capitalist, and ordinary capitalist bureaucratic spirit permeates all industries including the nationalized ones. We hear a lot of grumbling about 'bureaucracy on the railways' or in the coal mines. During a recent strike television presented some railwaymen who said 'things are not as they used to be': before the nationalization of the railways they could maintain a more personal relationship between themselves and their employers, while now the industry has become so anonymous that there is no personal link between the workingmen and this vast nationwide enterprise. This 'personal link' was, of course, a figment of the workers' imagination. What sort of personal relationship was there between the footplate man and the boss of one or another of the five huge railway companies? But politically it was important that this railwayman really believed that in the Southern or Midland or Western Railway he was more than a mere cog. Now he feels 'alienated' from that vast entity into which he has to fit, for which he has to go to work. And this 'alienation', as the word goes, is a problem common to all sorts of bureaucratic establishments, no matter what their broader social framework, and I would be the last to deny that there are certain common features between bureaucracy in a capitalist and in a post-capitalist system.

Now I would like to touch upon those special problems of bureaucracy which arise in a fully nationalized industry after a socialist revolution, under a regime which, at least in its beginnings, is in every sense a proletarian dictatorship. Clearly this problem affects one-third of the world, so it is weighty enough; and I am pretty sure that it will acquire validity over at least two-thirds of the world.

As I looked through some of the classical Marxist writings on bureaucracy, I was struck by how relatively optimistically — one might say lightmindedly — Marxists approached the problem. To give one illustration: Karl Kautsky once asked himself whether a socialist society would be threatened with all the evils of bureaucracy. In *The Foundations of Christianity* Kautsky discusses the process by which the Christian Church was transformed from a faith of the oppressed into a great imperial bureaucratic machine. This transformation was possible against the background of a society which lived on slave labour. The slaves of antiquity, devoid of any active class consciousness, were liable to become slaves of bureaucracy. But the modern working class, mature enough to overthrow capitalism, maintained Kautsky, will not allow a bureaucracy to rise on its back. This was not just an individual judgment of Kautsky, who for over two decades between Engels's death and the outbreak of the First World War was the most authoritative spokesman of Marxism and was considered a real successor to Marx and Engels. Engels himself in various of his works, and especially in *Anti-Dühring*, committed himself to a view which almost ruled out in advance the possibility of bureaucracy under socialism: 'The proletariat seizes the state power and turns the means of production in the first instance into state property. But in doing this it puts an end to itself as proletariat, puts an end to all . . . class antagonism.'[4]

Former societies needed the state as an organization of the exploiting class, as a means of holding down the class that was exploited —slaves, serfs, or wage labourers. In socialism the state, when it becomes truly representative of society as a whole, makes itself superfluous. And with the full development of modern productive forces, with the abundance and superabundance of goods, there will be no need to keep men and labour in subjection.

I think it was Trotsky who used a very plain but very telling metaphor: the policeman can use his baton either for regulating traffic or for dispersing a demonstration of strikers or unemployed. In this one sentence is summed up the classical distinction between administration of things and administration of men. If you assume a society in which there is no class supremacy, the bureaucracy's role is reduced to the administration of things, of the objective social and productive process. We are not concerned with the elimination of *all* administrative functions — this would be absurd in an industrially developing society — but we are concerned with reducing the policeman's baton to its proper role, that of disentangling traffic jams.

When Marx and Engels analysed the experience of the Commune of Paris they were as if half-aware of the bureaucratic threat that could arise in the future, and they were at great pains to underline the measures that the Commune had taken in order to guarantee a socialist revolution against the recrudescence of bureaucratic power. The Commune, they stressed, had taken a number of precautions which should serve as a pattern and a model for future socialist transformations: it was elected in a general election and established an elected civil service, every member of which could be deposed at any time at the demand of the electorate. The Commune abolished

[4]F. Engels, *Anti-Dühring*, London 1943, p. 308.

the standing army and replaced it with the people at arms; it also established the principle that no civil servant could earn more than the ordinary worker. This should have abolished all privileges of a bureaucratic group. The Commune, in other words, set the example of a state which was to begin to wither away as soon as it was established. It was no matter of chance that only a few weeks before the October Revolution Lenin made a special effort to restore this, by then almost forgotten, part of Marxist teaching about state, socialism and bureaucracy. He expressed his idea of the state in that famous aphorism: under socialism or even in a proletarian dictatorship the administration should become so simplified that every cook should be able to manage state affairs.

In the light of all the painful experience of the last decades it is all too easy to see how very greatly the representatives of classical Marxism had indeed underrated the problems of bureaucracy. There were, I think, two reasons for this. The original founders of the Marxist school never really attempted to portray in advance the society which would emerge after a socialist revolution. They analysed revolution, so to say, in the abstract; in the same way as Marx in *Das Kapital* analysed not any specific capitalist system but capitalism in the abstract, capitalism *per se*; they also thought of socialist or post-capitalist society in the abstract. If one considers that they carried out their analysis so many decades before the actual attempt, their method was scientifically justified. The other reason is, so to say, psychological. They could not help viewing the future revolution on the pattern of the greatest revolutionary experience in their own life, that of 1848. They saw it as a chain reaction of revolutions, as 1848 was, spreading at least over Europe more or less simultaneously. (Here was the germ of the idea of permanent revolution, which in this respect was not the original creation of Trotsky; it was indeed very deeply embedded in the thought of classical Marxism.) An all-European socialist revolution would have been relatively secure immediately after its victory. With very little social tension there would be hardly any civil strife, and without wars of intervention there would have been no need for the re-creation of standing armies, which are an important factor of bureaucratization. They also assumed that, at least in the highly industrialized societies of Western Europe, the very considerable proportion of the working class would provide a strong mass support for the revolutionary government. They also trusted that once the majority of the European working class had been won for the revolution it would, as it were, remain faithful and loyal to the revolution. This, together with the existing democratic tradition, would form the strongest guarantee against any revival of the bureaucratic machine or the formation of a new one.

When we are tempted to reproach the founders of the Marxist school with underrating the dangers of bureaucracy in post-revolutionary society, we must bear in mind the fact that they took the abundance of goods as the first condition, a precondition and *raison d'être* of a socialist revolution. 'The possibility of securing for every member of society, through social production, an existence not only fully sufficient materially . . . but guaranteeing to all the free development and exercise of their physical and mental faculties — this possibility is now . . . here . . . *it is here,*' stated Engels emphatically in his *Anti-Dühring* nearly ninety years ago.[5] It is only in the middle of this century that we are faced with attempts at socialist revolution in countries where a desperately insufficient production makes any decent material existence quite impossible.

There was undoubtedly in Marxism an ambivalent attitude toward the state. On the one hand — and this Marxism had in common with anarchism — there was a conviction based on a deeply realistic historical analysis that all revolutions are frustrated as long as they do not do away with the state; on the other, there was the conviction that the socialist revolution has need of a state for its own purpose, to smash, to break the old capitalist system and create its own state machine that would exercise the proletarian dictatorship. But that machine, for the first time in history, would represent the interests not of a privileged minority but of the mass of toilers, the real producers of society's wealth. 'The first act by virtue of which the state really constitutes itself the representative of the whole of society' — the taking possession of the means of production — 'is at the same time its last independent act as a state.'[6] From then on the interference of the state in social relations becomes superfluous. The government of persons is replaced by the administration of things. The political function of the state disappears; what remains is the direction of the process of production. The state will not be abolished overnight, as the anarchists imagine; it will slowly 'wither away'.

The reality of the Russian Revolution was in every single respect a negation of the assumptions made by classical Marxism. It was certainly not revolution in the abstract — it was real enough! It did not follow the 1848 pattern, it was not an all-European upheaval; it

[5]Ibid., p. 311.
[6]Ibid., p. 309.

remained isolated in one country. It occurred in a nation where the
proletariat was a tiny minority, and even that minority disintegrated
as a class in the process of world war, revolution and civil war. It was
also an extremely backward, poverty-stricken country where the
problem immediately facing the revolutionary government was not
to build socialism, but to create the first preconditions for any
modern civilized life. All this resulted in at least two political developments which inevitably led to the recrudescence of bureaucracy.

I have described how the political supremacy of bureaucracy
always followed a stalemate in the class struggle, an exhaustion of all
social classes in the process of political and social struggles. Now,
mutatis mutandis, after the Russian Revolution we see the same
situation again: in the early 1920s all classes of Russian society —
workers, peasants, bourgeoisie, landlords, aristocracy — are either
destroyed or completely exhausted politically, morally, intellectually. After all the trials of a decade filled with world war,
revolution, civil wars and industrial devastation no social class is
capable of asserting itself. What is left is only the machine of the
Bolshevik Party, which establishes its bureaucratic supremacy over
society as a whole. However, *cela change et ce n'est plus la même
chose:* society as a whole has undergone a fundamental change. The
old cleavage between the men of property and the propertyless
masses gives place to another division, different in character but no
less noxious and corrosive: the division between the rulers and the
ruled. Moreover, after the revolution it acquires a far greater force
than it had before when it was as if submerged by class distinction and
class discord. What again comes to the fore is the perennial, the oldest
split between the organizers and the organized. The prelude to class
society appears now as the epilogue. Far from 'withering away' the
post-revolutionary state gathers into its hands such power as it has
never had before. For the first time in history bureaucracy seems
omnipotent and omnipresent. If under the capitalist system we saw
that the power of bureaucracy always found a counterweight in the
power of the propertied classes, here we see no such restrictions and
no such limitations. The bureaucracy is the manager of the totality of
the nation's resources; more than ever before it appears independent,
separated, indeed set high above society. Far from withering away,
the state reaches its apotheosis, which takes the form of an almost
permanent orgy of bureaucratic violence over all classes of society.

Let us now go back for a moment to the Marxist analysis of the
revolution in the abstract and see where and in what way the picture

of post-revolutionary Russia contradicts this analysis. Had there been a European revolution in which proletarian majorities would have won swiftly and decisively and spared their nations all the political and social turmoil and slaughter of wars and civil strife, then very probably we would not have seen that fear-inspiring apotheosis of the Russian state. Nevertheless, the problem would still have existed to a degree which classical Marxism did not envisage. To put it in a nutshell: it seems that the thinkers and theoreticians of the nineteenth century tended to telescope certain stages of future development from capitalism to socialism. What classical Marxism 'telescoped' was the revolution-and-socialism as it were, whereas between the revolution and socialism there was bound to lie a terribly long and complicated period of transition. Even under the best of circumstances that period would have been characterized by an inevitable tension between the bureaucrat and the worker. Some prognosis of that tension can be found in Marxism, however. In his famous *Critique of the Gotha Programme* Marx speaks about two phases of communism, the lower and the higher.[7] In the lower one there still prevails the 'narrow horizon of bourgeois right', with its inequality and its wide differentials in individual incomes. Obviously, if in socialism, according to Marx, society still needs to secure the full development of its productive forces until a real economy of wealth and abundance is created, then it has to reward skill and offer incentives. The bureaucrat is in a sense the skilled worker, and there is no doubt that he will place himself on the privileged side of the scale.

The division between the organizers and the organized acquires more and not less importance precisely because the means of production having passed from private to public ownership, the responsibility for running the national economy rests now with the organizers. The new society has not developed on its own foundations, but is emerging from capitalism and still bears all the birthmarks of capitalism. It is not yet ripe, economically, morally and intellectually, to reward everyone according to his needs; and as long as everyone has to be paid according to his work, the bureaucracy will remain the privileged group. No matter what the pseudo-Marxist terminology of present Russian leaders, Russian society today is still far from socialist — it has only made the very first step on the road of transition from capitalism toward socialism.

The tension between the bureaucrat and the workers is rooted in

[7] Karl Marx, *Critique of the Gotha Programme*, London 1933, p. 106.

the cleavage between brain work and manual labour. It simply is not true that today's Russian state can be run by any cook (although all sorts of cooks try to do it). In practice it proved impossible to establish and maintain the principle proclaimed by the Commune of Paris which served Marx as the guarantee against the rise of bureaucracy, the principle extolled again by Lenin on the eve of October, according to which the functionary should not earn more than the ordinary worker's wage. This principle implied a truly egalitarian society — and here is part of an important contradiction in the thought of Marx and his disciples. Evidently the argument that no civil servant, no matter how high his function, must earn more than an ordinary worker cannot be reconciled with the other argument that in the lower phase of socialism, which still bears the stamp of 'bourgeois right', it would be utopian to expect 'equality of distribution'. In the post-revolutionary Russian state, with its poverty and its inadequate development of the productive forces, the scramble for rewards was bound to be fierce and ferocious; and because the abolition of capitalism was inspired by a longing for egalitarianism, the inequality was even more revolting and shocking. It was also inequality on an abysmally low level of existence, or rather inequality below subsistence level.

Part of the Marxist theory of the withering away of the state was based upon a certain balance between its centralist organization and the universal element of decentralization. The socialist state was to have been a state of elected communes, local municipal councils, local governments and self-governments, yet they were all to form a unified organism which was necessary for a rational nationalized mode of production. This concept also presupposed a highly developed society, which Russia at the beginning of the century was not.

In the development of post-capitalist society the tension between the worker and the bureaucrat may yet prove to have some essentially creative elements. The worker and the bureaucrat are equally necessary for the transition toward socialism. As long as the working masses are still in that stage of intellectual pauperism left over from the centuries of oppression and illiteracy, the management of the processes of production must fall to the civil servant. On the other hand, in a truly post-capitalist society the workers constitute the basic social class, and socialism is the workers' and not the bureaucrats' business. The dynamic balance between the official and the worker will find its counterpart in the authority of the state and the control of the masses over the state. This will also assure the necessary equilibrium between the principle of centralization and that of decentralization. What we have seen in Russia has been an utter disequilibrium. As a result of objective historic circumstances and subjective interests, the balance swung heavily, decisively, absolutely to the side of bureaucracy. What we saw in Hungary and Poland in 1956 was a reaction against this — Stalinist — state of affairs with an extreme swing of the pendulum in the other direction and the workers' passionate, violent, unreasoning revolt against bureaucratic despotism — a revolt no doubt justified by all their experiences and grievances, but one which in its consequences led again to a grave and dangerous imbalance.

How then do I see the prospects and how do I see the further development of that tension between the worker and the bureaucrat?

I have indicated before all the faults of the historical perspective in the classical Marxist view of bureaucracy. Yet, I think that fundamentally this view helps to cope with the problem of bureaucracy far better than any other I have encountered.

The question we have to answer is this: has the bureaucracy, whose apotheosis after the revolution I have described, constituted itself into a new class? Can it perpetuate itself as a privileged minority? Does it perpetuate social inequality? I would like first of all to point out one very obvious and important but often forgotten fact: all the inequality that exists in today's Russia between the worker and the bureaucrat is an inequality of consumption. This is undoubtedly very important, irritating and painful; yet with all the privileges which the bureaucrat defends brutally and stubbornly, he lacks the essential privilege of owning the means of production. Officialdom still dominates society and lords over it, yet it lacks the cohesion and unity which would make of it a separate class in the Marxist sense of the word. The bureaucrats enjoy power and some measure of prosperity, yet they cannot bequeath their prosperity and wealth to their children. They cannot accumulate capital, or invest it for the benefit of their descendants: they cannot perpetuate themselves or their kith and kin.

It is true that Soviet bureaucracy dominates society — economically, politically and culturally — more obviously and to a greater extent than does any modern possessing class. Yet it is also more vulnerable. Not only can it not perpetuate itself, but it has been unable even to secure for itself the continuity of its own position, the continuity of management. Under Stalin one leading group of bureaucrats after another was beheaded, one leading group of managers of industry after another was purged. Then came

Khrushchev, who dispersed the most powerful centre of that bureaucracy: all the economic ministries in the capital were scattered over wide and far-flung Russia. Until this day the Soviet bureaucracy has not managed to acquire that social, economic and psychological identity of its own which would allow us to describe it as a new class. It has been something like a huge amoeba covering post-revolutionary society with itself. It is an amoeba because it lacks a social backbone of its own; it is not a formed entity, not a historic force that comes on the scene in the way in which, for example, the old bourgeoisie came forth after the French Revolution.

Soviet bureaucracy is also hamstrung by a deep inherent contradiction: it rules as a result of the abolition of property in industry and finance, as a result of the workers' victory over the *ancien régime*; and it has to pay homage to that victory; it has to acknowledge ever anew that it manages industry and finance on behalf of the nation, on behalf of the workers. Privileged as they are, Soviet managers have to be on their guard: as more and more workers receive more and more education, the moment may easily come when the managers' skill, honesty and competence will come under close scrutiny. They thrive on the apathy of the workers who so far have allowed them to run the state on their behalf. But this is a precarious position, an incomparably less stable foundation than that sanctified by tradition, property and law. The conflict between the liberating origin of bureaucracy's power and the use it makes of that power generates constant tension between 'us', the workers, and 'them', the managerial and political hierarchy.

There is another reason for the lack of stability and cohesion in the managerial group, no matter how privileged it has become. Over the last decades Soviet bureaucracy has all the time been in a process of stupendous expansion. Millions of people from the working class, and to a lesser extent the peasantry, have been recruited into its ranks. This continuous expansion militates against the crystallization of the bureaucracy not only into a class but even into a cohesive social group. I know, of course, that once a man from the lower classes is made to share in the privileges of the hierarchy, he himself becomes a bureaucrat. This may be so in individual cases and in abstract theory, but on the whole the 'betrayal of one's class' does not work so very simply. When the son of a miner or a worker becomes an engineer or an administrator of a factory, he does not on the morrow become completely insensitive to what goes on in his former environment, in the working class. All surveys show convincingly that in no other country is there such a rapid movement from manual to non-manual, and to what the Americans like to call 'elite strata', as there is in the Soviet Union.

We must also realize that the privileges of the great majority of bureaucrats are very, very paltry. The Russian administrator has the standard of living of our lower middle classes. Even the luxuries of the small minority high on top of the pyramid are not especially enviable, particularly if one considers the risks — and we all know how terrible these were under Stalin.

Of course, even small privileges contribute to the tension between the worker and the bureaucrat, but we should not mistake that tension for a class antagonism, in spite of some similarities which on closer examination would prove to be only very superficial. What we observe here is rather the hostility between members of the same class, between, say, a skilled miner and an unskilled one, between an engine driver and a less expert railwayman. This hostility and this tension contain in themselves a tremendous political antagonism, but one that cannot be resolved by any upheaval in society. It can be resolved only by the growth which would make it possible to satisfy the minimum needs of the broadest masses of the population and more than that. It can be resolved by the spread and improvement of education, because it is the material and intellectual wealth of society that leads to the softening of the age-old division — now renewed and sharpened — between the organizers and the organized. When the organized is no longer the dumb and dull and helpless *muzhik*, when the cook is no longer the old scullion, then indeed the gulf between the bureaucrat and the worker can disappear. What will remain will be the division of functions, not of social status.

The old Marxist prospect of the 'withering away' of the state may seem odd to us. But let us not play with old formulas which were part of an idiom to which we are not accustomed. What Marx really meant was that the state should divest itself of its oppressive political functions. And I think this will become possible only in a society based on nationalized means of production, free from slumps and booms, free from speculations and speculators, free from the uncontrollable forces of the whimsical market of private economy. In a society in which all the miracles of science and technology are turned to peaceful and productive uses; in which automation in industry is not hampered by fear of investment on the one side and fear of redundancy on the other; in which working hours are short and leisure civilized (and completely unlike our stultifying commercialized mass entertainment!); and — last but not least — in a society free from cults, dogmatism and orthodoxies — in such a society the antagonism between brain work and manual labour really will wither away, and so will the division between the organizers and the organized. Then, and only then, will it be seen that if bureaucracy was a faint prelude to class society, bureaucracy will mark the fierce, ferocious epilogue to class society — no more than an epilogue.

At the beginning of 1960 Isaac Deutscher delivered three lectures on the subject of bureaucracy to a graduate seminar at the London School of Economics. 'The Roots of Bureaucracy' originally published in the autumn 1969 issue of *Canadian Slavic Studies*, is a shortened version of these lectures.

2
Marxism in our Time

What is our time, for a Marxist and for Marxism? Is it a time of the ascendancy of Marxism? Or is it an epoch of the decline of Marxism? In those countries where Marxism is supposed to be the ruling doctrine, the official answer is, of course, that this is a time of an unseen, unheard of, unprecedented flourishing of Marxism in theory and practice. Here in the West, especially in our Anglo-Saxon countries, we are told day in and day out, goodness knows from how many academic and other platforms, that Marxism has not only declined, but that it is irrelevant — that it bears no relation to the problems of our epoch. From my native country, Poland, comes the voice of a brilliant young philosopher, but a very poor political analyst, who tells us that it is no use discussing Marxism any longer because Marxism has already gained and won and conquered the human mind to such an extent that it has become an organic part of contemporary thinking, and this marks the end of every great doctrine — when it becomes the organic part of human thought. This young philosopher lived in Warsaw after an epoch of Stalinism during which he and people of his generation identified Stalinism and Marxism. They knew Marxism only in the Stalinist form; they were served, and they accepted, the official Marxism as Stalinism and Stalinism as Marxism. Now they want to get away from Stalinism, and this — as they equated Stalinism and Marxism — means for them getting away from Marxism. It seems to me — such is the bitter dialectic of our epoch — that Marxism is in ascendancy and decline simultaneously.

Since the beginning of my adult life (that is, over forty years ago), I have been a Marxist, and I have never for a moment hesitated in my — I wouldn't say allegiance because it is not a matter of 'allegiance' — I have never hesitated in my Marxist *Weltanschauung*. I cannot think otherwise than in Marxist terms. Kill me, I cannot do it.

I may try; I just cannot. Marxism has become part of my existence. As someone who owes this kind of 'allegiance' to Marxism, I would not like to give any of you, who perhaps only recently made an acquaintance with Marxism, the idea that this is one of the golden ages of the Marxist doctrine. Far from it. This is a time of triumph for Marxism only insofar as this is an age of revolution which develops an anti-capitalist, a post-capitalist kind of society. But it is also an age of degeneration of Marxist thought and of intellectual decline for the labour movement at large. Precisely because the modern labour movement cannot find another creative and fertile doctrine except Marxism, all its intellectual standards decline catastrophically whenever and wherever Marxism becomes ossified. We have an expansion in Marxist practice and a shrinkage and degeneration in Marxist thinking. There is a deep divorce between the practical experience of revolution and the whole Marxist theoretical framework within which that revolution has been anticipated, within which that revolution has been justified on philosophical, historical, economic, political, cultural and, if you like, even moral grounds.

For a student of philosophical or historical schools of thought and doctrines this is not an extraordinary statement. Almost every really great school of thought that dominated the thinking of generations has known its periods of great expansion, awakening and development, and its periods of decadence and decline. In this respect the only other school of thought that comes to mind is the Aristotelian school, which dominated human intellect for nearly two thousand years. In the course of this series of epochs it went through various phases of great creative interpretation and creative influence, and also epochs in which it found its triumph in a parody of itself, in the medieval Catholic scholasticism which, although based on Aristotelian philosophy, yet bore to it the same relationship which caricature bears to the real picture of an original object. This did not deprive the Aristotelian philosophy even in the Middle Ages of its *raison d'être*, of its creative phases, of its stimuli which still existed and later helped medieval Europe to overcome the scholastical degeneration. In this respect Marxism stands comparison with the Aristotelian philosophy as a way of thinking that epitomizes and generalizes the entire social, economic and, to some extent, political experience of the world under capitalism and exposes the inner dynamism of the historical development which is bound to lead from capitalism to some other post-capitalist order, which we have agreed to describe as a socialist order.

Marxism is not an intellectual, aesthetic or philosophical fashion, no matter what the fashion-mongers imagine. After having been infatuated with it for a season or two they may come and declare it to be obsolete. Marxism is a way of thinking, a generalization growing out of an immense historical development; and as long as this historic phase in which we live has not been left far behind us, the doctrine may prove to be mistaken on points of detail or secondary points, but in its essence nothing has deprived it, and nothing looks like depriving it, of its relevance, validity and importance for the future. But at the same time we face the problem of degeneration in Marxist thinking. We have the divorce between theory and practice, and we have a striking, and to a Marxist often humiliating, contrast between what I call classical Marxism — that is, the body of thought developed by Marx, Engels, their contemporaries, and after them by Kautsky, Plekhanov, Lenin, Trotsky, Rosa Luxemburg — and the vulgar Marxism, the pseudo-Marxism of the different varieties of European social-democrats, reformists, Stalinists, Khruschevites, and their like. I am speaking here of a contrast between classical and vulgar Marxism by analogy with the way in which Marx spoke of classical and vulgar economy. You know that for Marx the term 'classical economy' has a different meaning from the one it has in your textbooks at the London School of Economics. According to your textbooks, if I am not mistaken, classical economy lasts till the very end of the nineteenth and even the beginning of the twentieth century, and Marshall still forms part of it. To Karl Marx classical economy ends practically with Ricardo. All that follows is for him the vulgar economy of the bourgeoisie, and for a very good reason. In the classical economy, in Ricardo and Smith, Marx saw the main elements out of which he developed his own theory, especially the labour theory of value — of value based on human labour. This was the revolutionary element in the classical bourgeois political economy. For this revolutionary element the bourgeoisie had no use later on and, moreover, was afraid of it. Post-Ricardian economy wants to deduce value from anything *but* human labour. Later schools of vulgar economy deduce value from circulation; still later they 'dismiss' value altogether and build a political economy without it because in this concept of value created by human labour was the seed of revolution. And bourgeois thinking instinctively shied away from it and, frightened, turned in other directions. Classical economy, the economic thinking of Smith and Ricardo, Marx argued, had given an insight into the working of capitalism that far exceeded the practical needs of the bourgeois class.

Ricardo, who understood capitalism so well, knew that the bourgeoisie neither wished nor could afford to understand the workings of its own system, and therefore it had to get away from the labour theory of value in the first instance. This phenomenon of a doctrine and a theory that offers insights into the working of a social system far greater than are the practical requirements of the social class for which it is meant— this phenomenon occurs sometimes in history. And it has occurred with Marxism. The body of classical Marxist thought gave such profound, immense, and till this day unexhausted and unexplored riches of insight that the working class for its practical purposes seemed not to need it. This idea was once expressed by Rosa Luxemburg on the occasion of the publication of the second and third volumes of *Das Kapital*. She said that the social-democratic movement in Europe had conducted its propaganda and agitation in the course of thirty or forty years on the basis of the first volume of *Das Kapital* — that is, on the basis of a fragment of Marx's economic theory; then came the second and the third volume and the huge structure was rising before our eyes — yet the labour movement did not at all feel that it conducted its practical and theoretical activities on an inadequate foundation: the intellectual content even of the fragment of *Das Kapital* was quite sufficient to keep, so to speak, the labour movement intellectually alive for decades.

Marx created a body of thought far in excess of the narrow practical needs of the movement for which he intended his work to serve. Then came the vulgarization, which was in sharp contrast with the original doctrine but which reflected the requirements of the labour movements and of the revolutions that were coming under the banner of Marxism. I hope I have explained in what sense I am using these terms — classical Marxism and vulgar Marxism. I shall perhaps sum up my argument: classical Marxism offers deep historical insight into the working of capitalism, into the prospects of the dissolution of capitalism, and, broader still, into man's relation under this system with other men, with his own class and other classes, his relationship and attitude towards the technology of his age. Vulgar Marxism does not need all that insight; it is fully satisfied with a small fraction of all that understanding, which it places in the severely limited orbit of practical needs, practical strivings, and practical tasks. We have here a historic hypertrophy of practice and an atrophy of thought. Practice is sometimes the enemy of thought; thought sometimes suffers from contact with practice. Here is the dialectic in its crystalline form: practice cannot in the long run ignore theory. Nevertheless there are temporary, transitional periods of unresolved tensions between theory and practice, and it is in such a period that we have been living these last decades. These unresolved tensions affect the whole structure of Marxist thinking.

The intellectual structure of classical Marxim was entirely based on the assumption of a socialist revolution taking place within a mature capitalist bourgeois society. The vulgar Marxism of our decade, by which I mean the Marxism that comes from the post-capitalist third of the world, is all based on the fact of revolutions occurring within underdeveloped societies. Now, how does this affect the structure of Marxist thinking?

If a revolution takes place in a mature bourgeois society, then what you assume, and what would in fact follow, would be first of all a material abundance, an abundance of goods, an abundance of means of production and a relative or even an absolute abundance of means of consumption, an abundance of human skills, of tools, of abilities, of experience, of resources, an abundance of culture. If the revolution takes place in underdeveloped societies, then the basic, decisive and determining factor with which we have to reckon is the all-round scarcity: scarcity of means of production, of means of consumption, of skills, of abilities, of schools, scarcity of civilization and of culture — scarcity all round — only an abundance or super-abundance of revolutionary elements. If abundance is the basis of the whole structure of the revolution and of Marxist thinking within the revolution, political freedom is the element which you take for granted. Even if a revolution entails civil war and the dictatorship of the proletariat, this is viewed as a transitory phase during which the dictatorship is to serve only one immediate purpose: the breaking down of the armed resistance of the former possessing classes, but not the disciplining or forcing into obedience of the working classes or even the middle classes of one's own society. Marx rarely, if ever, spoke about 'political freedom'. Precisely because he assumed a revolution amid the abundance of a mature bourgeois society, he took political freedom so much for granted that he discussed only, so to say, the higher mathematics of freedom, those refinements of genuine freedom of which only a socialist society would be capable. On the basis of material scarcity there is no freedom. On the basis of abundance there would be no need for those sharply differentiated wage scales, the Stakhanovism[7] and other systems and tricks which result in the re-creation of revolting inequality. This inequality was inevitable in a society like the Russian one where — as I used to

---

[7]Soviet worker-incentive system named after the miner Alexei Stakhanov, who devised it in 1935.

argue in the old days — fifty million pairs of shoes were produced for a nation of one hundred and sixty million. This was my old argument and old simile; but it is still valid, in one way or another, if applied to nearly all the underdeveloped countries.

In a revolution which takes its course amid abundance and growing equality, there is no question of constraint in cultural matters. This coercion and constraint is presented to you as prole-tarian culture, as socialist culture. The constraint in the cultural field comes from nothing else but political fear. Censors confiscate poems because they are afraid that these poems may become political mani-festoes. When the censors call for novels of 'social realism', they wage a preventive battle against political manifestoes of opposition or revolution that might come not even from the poets, but from very prosaic young men somewhere in factories or universities. Intel-lectual constraint goes together with political constraint, with scarcity, with inequality.

Classical Marxism never envisaged 'socialism in a single country' — in Germany, or in France, or in England. Its ground was always Europe, at the very least Western Europe. It was always international in its outlook; yet in the actual historical development it became national in scale. It became national in the sense in which Stalin viewed socialism within the framework of a single state on the basis of economic and even cultural self-sufficiency. This was a profoundly anti-Marxist view. It was the reflection of the false consciousness of the isolated Russian Revolution. Till this day in the East — in Russia, in China, among the foremost Stalinists in Eastern Europe — the whole way of thinking is still shaped by the tradition, the implications and the tacit assumptions of 'socialism in a single country', that is, of autarkic socialism, closed within itself. And of course, while you have scarcity, lack of freedom, inequality, cultural and intellectual coercion, and socialism on a national scale, and consequently the renewed struggle of nationalisms, you have a new form of what it is now fashionable to call, after the youthful Marx, *alienation*. This is a new form of alienation; man feels estranged from society; he is the plaything of what looks to him like blind social forces. He himself forms part of these forces, which are of his own making, and yet he is their victim. To Marx this estrangement from society was unthinkable in a socialist society, a society which was to grow out of the rich soil of mature capitalist civilization. However, contrary to Marx's expectations the revolution did not develop in Europe, in countries which we like to describe as the cradles of Western civilization, but in the East. And there, in the East, Marx's socialism could not be built. How could it, if no material basis for it existed? People there could only engage in the primitive accumulation of the preconditions of socialism; and this they are achieving. Let us not be supercilious, and let us not belittle their immense task and their immense achievement. They are learning with long delays what the Western European nations learned generations earlier, but they also know what the nations of the West never learned. The development is combined. There is backwardness and there is tremendous progress — it would be unrealistic ever to leave out of sight any one of these contradictory aspects of history.

'Why then did the West not respond to the appeal of Marxism?' I will be asked. The revolution first won in a country which was underdeveloped and backward in 1917; underdeveloped and backward in its whole social structure despite its brilliant and fantastic artistic-literary achievement. The whole edifice was going up on unstable, unhealthy foundations and in the process became as if adjusted to these existing conditions of backwardness. Full of gallows humour, old communists used to sigh: 'Couldn't God help us to start the upheaval in a more suitable country than this Russia of the *muzhiks*?' No, God did not help. Hence, the incongruity of a modern revolution against the background of murky age-old traditions. This had its negative impact on the possibilities of revolutionary development in the West. The revolution in a pre-capitalist society, which nevertheless aspired to achieve socialism, produced a hybrid which in many respects looked like a parody of socialism. The Western worker, however seemingly non-political, followed events very carefully and was quite aware of the famines, the hunger and the deprivation that the people of Russia suffered after the revolution; he was aware of the terror and persecution they were subjected to. And, unsophisticated as he was, the British worker, the German worker, and even the French one, often wondered: Is this socialism? Have we perhaps in our century-old allegiance to socialism followed a dangerous will-o'-the-wisp? Workers have been asking themselves these questions. Uncertain, hesitant, the Western European worker has preferred to wait and see. The Russian Revolution has acted as a deterrent to revolution in the West.

By and large we must look at the developments in the West and the relation of Marxism to the course of the class struggle in the West as upon a war which has lasted for generations — for a century and a half. And this class war has had its ups and downs, its intervals, its pitched battles, its long lulls between battles and campaigns. Anyone may say during a lull between two pitched battles: 'Ah, your Marx said history is the history of class struggle and there is no class struggle!' Of course, when Marx wrote in the *Communist Manifesto* that the history of mankind is the history of class wars, he knew perfectly well that there were times during which the war of the classes was at a very low ebb, almost stagnant. Churchill once wrote that the history of mankind is the history of wars — perhaps an unconscious plagiarism from Marx? The difference, of course, is that for Marx it is the history of class war, and for Churchill it is the history of war *tout court*. But Churchill also knew that wars are not fought ceaselessly; and Marx also knew that class wars have their time of truce, of open struggle, latent struggle, doldrums and intervals.

We have had a war against capitalism lasting many generations. There was 1848, 1870, 1905, 1917–18, 1945–46: all great battles, concluded partly with a victory of revolution in the East, and with heavy defeats of the revolution in the West. Marx never promised victories for the revolutions at any definite date of the calendar. All that he forecast was that there was going to be a struggle, a heavy, at times a bloody struggle, between classes and peoples, a struggle that would go on for generations and which should — if civilization did not in the meantime collapse into barbarity — lead to the dissolution of capitalism and the emergence of socialism. And, of course, parallel with this there has also been a mobilization of all the forces of the counter-revolution. Those who like to speak now about the unfulfilled prophecies of Marx — do they imagine (how shall I put it?), do they imagine that Marx was as shallow as his critics and saw the road towards socialism without the barricades of counter-revolution? We have had the mobilization of counter-revolution all over the world, in all its various forms, from fascism to the most refined social-democratic reformism, all mobilized in the defence of the existing social order. Those forces have benefited from every difficulty, from every wound in the body of socialism. Never yet, except in extra-ordinary moments like the Commune of Paris, has the working class mobilized itself even to a fraction of that intensity and strength at which the possessing and ruling classes have maintained their mobilization on an almost permanent footing. Even during the Commune the insurgents never really mobilized for a life-and-death struggle — we have all the descriptions showing their light-mindedness, their good-humoured and good-tempered optimism.

When I speak of classical Marxism and of its validity, I have in mind what is essential in Marx. Marx was politically active in 1847–48, in 1868, and 1878; he wrote letters to his friends and to Engels in which he expressed his hope that perhaps the labour movement would take a revolutionary impetus in a year's time, in two or three years. And then Engels, after his friend's death, was writing to his disciples — and there were many of them in Western Europe — communicating to them his hope still to live and see the coming together of the workers of Britain and France and Germany. It was only natural that they had all these sanguine expectations, but they were also thinkers who could step back from their immediate and tactical involvements and look at the historical perspective. There was Marx who laid the foundations of the First International and hoped that soon, very soon, that International would be able to produce some great upheaval. But there was also Marx who was writing *Das Kapital,* and he did not commit himself in this severely scientific and historical work to any forecast or any prophecy except to a conclusion which followed from his profound, detailed and meticulous analysis of capitalism — the conclusion that this system must collapse because its inner contradictions would not allow it to function in the long run. When it will dissolve and collapse — into this he never entered, not because (as so many of his clever critics suggest) he was so clever, but because he had a sense of responsibility. A politician may have to bank on certain events occurring within a certain time; he can rally for the coming struggle his own strength and that of his friends and followers. The historical thinker cannot do this; nor can he foresee the complications of history or map out its exact route.

I said that I shall concentrate on what is essential in Marx and I have slipped into what is inessential, so allow me just to touch on another problem which is marginal, namely the problem whether the working class under capitalism is condemned to absolute im-poverishment. This has long been passionately discussed in the European, and especially in the French, Communist Parties. Well, you can find in Marx some support for such a theory and you can find some refutation of it. Marx's mind was too rich and complex to play with narrow formulae. In Marx's time, in Western Europe, there certainly were empirical facts which pointed to progressive and absolute impoverishment.

But let us return to the very essentials in the Marxist critique of capitalism. When people say that Marxism was a doctrine, highly elaborate and realistic for the nineteenth century but now obsolete, may we ask: obsolete in what? In its essentials? There is one, only one, essential element in the Marxist critique of capitalism. It is very simple and very plain, but in it are focused all the many-faceted analyses of the capitalist order. It is this: there is a striking contradiction between the increasingly social character of the process of production and the anti-social character of capitalist property. Our mode of existence, the whole manner of production, is becoming more and more social in the sense that the old freelance producers can no longer go on producing in independence from each other, from generation to generation, as they did in the pre-capitalist system. Every element, every fraction, every little tiny organ of our society is dependent on all the rest. The whole process of production becomes one social process of production — and not only one national process of production but one international process of production. At the same time you have an anti-social kind of property, private property. This contradiction between the anti-social character of property and the social character of our production is the source of all anarchy and irrationality in capitalism.

This contradiction cannot be reconciled *à la longue*. The collision must come. That was all that Marx said. Now, has this essential critique of capitalism become obsolete? We are told that it has, that since Keynes capitalism knows how to plan the economy. For eighty years planning was supposed to be a bee in Marx's bonnet. Now that bee has been elevated almost to a divine insect, and we are told that capitalism can also plan. Has it ever planned except for war purposes? If it has, I have not yet heard of such a case. But suppose that it can. Is planning congenial to capitalism? Some capitalist enterprises were, after all, conducted on a feudal basis; one can also, I suppose, create a simulacrum of socialism on a capitalist basis. But is this congenial to capitalism? And can capitalism, even when it plans, achieve the rate of growth that planning in a really publicly owned economy has achieved? Of course not, because if there is national or international planning, then national or international ownership and organization are the congenial and natural conditions for planning. You can, of course, put planning into capitalism, but it is almost like putting a motor engine into a horse-drawn *drozhka*. And can capitalism create international societies? You will say: What about the Russians and the Chinese? Have they created an international society? Of course not. The way in which the Russians and the Chinese conduct their affairs is still a reflection of a capitalist way of thinking. But there it is a reflection of capitalism, a projection of capitalism into a post-capitalist structure of society, while here it is historically inherent in the whole working of the capitalist order. Wherever capitalism tries to break out of its national crust, it always does so in a catastrophic way, by staging world wars, by swallowing smaller and weaker nations or competitors.

If you look at the nearly two decades of post-war capitalist prosperity, what do you see? A refutation of Marxism? This is not the first time in history that we have seen twenty years running their course without the old-type slump and boom that have been characteristic of capitalism from at least 1825 to the Second World War. After the Franco–Prussian War of 1870–71 there were twenty-five years of Germany's tremendous industrialization, of capitalist development without a real crisis. At the end of these twenty-five years came the revisionists, the friends and disciples of Marx and Engels, who said: 'The masters must have been mistaken. They said there would be a collapse, there would be crises, there would be slumps. There are no slumps. From now on capitalism will develop smoothly in an evolutionary manner.' And after only a few years, in 1907, came the tremendous collapse. Then the next tremendous slump led into the First World War.

I don't want to be a Cassandra, but I cannot say that I have confidence in the further smooth, evolutionary development of Western capitalism, or in the perpetuation of its so-called prosperity. After these twenty years of prosperity, what do we see in Western society? We see an intensification of all those trends which Karl Marx diagnosed as the trends leading to the further development of capitalism and its doom. We see all over the West the disappearance of those middle classes that were supposed to constitute the conservative foundation of capitalism; of the small-owning, small-holding peasantry. The peasantry that was the mainstay of French conservatism is vanishing, and France has ceased to be a peasant country. So have most Western European countries. America has no peasants, and only a small percentage of its population is engaged in farming. That was what Marx prophesied: what will be left will be the bourgeoisie and the propertyless working class. For decades it seemed that this particular prognostication was not coming true. Karl Kautsky wrote a very learned and voluminous work on the agrarian problem, in which he explained why in agriculture there was no such concentration of capital as there was in industry. Nevertheless, he maintained, the Marxist prognosis was correct. Lenin accepted Kautsky's argument and pointed out that the peasantry remained in existence although it was getting progressively impoverished. Now this peasantry is vanishing! The proletariat is growing in numbers. Proletarianization, that horror of the bourgeoisie, is progressing with every year of our prosperity, with every year of our welfare state. The processes of production are becoming larger and larger in scale, centralized, social in character, calling more and more for social control, for social ownership. The productive forces of our countries cry out against the national self-sufficiency in which tradition and the ruling classes have kept them. That is the Marxist inferno coming true, almost invisibly, almost unnoticed, in the midst of this welfare-state paradise.

In the meantime, one feels as if the whole development of class struggle here in the West has become arrested for a while, waiting for some great chapters to come to a close. There is one great trend in the historic development which promises — but this is only a promise — to turn the whole tide of Marxism and socialism: the growth of the productive forces of the Soviet Union, and with it that of the other post-capitalist countries. The process of primitive socialist accumulation, which has caused such tremendous distortion in the intellectual and moral structure of Marxism, does not have long to run. I do not know whether this is a matter of another decade or two, but the development will come full circle when Russia, this underdeveloped and backward country, and with it the other countries, will at last turn fully into modern, industrial nations — when the educated countries (with a socialist tradition surviving in them in spite of everything) realize in their midst those preconditions for socialism of which Marx and Engels and generations of socialists had dreamed: the material and cultural abundance, the lack of constraint in politics and in culture, the growing equality, the growing internationalism.

I have no doubt that despite the very ugly scenes between Moscow and Peking, the social systems of those countries are more intelligent and more progressive than their leaders. The social systems will force the leaders into internationalism even if they are the most chauvinistic idiots under the sun; they will push and drive them aside and bring out new people who will be capable of following the call of internationalism that comes today from the whole of mankind. And when this happens the development of those countries will not only catch up with classical Marxism, but it will probably surpass it. So, I think, we can confidently look forward to the prospect, even if it is not an imminent one, that theory and practice in Marxism will come together again. You and people of your generation should look whole-heartedly to this perspective, when Marxism will no longer be the Marxism with which we had to live — the Marxism projected through the distorting prism of backwardness, of backward civilization and backward societies. Your generation, I hope, will see this new upsurge, this new ascendancy of Marxism undimmed by any intellectual decline.

Marxism and socialism have been the products of Western Europe. They have gone out of Western Europe to conquer the world and they have lost ground in Western Europe. When will they come back? The country in medieval Europe from which the rest of Europe learned the arts of capitalism was Italy. The Italian cities, the Italian economists, the Italian bankers were the foremost in Europe. And then, in the nineteenth century, when nearly the whole of Europe had already gone bourgeois, Italy had not yet achieved its own capitalism. Capitalism came back to Italy belatedly, after the whole of Europe had accepted it. Is Western Europe going to be the Italy of socialism? Are we going to wait until Marxism and socialism have conquered the world, and then stand there, last in the queue, waiting for its return to us? Or shall we save ourselves from our own increasing and terrifying backwardness?

'Marxism in Our Time' is an edited manuscript of a lecture given in February 1965 at the London School of Economics.

3
Violence and Non-violence

There is a whole dialectic of violence and non-violence implied in the Marxist doctrine from its beginnings and throughout all its historic metamorphoses from 1848 to 1966. As Marxists we have always preached proletarian dictatorship, and the need to overthrow capitalism by force. We have always tried to impress on the working classes of all countries that they would have to be prepared to struggle, even in civil wars, against their oppressing and ruling classes. We were quite devastating in our rejoinders to all those who doubted the right or questioned the need for all those preachings. But here is the dialectical contradiction; after all, what has been the idea of Marxism? That of the classless society in which man is no longer exploited and dominated by man, a stateless society. So many people of the left consider this the utopian element in Marxism, the aspiration to transform societies in such a way that violence should cease forever as the necessary and permanent element in the regulation of the relationship between society and individuals, between individuals and individuals.

In embracing the vision of a non-violent society, Marxism, I maintain, has gone further and deeper than any pacifist preachers of non-violence have ever done. Why? Because Marxism laid bare the roots of violence in our society, which the others have not done. Marxism has set out to attack those roots; to uproot violence not just from human thoughts, not just from human emotions, but to uproot it from the very bases of the material existence of society. Marxism has seen violence fed by class antagonism in society — and here Marxism should be assessed against the two-thousand-year record of futile Christian preaching of non-violence. I say futile in the sense that it has led to no real consequences, to no real diminution of violence. After two millennia of 'love thy brother' we are in this situation: that those who go to church throw the napalm bombs and the others who were also brought up in a Christian tradition, the Nazis, have sent six million descendants of Christ's countrymen to the gas chambers. After two millennia the preaching of non-violence has led to this! One of the reasons for this is that the roots of violence have never been attacked, never been dug up. Class society has persisted and therefore these preachings, even when most sincere, even when the Christian teacher puts both his heart and soul in them, were bound to be futile, because they attacked only the surface of the violence. But then the dialectic of Marxism has also been at fault — Marxism itself, throughout its history of deep and tragic contradictions. How strong the dream of non-violence lay at the root of the Russian Revolution one can find out if one studies Lenin's statement on revolution, which is written seemingly in a very dogmatic form, almost like an ecclesiastical text interpreting biblical verses. Behind these somewhat ecclesiastical formulae there is the dream of the stateless society constantly welling up. The October insurrection was carried out in such a way that, according to all the hostile eyewitnesses (such as the Western ambassadors who were then in Petrograd), the total number of victims on all sides was ten. That is the total number of victims of that great revolutionary October insurrection. The men who directed this insurrection — Lenin, Trotsky, the members of the military revolutionary committee — gave some thought to the question of violence and non-violence and organized this tremendous upheaval with a very profound although unspoken concern for human lives, for the lives of their enemies as well as for their own people. The Russian Revolution, in the name of which so much violence has been committed, was the most non-violent act of this scale in the whole history of the human race!

The revolution was won not with guns, but with words, with argument, persuasion. The words were very violent, the words were terribly forceful, but this is the violence of emotion in the revolt against the actuality of violence, of a world war which cost millions of human beings. All those people nowadays who take it upon themselves to preach morality to the makers of the Russian Revolution assume, of course, that there was a kind of good and angelic status quo, an angelic non-violence which was upset by those Dostoevskian possessed fiends the revolutionaries, who appropriated to themselves the right to dispose of human lives. Nearly ten million people had perished in the trenches of the First World War when the Bolsheviks carried out that great revolution which cost ten victims.

The deep universal humanism inherent in what you call the challenge of non-violence has been there in Marxism as its most essential element. We were a little more shy about talking about humanism; we are more shy about this because what scoundrel in history hasn't spoken about humanism — hasn't Stalin, hasn't Hitler, hasn't Goebbels? I always get more than a little shocked when I hear left-wingers and ex-Marxists suggest that Marxism needs to be supplemented by humanism. Marxism only needs to be true to itself.

But what happened really after this very promising beginning of the Russian Revolution, after Lenin had written *The State and Revolution,* which is the great revolutionary dream about non-violence expressed in Marxist terms, what happened? The others who preached non-violence, for instance Kerensky, preached non-violence to the oppressed by reintroducing the death penalty for soldiers who were refusing to fight on the front. Perhaps in the nature of people who really detest violence there is a greater shyness about speaking about non-violence. I distrust those who have so many noble words on their lips. I very often trust more those who speak frankly and even brutally about the necessities of the political struggle as long as they don't get carried away by their own righteousness.

Then came the intervention, the civil war. Violence had to be used on an increasing scale, just as the Viet Cong today have to use violence on an increasing scale. They can't help it; either they go under or they use violence. But even in the civil war what did the Bolsheviks do? Again they tried to keep a balance between argument, persuasion and violence; a balance in which they still attached far greater importance to persuasion and argument than to the gun. In sheer arms they were infinitely inferior to the British, the French and the Americans (who sent both troops and munitions for the White armies in Russia). The Red Army, led by Trotsky, at that time was far inferior. What happened? They agitated, they appealed to the consciousness of the soldiers, of the workers in uniform in those interventionist armies. The French navy, sent to suppress the revolution, rose in mutiny in Odessa and refused to fight against the Bolsheviks: another triumph of non-violence in the civil war. This revolt of the sailors was the result of what was called Bolshevik propaganda, but this 'subversion' prevented violence. (In Britain in 1920 during the intervention, during the Russo–Polish war, the dockers of London struck and refused to send arms against Russia and the docks of London were immobilized — this was non-violence.)

Then comes the great tragedy of the isolation of the Russian Revolution; of its succumbing to incredible, unimaginable destruction, poverty, hunger and disease as a result of the wars of intervention, the civil wars, and of course the long and exhausting world war which was not of Bolshevik making. As a result of all this, terror was let loose in Russia. Men lost their balance. Even the leaders lost the clarity of their thinking and of their minds. They acted under overwhelming and inhuman pressures. I don't undertake to judge them, to blame them or to justify them. I can only see the deep tragedy of this historic process, the result of which was the glorification of violence.

But what was to have been but a glassful of violence became buckets and buckets full, and then rivers of violence. That is the tragedy of the Russian Revolution. The dialectics of violence and non-violence in Marxism were so upset that in the end the non-violent meaning of Marxism was suppressed under the massive, crushing weight of Stalinism. It wasn't a matter of chance that Stalin implicitly denounced the Leninist and Marxist idea of the withering away of the state. It was in that idea that the whole Marxist non-violence was epitomized. The Stalinist regime couldn't tolerate, couldn't bear the survival of that dream. It had to crush it out of human minds in order to justify its own violence. I'm not saying this to blame the whole thing on single individuals. It was more than that. It was the tragedy of an isolated and poverty-ridden revolution incapable of fulfilling its promise in isolation and poverty: a revolution caught in this tragic situation — of the irreconcilable contradiction between promise and fulfilment, between dream and reality, sunk into irrationality.

To what extent is Marxism, as such, responsible for this? It would be wrong to identify Stalinism with Marxism, and to blame Marxism for the things that have been done under Stalinism. On the other hand, it would show a lack of moral courage in Marxism to draw the formal line of dissociation and say that we are not responsible for Stalinism, that that wasn't what we aimed at. You see, in a way Marxism is as responsible for Stalin as Christianity was responsible for the Borgias. The Borgias are not Christianity, but Christianity cannot bleach the Borgias from its records. We cannot delete Stalinism from our records although we are not responsible for Stalinist crimes. To some extent we (and when I say 'we', I mean that generation of Marxists with which I as an individual identify morally, I mean Lenin, Trotsky, Bukharin, Zinoviev, the early Communist leaders in Europe) participated in this glorification of violence as a self-defence mechanism. Rosa Luxemburg understood this when she criticized the first faint signs of this attitude.

But the issue is larger and deeper than just human intentions. The violence isn't rooted in human intentions. The human intentions are, shall we say, the mechanism, the psychological, the ideal mechanism through which material factors and material necessities transmit their pressures. Marxism had not made any allowances for the possibility of such a tremendous outgrowth of violence, of such tremendous abuse of violence that would be done in the name of Marxism, for a simple reason. Marxism assumed that revolution would always be an act of change in society carried out violently, but with the support of immense popular majorities. It assumed revolution in an industrialized West carried out by working classes committed to socialism, supporting the revolution with all their heart and confronting as their enemies a really small minority consisting of the exploiters. In such a confrontation of revolutionary majorities with counter revolutionary minorities, the need to use violence would indeed have been very limited and the dream of non-violence would have had all this hope of fulfilment.

It is said that Marxism suits the underdeveloped countries but not the advanced and industrial West. I still maintain that the original dream of Marxism and the real original inspiration and hope of Marxism still suits the industrial West much better than it can suit the underdeveloped countries, even if revolution in certain phases is the job of great majorities as it was in Russia in 1917, as it was in China in 1949, as it is in Vietnam today. In underdeveloped countries there comes a moment after the revolution when again there is a breach between promise and fulfilment. Therefore there come frustrations, explosive dissonances and the desire of the post-revolutionary rulers to secure the revolution as they understand it and are able to secure it. The more underdeveloped the country, the more is bound to come, after the revolution, a moment of bitter truth and violence.

However, I think that the violence in China already is much smaller than it was in Russia. The irrationality of the Chinese Revolution, though goodness knows there is a lot of irrationality, so far is much less, I think, than what came to the top in the Russian Revolution. But then the Chinese Revolution wasn't the first pioneer, wasn't the *isolated* revolution: it was already assisted by Stalinist Russia, and this reduced the amount of irrationality. I think that with the spread of revolution, with the advance of the industrial and technological aspects of revolutionary societies, with the growth of their wealth, with the rise in their standards of living, with a relative contentment in the popular masses, the irrational element will decrease. The final vindication of the dream of non-violence in Marxism will come with socialism gaining the advanced countries.

That is my belief, and it is not a belief of wishful thinking; it is the whole theoretical structure of Marxism that leads me to this conclusion. I think that the de-Stalinization carried out in Russia, partial, self-contradictory, inadequate, hypocritical as it has been, has already somewhat re-established the balance between the contradictory elements in the Russian Revolution by reducing the violence and giving more scope to the non-violent element in Marxism.

You have asked me what I meant when I spoke about the negative effect on the Communist world of the war in Vietnam. The war in Vietnam may or may not be a prelude to new confrontations of violence surging back from the Western world and flooding the world again. The fear of the ultimate violence promotes a recrudescence of the authoritarian and violent trend within Russia and in China. I made an analogy between the effects of the Vietnamese War in the Communist part of the world and the repercussions of the Korean War in the last years of Stalin's era. The fears and panics let loose by the Korean War expressed themselves in Russia in the insanity of Stalin's rule in the last years, in the repetition of the witches' sabbath of the thirties. I don't foresee and I'm not afraid of something as terrible as that in Russia in response to the American aggression in Vietnam, but we have already seen some recrudescence of the authoritarian trend. The Twenty-third Congress of the Communist Party testifies to this. The trials of Daniel and Sinyavsky were symptomatic of the partial return of the authoritarian trend.

On the other hand I don't think that one can say that the Korean War had only one effect, i.e. the encouragement of domestic violence in the Soviet Union and China. It also had a positive effect parallel to the effect that it had in our part of the world. It gave one a sense of human solidarity with a small nation so ruthlessly attacked, so ruthlessly crushed by the most powerful, the greatest, the richest nations in the world. The Korean War disposed of certain illusions which Khrushchevism spread; namely, the illusion about the possibility of the peaceful transition from capitalism to socialism in such countries as France or Italy. Try to go now to French and Italian workers and tell them that they can accomplish this miracle when in such small nations as Korea and Vietnam it is so resisted by the great capitalist powers.

As Marxists, whenever we are driven to use violence we must know and tell those people on whom we shall call to act, that violence is a necessary evil. And the emphasis will be on both the adjective and the noun, on the necessary and on evil. To preach non-violence to those always the object of violence may even be false. I say the lesson we should learn from Soviet history is that we can't overemphasize the evil of violence. But if I were a Vietnamese and also in the ranks of the Viet Cong I would try to tell my comrades-in-arms that we should not make a virtue of the bitter and terrible necessity of violence. But we are acting in the West — where this argument has much more chance of being understood and accepted.

In the West on the left we must foster a way of thinking which would not shirk realities. We share with anarchists the dream of stateless society, but we ask: how do you arrive at it? And it is here that Marxism parts from anarchism and pure pacifism. You accept the view that the Vietnamese war is not an accident of history; that it expresses the structure of your society, expresses the imperialist character in your relationship to the outside world. If you accept this, you imply that the social order has to be changed. How is it to be changed? How is it going to be changed by non-violent methods when those who refuse to give an inch in Vietnam to their class enemies — will they yield the territory of the United States to socialism without defending the status quo? Can you imagine this? I can, but only under one condition. That is when you have the overwhelming number of Americans ready to use violence in order to bring about socialism, only then may socialism conquer the United States without the use of violence. The revolution's capital is its moral supremacy. You see, if you achieve for socialism a moral supremacy in American society comparable to that of the Russian Revolution, then you might have to use only an infinitesimal amount of violence. But — here again is the dialectic — only if you're ready to use violence without making a virtue of it.

'Violence and Non-violence' is an edited version of a contribution to a discussion organized by D. Dellinger, in Berkeley in 1966, in connection with the Vietnam Day of Protest.

4

On Socialist Man

I have been asked to address you on 'Socialist Man'. This is a theme so wide, and requiring so many approaches from various angles, that I must beg you to excuse me if what I am going to say resembles a somewhat rambling *causerie* in form, rather than a systematic lecture.

Marxists have as a rule been reluctant to speak about socialist man; and I must confess that I myself felt something of that reluctance when the subject for this lecture was first suggested to me. Any attempt to give a positive description of socialist man, i.e. to portray the member of the future classless society, is bound to have a utopian flavour about it. This was the domain of the great visionaries of socialism, especially of Saint-Simon and Fourier, who, like the French rationalists of the eighteenth century, imagined that they — and through them Reason — had at last discovered the ideal man and that once the discovery had been made, the realization was bound to follow. Nothing was further from Marx and Engels and the outstanding Marxists of later generations than such a thought. They, indeed, did not tell mankind: 'Here is the ideal, go down on your knees before it!' Instead of giving us a blueprint of the society that is to come, they devoted their work to a profoundly realistic analysis of society as it was and is, of capitalist society; and, facing the class struggles of their time, they committed themselves irrevocably to the cause of the proletariat.

In attending to the needs of their age, however, they did not turn their backs upon the future. They did try at least to guess the shape of things to come; but they formulated their guesses with remarkable reserve and they did so only incidentally. In all their voluminous writings Marx and Engels have left us only a few scattered hints about the subject of our discussion, hints meaningfully interrelated and suggesting immense new horizons, but only hints. No doubt Karl

Marx had his conception of socialist man, but this was an analyst's working hypothesis, not a visionary's brainwave; and although he was convinced of the historic realism of his anticipations, he treated them with a certain dose of scepticism.

Marx scrutinized, to paraphrase his own saying, the embryo of socialism within the womb of capitalism — he could therefore see only the embryo of socialist man. At the risk of disappointing some of you, I must say that this is all that we can do even now. After all the revolutions of our age and despite all that we have learned about society since Marx, we are not at all ahead of him in this respect: in discussing socialist man we cannot yet go beyond the rudiments of the problem. Anything we can say about it is bound to be very general, fragmentary and, in a sense, negative. We can easier see what socialist man cannot be than what he will be. To the extent, however, that negation implies also assertion, our negative characterization of socialist man foreshadows some of his positive features as well.

Marxism has seen the chief contradiction of bourgeois society, the deepest cause of its anarchy and irrationality, in the conflict between the growing socialization of the modern productive process and the unsocial character of the control that private property exercises over that process. Modern technology and industry tend to unite society, while private property in the means of production disunites it. The socialized productive process, that rudimentary element of collectivism contained within the capitalist and, if you like, within the neo-capitalist economy, needs to be released from the bourgeois property relations which constrict and disorganize it. For more than a century bourgeois economists were blind to this contradiction until Keynes and his followers recognized it in their own eclectic way, thus paying an unavowed tribute to the Marxist critique.

But all that Keynesianism and neo-capitalism, more than ever haunted by the spectre of communism, have tried to do is to introduce, on the basis of private property (i.e., of monopolistic capitalist corporations) a kind of pseudo-social control over the socialized productive process. This is not the first or the last time that men have desperately struggled to ensure the survival of archaic institutions or ways of life into an age that has no need and no use for them. I once saw in my native country, Poland, a peasant who by chance acquired an old motor car and then insisted on harnessing his horses to it. Keynesianism and neo-capitalism are keeping the horses of private property harnessed to the nuclear-driven vehicles and space ships of our time — and they threaten to shake heaven and earth to prevent us unharnessing them.

To return to my proper subject: our idea of socialism is not an arbitrary intellectual construction but a careful extrapolation and projection into the future of those elements of rational social organization that are inherent in capitalist society but are constantly thwarted and negated by it. Similarly our idea of socialist man is but a projection of the social man who already exists within us potentially, but is distorted, crushed and stultified by the condition in which he lives. (The germ of socialist man is present even in the alienated worker of our time in those rare moments when he rises to a genuine awareness of his role in society and to class solidarity and when he struggles for his emancipation.) It is here that our aspirations are rooted in the realities and are sustained by them, but all too often are also imprisoned in them.

We know, I repeat, what socialist man cannot be and will not be: he cannot be the product of antagonistic society; he cannot be the collective producer who is controlled by his product and social environment instead of controlling them. He cannot be the plaything of the blind forces of the market, nor the robot of a state-managed neo-capitalist war economy. He cannot be the alienated and cowed proletarian of earlier days, nor the dull counterfeit copy of the petty bourgeois into which our so-called welfare state is turning the worker. He can be himself as collective worker only in a most highly developed and collectivist society. Only such a society will enable him to reduce his socially necessary labour to the unburdensome minimum which the new technology already permits. Only in such a society will he be able to satisfy his material and spiritual needs securely, not haphazardly; rationally, not whimsically. Only in such a society will he guide himself in the satisfaction of his needs and the use of his leisure by educated discernment and intelligent choice, not by any silent or vociferous persuaders of commercial advertisement. Only in a socialist community will man be able to develop all his biological and spiritual capacities, to expand and integrate his personality, and free himself of the dark heritage of millennial material scarcity, inequality and oppression. Only in such a community can man overcome finally the divorce between physical and intellectual labour, the divorce that has been at the root of man's estrangement from man, of mankind's division into rulers and ruled and into antagonistic classes — the divorce that our advanced technology even now is rendering superfluous while capitalism and neo-capitalism do what they can to perpetuate it. Socialist man can rise to his full stature only at the summit of our culture and civilization, a summit which is within our sight but toward which our property relationships, our social institutions, and deeply ingrained inertia do not allow us to advance as firmly and rapidly as we might advance.

Our idea of socialist man has often been criticized for its un-abashed optimism. We are told that we too are utopians and that our historical-philosophical and psychological assumptions are unten-able. We are told that the 'paradise on earth' of which propagandists of socialism have spoken is as unattainable as was the paradise in heaven the theologians had promised. We must listen with open minds to these criticisms — we sometimes find grains of truth in them. We must admit that we have more than once taken too opti-mistic a view if not of socialism itself, then of the roads leading to it. But we must also realize that many of these criticisms express only the sense of doom permeating bourgeois society and its ideologues, or else irrational forms of disillusionment in our own camp.

Thus some of the existentialists tell us that we are trying to escape from the basic predicaments of the human condition and that we are glossing over the inherent absurdity of our destiny. It is extremely difficult to engage in any fruitful debate with opponents who argue *sub specie aeternitatis* and from purely teleological premises. The pessimistic existentialist asks the old question: What is the purpose or the aim of man's existence and activity when set against the infinity of time and space? To this question we have, of course, no answer — nor has the existentialist. But the question itself is absurd, for it postulates the need or necessity of an ultimate, metaphysical purpose of human existence, a purpose valid for all eternity. We have no such purpose, and we have no need for it. We see no metaphysical sense in our existence and therefore we see no absurdity in it either — absurdity and sense are only the obverse sides of the same coin: only when you postulate sense can you speak of absurdity.

The human condition with which we are concerned is not man's loneliness in the infinity of space and time — in that infinity even the terms 'loneliness' and 'absurdity' are meaningless. We are concerned with man's condition in society — which is his own creation and which he is capable of changing. The argument *sub specie aeternitatis* is philosophically arid and socially reactionary; it is as a rule an argument for moral indifference and political quietism, an argument for resigned acceptance of our social conditions as they are. Happily, existentialists, as Sartre's remarkable example shows, can be philo-sophically inconsistent and can accept the idea of socialist man despite their view of the absurdity of the human condition.

More specific to some extent is the criticism of socialist and Marxist aspirations that Sigmund Freud makes in *Civilization and its*

Discontents. To our view of what man can and probably will be in a classless and stateless society, Freud replies with the old adage: *Homo homini lupus.* Human beings, he says, will always remain aggressive and hostile to each other; their aggressive instincts are biologically predetermined and are not significantly affected by any changes in the structure of society. 'The communists', Freud says, 'believe that they have found the path to deliverance from our evils. According to them, man is wholly good and well-disposed to his neighbour, but the institution of private property has corrupted his nature. The ownership of private wealth gives the individual power and with it the temptation to ill-treat his neighbour; while the man who is excluded from possession is bound to rebel in hostility against his oppressor. If private property were abolished, and wealth held in common, and everyone allowed to share in the enjoyment of it, ill-will and hostility would disappear among men. Since everyone's needs would be satisfied, no one would have any reason to regard another as his enemy; all would willingly undertake the work that was necessary.'[1]

Before I proceed, let me first check whether Freud's summary of the Marxist view is correct. Do we really consider man to be 'wholly good' by nature and 'well-disposed' to his neighbour'? Freud, who was rather ill-informed about Marxist theory, certainly came across some such statements in the popular communist or social-democratic propaganda, where they did indeed occur. Serious Marxist theory, however, does not make any such assumptions about human nature — at the most such assumptions may be traced in Marx's youthful, Feuerbachian writings. I remember that this problem occupied me strongly when, as a very young man, I was acquainting myself with Marxist theory and was trying to obtain clarity about the conception of human nature underlying it. Working through the writings of Marx, Engels, Kautsky, Plekhanov, Mehring, Rosa Luxemburg, Lenin, Trotsky and Bukharin, I arrived at the conclusion that their assumptions about human nature were essentially, so to speak, neutral. They did not see man as 'wholly good' or 'wholly evil', as 'well-disposed' or 'ill-disposed toward his neighbour'; they refused to accept the metaphysical notion of an immutable human nature unaffected by social conditions. I still think that the conclusion I then drew forty years ago was correct.

Man is the creature of nature, but more particularly of that part of nature which, as human society, distinguishes itself from nature and

---

[1] *Civilization and Its Discontents*, London 1963, pp. 49–50.

partly opposes itself to it. Whatever the biological basis of our being, social conditions play the decisive part in shaping our character — even the biological factors refract themselves through, and are partly transformed by, our social personality. To some extent man's nature, including his instincts, has so far been submerged and distorted by his social conditions, and only when these conditions lose their oppressive and distorting quality may we be able to take a clearer and more scientific view than we have had so far of the various biological and social elements in man's nature.

The main criticism of Freudianism that a Marxist is bound to make — and I am speaking as one who wholeheartedly recognizes Freud's fundamental and revolutionary contribution to our understanding of psychology — is that Freud and his disciples all too often fail to make allowance for this refraction and transmutation of man's instinctual drives through his changing social identity — and yet it is Freud who has made us aware of the processes which are nothing but the mechanisms of sublimation! Psychoanalysis has so far been able to deal only with bourgeois man, the bourgeois man of the epoch of imperialism, whom it has tended to present as man at large, treating his inner conflicts in a supra-historical manner as conflicts besetting human beings in all epochs, under all social orders, as conflicts inherent in the human condition. From this point of view socialist man can be seen only as a variation of bourgeois man. Freud himself makes this point: 'In abolishing private property we deprive the human love of aggression of one of its instruments, certainly a strong one, though certainly not the strongest; but we have in no way altered the differences in power and influence which are misused by aggressiveness nor have we altered anything in its nature.'[2]

Then Freud makes this even more categorical assertion: 'Aggressiveness was not created by property; it reigned almost without limit in primitive times, when property was still very scant, and it already shows itself in the nursery almost before aggressiveness has given up its primal, anal form . . . If we do away with personal rights over material wealth, there still remains prerogative in the field of sexual relationships, which is bound to become the source of the strongest dislike and the most violent hostility among men who in other respects are on an equal footing.'[3] Thus we are warned that socialist man will be, not less than bourgeois man, aggressive and hostile toward fellow beings, and that his aggressiveness will show itself

[2] *Ibid.* p. 50.
[3] *Loc. cit.*

even in the nursery.

Note that while Freud recognizes in private property a strong instrument of aggression, he asserts in the most dogmatic manner that it is not the strongest of those instruments. How does he know it? How does he measure the relative strength of the various instruments of aggression? We, Marxists, are more modest here and less dogmatic: we do not claim to have made such precise comparative measurements as would allow us to weigh sexual drives and instinctual aggression against social needs, interests, and compulsions. The instinctual drives will undoubtedly be there in socialist man as well — how could it be otherwise? — but we do not know how they will refract themselves through his personality. We can only guess that they will affect him in a different manner than they affect bourgeois man. (I even suppose that socialist man will offer the psychoanalyst far richer and more reliable material for research and conclusions, because in him a future Freud will be able to watch the working of the instinctual drives directly, not through a glass darkly, not through the distorting prisms of the analyst's and the patient's class psychology.) Nor is Freud right in saying that property is only an instrument of our aggressive instincts — on the contrary, property often uses those instincts as its instruments and generates its own varieties of aggressive drives. After all, throughout history men organized into armies have slaughtered each other over property or claims to property; but they have not so far, except in mythology, fought wars over 'prerogative in the field of sexual relationships'.

And so, when Freud maintains that the abolition of property will not alter 'the differences in power and influence which are misused by aggressiveness' and will not 'alter anything in the nature of human aggression', he simply begs the question. And when he goes on to say that 'aggressiveness . . . reigned almost without limit in primitive times, when property was still very scanty', he does not even suspect that it was precisely the scantiness of property, i.e., material scarcity, that destroyed the unity of primitive society, by giving rise to savage scrambles over scanty resources, scrambles that split society into mutually hostile classes. That is why we maintain that socialist man is conceivable only against the background of an unprecedented abundance of material and cultural goods and services. This is the ABC of Marxism. A friend of mine, an old and wise psychoanalyst, often says with a sigh: 'Oh, if only Freud had read Engels's *The Origin of the Family, Private Property and the State* — he would have avoided so many false trails and errors!' He might also have avoided supplying ammunition to people for whom *homo homini lupus* is the battle cry against progress and socialism, who operate the bogey of the *eternal* human *lupus* in the interest of the real and bloody *lupus* of *contemporary* imperialism.

We may well grant that the aggressiveness of socialist man will show itself in the nursery 'in its primal, anal form' and in other more developed manifestations. Yet much will depend, *inter alia*, on the character of the nursery: do we imagine it as an individual nursery within the family unit as we know it? Or as a communal nursery after the dissolution of this family unit? In our hypothesis about socialist man we assume that he will not live within anything like the present family, with its money nexus and its dependence of woman and child on father. We suppose that socialist man will in childhood be far less subjected to paternal authority than his predecessors have been, or that he will not know it at all; and that as an adult he will be free in his sexual and erotic life, or, at any rate, that he will be incomparably freer than bourgeois man is to follow his emotional urges and need of love without coming into conflict with society. His instinctual drives will be refracted through his personality in a manner which we cannot predict but which certainly will not be the manner Freud takes for granted.

Should one, for instance, take it for granted that socialist man will be subject to the Oedipus complex? Will this complex that has worked so powerfully in our psyche, at least since matriarchy gave place to patriarchal society, still be there if and when mankind has moved beyond the bourgeois form of the patriarchal family? And one may wonder what the superego may be like in socialist man, the superego that works in us as our unconscious moral censor and our father within us? Freud, who confuses fatherhood, which is a biological category, with paternal authority, which is a social institution, takes it for granted that the superego and the Oedipus complex and other reflections of paternalistic society in the individual's mind, are there forever.

True, he seems to have had a momentary premonition of other possibilities. He says: 'If we were to remove this factor too [i.e., prerogative in the field of sexual relationships] by allowing complete freedom of sexual life and thus abolishing the family, the germ cell of civilization, we cannot, it is true, easily foresee what new paths the development of civilization could take.'[4] He cannot, however, visualize the prospect, for the monogamous family is to him the indispensable germ cell of civilization, and even in his thought he

[4]*Ibid*. p. 51.

cannot detach himself from his patient, the bourgeois, monogamous man lying in front of him on the couch. And so, although he grants uneasily that we cannot foresee what new paths the development of civilization could take without the present family unit, he is sure that the indestructible aggressiveness of human nature will pursue socialist man beyond class, society, state and family.

Here again we, Marxists, prefer a certain amount of agnosticism. We are, of course, concerned in the main with the cruelty and oppression which are generated directly by poverty, scarcity of goods, class society, and man's domination by man. Whenever Freud ventures into the fields of sociology and history, he lays himself open to the reproach that he speaks willy-nilly as an apologist for existing society. We have nevertheless learned from him something important about the reality of the destructive and aggressive elements in human nature. It is, of course, true that emperors, kings, warlords, dictators, governments and leaders of all sorts would not have been able to make men behave as aggressively as they have behaved if aggressiveness had not been there in human nature — our rulers have always appealed and still appeal to man's base instinctual drives. But the question of how much of the biologically or sexually conditioned aggressiveness will affect the non-biological relationship of socialist man must be left open.

We do not maintain that socialism is going to solve all predicaments of the human race. We are struggling in the first instance with the predicaments that are of man's making and that man can resolve. May I remind you that Trotsky, for instance, speaks of three basic tragedies — hunger, sex and death — besetting man. Hunger is the enemy that Marxism and the modern labour movement have taken on. In doing so they have naturally been inclined to ignore or belittle man's other predicaments. But is it not true that hunger or, more broadly, social inequality and oppression, have hugely complicated and intensified for innumerable human beings the torments of sex and death as well?

In fighting against social inequality and oppression we fight also for the mitigation of those blows that nature inflicts on us. I think that Marxism has tried and is trying to tackle from the right end the tasks confronting our society. The Freudians have concentrated on sex and ignored or belittled man's social problems. And what is the result? For all the theoretical importance of psychoanalysis, the practical benefits of its therapy are in our society available only to a tiny privileged minority. Our vision of socialist man, on the other hand, has inspired a huge segment of mankind; and although we have fought with varying success and suffered terrible defeats, we have nevertheless moved mountains, whereas all the psychoanalysis of the world cannot reduce by a single iota the aggressiveness with which our world is boiling over.

Yes, socialist man will still be pursued by sex and death; but we are convinced that he will be better equipped than we are to cope even with these. And if his nature remains aggressive, his society will give him immeasurably greater and more varied opportunities than bourgeois man has for sublimating his instinctual drives and turning them to creative uses. Even if socialist man may not be quite 'free from guilt or pain' as Shelley dreamed he would be, he may be still 'sceptreless, free, uncircumscribed, but man equal, unclassed, tribeless, and nationless, exempt from all worship and awe'. The average member of socialist society may yet rise, as Trotsky anticipated, to the stature of Aristotle, Goethe, Marx, who, whatever their sexual instincts and aggressive drives, embody some of mankind's highest achievements so far. And we assume that 'above these heights new peaks will rise'. We do not see in socialist man evolution's last and perfect product, or the end of history, but in a sense only the beginning of history. Socialist man may indeed feel the *Unbehagen*, the unease and discomfort, that civilization imposes upon the beast in man. Moreover, this may, indeed, be the most essential of his own inner contradictions and tensions that will impel him to evolve further and scale heights which are beyond our imagination.

These views are or ought to be truisms for any Marxist, and I ought perhaps to apologize for stating them at a Socialist Scholars' Conference. Unfortunately, in the present condition of the labour movement and of socialist thinking certain elementary truths need to be restated, for all too often they are forgotten or falsified for the sake of some dubious political convenience. I have heard it said, for instance, that the proper subject of my analysis ought to be the socialist man living in the USSR or China today. I would take this view only if I held that those countries have already achieved or that they have nearly achieved socialism. I do not accept this assumption, and I do not think that the typical or even the advanced member of Soviet or Chinese society today can be described as socialist man.

We all speak, of course, colloquially about the USSR, China and the associated and disassociated states as 'socialist countries', and we are entitled to do so as long as we intend merely to oppose their regimes to the capitalist states, to indicate their post-capitalist character or to refer to the socialist origins and inspiration of their governments and policies. But here I am concerned with a theoretically correct description of the structure of their society and the nature of human relationship evolving within that structure. You may remember that over thirty years ago Stalin proclaimed that the Soviet Union had completed the building of socialism; and until now, despite the so-called de-Stalinization and the demolition of so many Stalinist myths, this has remained a central tenet of official Soviet ideology. Moreover, Stalin's successors allege that the Soviet Union is now engaged in the transition from socialism to communism, or that it is entering into that higher stage of classless society that is to complete the cycle of socialist transformation opened up by the October Revolution.

Spokesmen of the People's Republic of China have been making similar claims for their country. Now, the Stalinist dogma about the achievement of socialism in the Soviet Union has significantly affected and changed the popular image of socialist man and even the thinking of quite a few socialist scholars. Yet one thing is, or ought to be, immediately obvious: the typical man of Soviet society, whether under Stalin or his successors, presents so striking a contrast to the Marxist conception of socialist man that either we must refuse to consider him as socialist man or we must throw the Marxist conception overboard, as the Stalinist school of thought has tacitly done. This is not a squabble over the letter of the Gospel, but an issue of the greatest theoretical and practical importance for us. If our aim is socialist man then our conception or image of him is vital to our theoretical thinking, to the moral-political climate of the labour movement, and to our own ability or inability to inspire our working classes.

Now, socialist man was envisaged by Marx, and all his followers up to Stalin, as a free associated producer working, even in the so-called lower phase of communism, under a rationally planned economy, no longer a buyer or seller trading products in the markets, but someone who turns out goods for society at large and receives them for personal consumption from society's common pool. By definition socialist man lives in a classless and stateless society, free from social or political oppression, even though he may at the beginning still carry a burden — a steadily diminishing burden — of inherited social inequality. The society in which he lives has to be so highly developed, so wealthy, educated and civilized that there is no objective need or necessity for it to allow any recrudescence of inequality or oppression.

This is what *all* Marxists before Stalin took for granted. This is the ideal that has inspired generations of socialists; without it socialism would have never come to life as the dynamic force of the century. Marxism has demonstrated the realistic character of this ideal by showing that the whole development of modern society, with its technology, industry and increasingly socialized productive process, tends toward this outcome. Now, the socialist man that Stalin and his successors have shown the world is a pitiful parody of the Marxist image of socialist man. True, the Soviet citizen has lived in a society where the state, not the capitalists, owns the means of production, and this circumstance is already reflected in certain progressive features of his mentality. Even the most backward of Soviet workers takes the social public ownership of the means of production for granted. Private ownership of a factory or of a coal mine seems to him to be a revolting relic of some barbarous past. He shudders at the mere thought of it. He looks upon it very much as the average member of any modern bourgeois society looks upon slavery, as a social condition degrading to man. Bur nevertheless these progressive features in the outlook of Soviet man — although they are there — are not the dominant features of his social psychology.

Soviet society has suffered and is still suffering from material scarcity, an extreme scarcity of consumer goods in the first instance, which has over the decades led to an inevitable recrudescence and aggravation of social inequalities, to a deep division between a privileged minority and a deprived majority, to a spontaneous reassertion of the economic forces of the market, and to a revival and a terrifying growth of the oppressive functions of the state.

The socialist man Stalin presented to the world was the hungry, ill-clad, ill-shod or even barefoot worker or peasant selling or buying a shirt, a piece of furniture, a few ounces of meat or even a piece of bread on black or grey markets, working ten or twelve hours a day under a barracks-like factory discipline and, sometimes, paying for any real or alleged offence with years of forced labour in a concentration camp. He did not dare to criticize a factory manger, let alone a party boss. He had no right to express any opinion on any major issue affecting his and the nation's destiny. He had to vote as he was ordered; and to let his dignity and personality be mocked by the so-called personality cult. These are the facts, now officially so described by the Soviet leaders and reflected in a vast Soviet literature with all the emphasis of authenticity. Although in recent years conditions have been greatly mitigated, the poverty, the inequality, the lack of political and intellectual freedom and the bureaucratic terror are still there.

My purpose in recalling all this is not polemical, if only because I see the main cause of these conditions not just in the rulers' ill-will, though there has never been any lack of this, but in objective circumstances, in the terrible inherited poverty that the Soviet Union (and now China) has had to overcome in isolation, amid blockades, wars and armament races. It was out of the question that a country like this should be able to achieve socialism in such circumstances. It had to devote all its energies to 'primitive accumulation', that is, to the creation under state ownership of the most essential economic preliminaries to any genuine building of socialism. Consequently the Soviet Union is even today a transitional society, finding itself some way between capitalism and socialism, combining features of the one and of the other, and showing marks even of its more primitive pre-capitalist heritage. The same is unfortunately true of China, Vietnam, North Korea and most of Eastern Europe. We in the West bear a heavy responsibility for the predicaments of those countries — our failure to promote socialism in the West has been the ultimate cause of their failure. But if we are to face our task anew and enable a new generation of socialists to resume the struggle, we must clear our own minds to the end of the misconceptions and myths about socialism that have grown up in the past decades. We must dissociate socialism once and for all not from the Soviet Union or China and their progressive achievement, but from the Stalinist and post-Stalinist parody of socialist man.

I cannot go here into the motives of dogma and prestige that led Stalin and his associates to proclaim that the Soviet Union had achieved socialism and that still cause his successors to keep up this pretence. I am concerned here only with the impact this dogma or boast has had on socialism in the West. The impact has been disastrous. It has demoralized our labour movement and confused socialist thinking. Our working classes have watched in their own shrewd way developments in the Soviet Union and have drawn their own conclusions. 'If this is the ideal of the socialist man', they have said in effect, 'then we will have nothing to do with it.' Many of our socialist intelligentsia have reacted likewise or have become so entangled in Stalinist mythology and scholasticism that they lost the élan and power of socialist conviction and have so disarmed themselves spiritually that they have been unable to struggle against the disillusionment and apathy in the working classes.

It was once said of the Jesuits that, having failed to raise earth to heaven, they dragged heaven down to earth. Similarly, Stalin and Stalinism, unable to raise a poverty-stricken and miserable Russia to socialism, have dragged down socialism to the level of Russian misery. It may be argued that they had to do it. Even if that were so, we have to do something else: We have to raise socialism back to its own height. We have to explain to our working classes and intelligentsia why the Soviet Union and China have not been able to produce and could not produce socialist man, despite their remarkable achievements which give them a right to our recognition and solidarity. We must restore the image of socialist man to all its spiritual splendour. We must restore it in our own minds first and then, fortified in our conviction and rearmed politically, we must carry socialist consciousness and the socialist idea back into the working class.

This speech, given to the second Socialist Scholars' Conference in New York in 1966, was published in pamphlet form by Merit Publishers, New York 1967.